Brenda W̶
74b
Mi

604-557-6220

Two Tracks — One Goal

How Alcoholics Anonymous Relates to Christianity

❧

by

Cal Chambers

Canadian Cataloguing in Publication Data

Chambers, Calvin H., 1925-
  Two tracks, one goal

  ISBN 0-92047-40-5

  1. Alcoholics Anonymous. 2. Alcoholism—
Religious aspects—Christianity. I. Title.
HV5186.C53 1992   362.29'286   C92-091628-7

©1992 by Calvin H. Chambers

ISBN 0-920479-40-5
(paperback)

Cover Design by
Neil Klassen

Scripture quotes are taken from:
Good News for Modern Man primarily
in addition to author's paraphrases

All given names in conversational narratives
have been changed

Alcoholics Anonymous has not reviewed
the contents of this publication.

Printed in Canada

CONTENTS

Preface

Acknowledgments

Dedication

Foreword

The Twelve Steps with the Christian Interpretation

CHAPTER ONE *Page 1*

Step One: We admitted we were powerless over alcohol and that our lives had become unmanageable. *(Alcoholics Anonymous)*

Track One: No one is ever made better by having someone else tell him how rotten he is, but many are made better by avowing the guilt themselves. *(Bishop Fulton Sheen)*

Track Two: Open confession is good for the soul. Get it out in the open. *(Handbook of Proverbs by H.G. Bohm p.471)*

CHAPTER TWO *Page 25*

Step Two: Came to believe that a power greater than ourselves could restore us to sanity. *(Alcoholics Anonymous)*

Track One: It is much more difficult than one thinks, not to believe in God. *(Andre Gide, Les Nouvelles, Nourtures 1936)*

Track Two: I doubt, therefore I believe. *(Marshall Fishwick)*

CHAPTER THREE *Page 55*

Step Three: Made a decision to turn my will and my life over to the care of God, as we understood Him. *(Alcoholics Anonymous)*

Track One: My wise and faithful maid said in response to the question of what keeps people from believing, "Too stiff to bend, I guess."
(Theodore P. Ferris)

Track Two: God as we understood Him.
(Alcoholics Anonymous)

CHAPTER FOUR   *Page 89*

Step Four: Made a searching and fearless moral inventory of ourselves. *(Alcoholics Anonymous)*

Track One: Let nothing stand between you and the light.
(Henry David Thoreau, letter March 7, 1848)

Track Two: Search me, O God, and know my heart, try my anxious thoughts, and see if there be any offensive way in me, and lead me in the way of everlasting [a new quality] life.
(Psalm 139: 23,24)

CHAPTER FIVE   *Page 113*

Step Five: Admitted to God, to ourselves and to another human being the exact nature of our faults.
(Alcoholics Anonymous)

Track One: They believed liberty to be the secret of happiness and courage to be the secret of liberty.
(Louis Bradeis, U.S. Supreme Court Justice 1856-1941)

Track Two: Confess your faults one to another, that you may be healed. *(James 5:16)*

CHAPTER SIX   *Page 131*

Step Six: Were entirely willing and ready to have God remove any defects of character. *(Alcoholics Anonymous)*

Track One: We would rather be ruined than change
We would rather die in our dread
Than climb the cross of the moment,
And let our illusions die.
(Wystan High Auden, The Age of Anxiety, 1948)

Track Two: This is the will of God, even your
             sanctification. *(1 Thessalonians 4:3)*

CHAPTER SEVEN   *Page 151*
Step Seven: Humbly asked Him to remove all our shortcomings.
             (Alcoholics Anonymous)
   Track One: The greatest friend of truth is time, her greatest
               enemy is prejudice, and her constant companion
               is humility. *(Charles Caleb Cotton 1780-1829)*
   Track Two: Humility is the most difficult of virtues to
               achieve. *(T.S. Eliot, Shakespeare and the
               Stoicism of Seneca)*

CHAPTER EIGHT   *Page 169*
Step Eight: Made a list of all persons we had harmed and
             became willing to make amends to them all.
             (Alcoholics Anonymous)
   Track One: It is part of the cure to wish to be cured.
               (Seneca)
   Track Two: Listen, I will give half my belongings to the
               poor and if I have cheated anyone, I will pay
               back four times as much.
               (Zacchaeus, Luke 19:8)

CHAPTER NINE   *Page 187*
Step Nine: Made amends to such people whenever possible,
             except when to do so would injure them or others.
             (Alcoholics Anonymous)
   Track One: The hearts of good men admit the need of
               atonement. *(Homer)*
   Track Two: If you come to the altar, prepared to give a gift
               to the Lord and there you remember that your
               brother or sister has something against you,
               leave your gift in front of the altar, and go and
               make peace and then come and offer your gift to
               God. *(Jesus, Matthew 5:24)*

CHAPTER TEN   *Page 199*

Step Ten: Continued to take personal inventory, and where we
were wrong, promptly admitted it.
(Alcoholics Anonymous)

Track One: Make yourself an honest man, and then you may
be sure there is one less rascal in the world.
(Carlyle)

Track Two: One thing I do, forgetting those things which
are behind, and stretching forward to those
things which are before, I press on toward the
goal unto the prize of the high calling of God in
Christ Jesus. *(Philippians 3:13, 14)*

CHAPTER ELEVEN   *Page 215*

Step Eleven: Sought through prayer and meditation to
improve our conscious contact with God,
praying only for the knowledge of his will and
the power to carry it out. *(Alcoholics Anonymous)*

Track One: Meditation is the life of the soul, action is the
soul of meditation.
(Francis Quarles, 1592-1644)

Track Two: He meditates on his law day and night.
(Psalm 1:2)

CHAPTER TWELVE   *Page 231*

Step Twelve: Having had a spiritual awakening as a result of
these steps, we tried to carry this message to
alcoholics and to practice these principles in all
our affairs. *(Alcoholics Anonymous)*

Track One: A Christian is a beggar telling another beggar
where he can find food. *(D.T. Niles)*

Track Two: I am not ashamed of the Gospel of Christ, for it
is the power of God unto salvation to everyone
who believes. *(The Apostle Paul, Romans 1:16)*

PREFACE

The fellowship of Alcoholics Anonymous is obliquely based upon the Christian understanding and concept of God. This understanding, integrated into a recovery program for millions of afflicted alcoholics, has resulted in their miraculous transformation. The founders of Alcoholics Anonymous, Dr. Bob (Robert Holbrook Smith) and Bill (William Griffith Wilson) were introduced to Christianity through the teachings and philosophy of the Oxford Movement. This interdenominational fellowship, now called Moral Rearmament, was founded by Frank Buchman and sought to bring about conversion through the Christian insights of confession, surrender, guidance and sharing. This led to the formulation of the four absolutes—absolute purity, absolute unselfishness, absolute honesty and absolute love. None of these absolutes were achievable through humanistic self-effort—only by the acknowledgment of one's complete dependency upon God Who has revealed Himself fully in Jesus Christ.

Bereft of power to combat their personal alcoholism, both Bill and Dr. Bob, under God, brought into existence an unparalleled movement of healing for thousands shipwrecked by alcohol abuse. Beginning in 1935, Bob and Bill, together with Sister Ignatia, guided some five thousand alcoholics to physical and spiritual recovery within fifteen years. Since then, this movement has spread to much of the Western world.

Some Christian people believe that Alcoholics Anonymous is not "Christian" enough, primarily because the name of Jesus Christ is not mentioned specifically. Similarly, some A.A. members believe there is no place for a specific Christian emphasis in this organization, espousing that A.A. is not interested in religion as such, but only in how spirituality can encourage sobriety.

This book will illustrate how Christianity undergirds the Twelve Steps in the Alcoholics Anonymous Program and that the God referred to seven times in these Twelve Steps is the same God Who has revealed Himself uniquely in the Man Jesus Christ. The book is also designed to help alcoholics become as open as possible to spiritual truth wherever it leads them. Step Eleven in the program encourages people, through prayer and meditation, to improve their conscious contact with God. Sincere attempts to move in this direction will undoubtedly succeed. "If you seek for me with all your heart you will surely find me, for I am always ready to be found of those who seek me earnestly" (Jeremiah 29:13).

Although I am not an alcoholic, I have enjoyed an intimate association with Alcoholics Anonymous in New Westminster, British Columbia, where I lived and ministered for twenty-four years. In 1960 I met a man in my congregation who found faith in Jesus Christ as well as sobriety through the program of A.A. He took me to my first A.A. meeting where I heard the Twelve Steps read and the testimonies of recovering alcoholics. Since then, I have initiated discussion groups for A.A. members interested in exploring the Christian Faith. In 1981, assisted by two A.A. members, I began a chapter of A.A. called "Good Samaritan." It was a special-interest group emphasizing the Third Step in A.A.—"Willing to turn my will and life over to the care of God, as I understand Him." Here Christian A.A. members named Christ as their Higher Power, the One through Whom God became real to them. Many A.A. members also wanted my assistance with the Fifth

Step—"Admitted to God, myself, and some other person the exact nature of my wrongs." In this role, I directed many alcoholics to consider the reality of Christ, whose forgiveness, love and grace could bring deeper dimension to spiritual life. Many of these people were eventually baptized and became practising Christians within the fellowship of the Church. I also ministered in the Maple Cottage Detoxification Center, sponsored by the government of British Columbia. Here I served as a volunteer counselor and chaplain, seeking to implement the A.A. program for those recognizing that their lives had become unmanageable because of alcohol.

I am completely committed to two facts: 1. God has revealed Himself personally and powerfully in Jesus Christ, whose life is chronicled in the New Testament. 2. God has raised up Alcoholics Anonymous as a ministry of love to help free anyone afflicted by the inordinate misuse of alcohol or any other artificial dependency that robs men and women of inner freedom.

The Bible describes Christ's ministry in people's lives as "salvation." This word literally means, "to make spacious, to liberate, to emancipate, to set free." Certainly millions of alcoholics have testified that life was "hell" and their deliverance from alcoholic addiction was miraculous. God is ever seeking to free us. As Christ Himself said about his ministry, "If the Son makes you free, you will really be free" (John 8: 36).

I ask alcoholics to read this book with an open mind toward the foundational beliefs of Christianity. I would like Christian people to become cognizant of God's saving power evidenced through Alcoholics Anonymous. Alcoholics need not regard the Christian Faith as suspect and Christians need not deny the powerful influence of A.A. Jesus once said, "He that is not for me is against me." I have personally found many alcoholics receptive to the Christian message if presented with a non-judgmental, loving attitude. Many alcoholics have been "turned off" by negative experiences within the church of their childhood. May this book build bridges between both alcoholics and Christians as together we explore the riches of Jesus Christ, Who came into the world not to condemn sinners, but to set them free.

ACKNOWLEDGMENTS

This book would never have been undertaken apart from the encouragement of the people I've met through years of involvement in Alcoholics Anonymous. Some of them have become my closest friends. Also deeply influenced by A.A., my wife Alice opened our home continually for recovering alcoholics to begin again in an atmosphere of love and acceptance. Her unqualified support and inspiration have seen this book project to completion. As I grappled with a suitable book title, my oldest daughter Janice, in a moment of inspiration said, "Dad, why not call it Two Tracks, One Goal?" I was immediately taken with her understanding of what I wanted to communicate. I am grateful for her important contribution.

Certainly Nancy and Terry Ruddell encouraged me to persevere when I was tempted to drop this project. Credo Publishing inspired me with their confidence that the book was worthy of publication and could meet a real need among alcoholics seeking more understanding of the Christian approach to God—especially Jocelyn Cameron, whose expertise helped refine and polish the manuscript for publication.

One of our favorite hymns written by Jean Vanier the founder of L'Arche homes for the mentally handicapped, has been my prayer:

> Lord Jesus of You, I will sing as I journey
> I'll tell all my brothers and sister about you
> wherever I go
> You alone are man's life and his peace and
> his joy
> Lord Jesus, of You I will sing as I journey.

DEDICATION

To Alice my dear wife
who shared the ministry of A.A. with me
and to all my friends in A.A.
from whom I learned so much.

FOREWORD

God has to change us before He uses us.

As I look back over the past thirty years of my involvement with Alcoholics Anonymous, I stand in awe at how God works his transformation of our mind-sets and then opens a door for ministry.

Brought up in a strict teetotaling family, I was taught to recite poems against the evils of alcohol, through the Women's Christian Temperance Union Recitation Contests. I proudly boasted winning bronze, silver and gold medals before I was fourteen. With my self-righteous attitude toward alcoholics, I thought nothing, as a child, of throwing stones at a poor drunk weaving his way home from a bar on a Saturday night.

You can imagine my chagrin when I was asked by Rev. Robert Barr, Minister of Knox Presbyterian Church, Toronto, to spend the summer of 1950 in Evangel Hall, a Presbyterian ministry on Queen Street, the worst juvenile-delinquency area at that time. I will always remember my anger as I walked along Queen Street toward the Mission, muttering to myself, "Who does Robert Barr think he is, asking a nice boy like me to go and live in a joint like this?" I did not in the least welcome the experience.

But as I began to live in this four-story Mission, taking part in the various activities, preaching at the evening services, and meeting the men and women who came to the Mission for help, I began to soften. In reflection I realized that the year before I went to Knox College, I had a life-changing encounter with the Holy Spirit, releasing my evangelistic gifts. My last year in university involved me in a student witness I had never had before. But I needed to be involved in social action also, an aspect of my Christian life yet undeveloped.

During those three years that I lived and served in Evangel Hall, God worked his miracle in me. The Holy Spirit began to release God's love in me, and I could identify with the alcoholic sufferer in a totally new way. Somehow God gave me the ability to "get under the skin" of the alcoholic, and deeply feel what they grappled with in their affliction.

In the Fall of 1960, I accepted a call to First Presbyterian Church, New Westminster, B.C. Within the first week, I met a man, Glen C. who had been introduced to faith in Christ through a friend, but had also begun to experience recovery from alcoholism through A.A. He invited me to my first meeting. I saw immediately the potential for sharing God's love in Jesus Christ. And so I began to attend meetings in New Westminster regularly. When it was discovered that I was a minister, I was asked to speak and share my life. I would usually take one of the Twelve Steps of Recovery and speak briefly about it. I would make some low-key statements about Christ, without going into any theological explanation. But I always prayed that God would put me in touch with someone at the meeting who sought something more than sobriety. Invariably, He did.

Over the next twenty-five years, I led a number of Discussion Group meetings, centering around the Third Step: "I was willing to turn my will and my life over to God, as I understand Him." Through these group meetings, many alcoholic men and women came into a living faith. Not all of them became part of the Church, because in so many instances, their experience of the Church had been negative in their youth, and they found it hard to believe they would be accepted. But a good number did, and before I left New Westminster in 1984 to minister in Ottawa, I could look out over the congregation on a given Sunday morning and count one third of the people as recovering alcoholics. I formed an A.A. Group called Good Samaritan, in which Christian members were encouraged to identify Christ as their Higher Power.

The door to ministry among alcoholics was opened once the Lord changed my attitudes and gave me a love and concern for them only He could have generated. The book I have written, *Two Tracks, One Goal*, shares my own insights on how the Christian Faith has inspired the Twelve Steps of Recovery in A.A., and how we as Christians can use the Twelve-Step Program to help them discover the God Who has always loved them, and can change them by his great power.

Many members of A.A. do not understand the dynamics of the Christian Faith, and many Christians do not understand the power at work in an A.A. meeting. Today we need people willing to identify with the alcoholic—where he or she lives and there, in a low-key way, share how the principles of A.A. flow out of the Christian Faith, and its understanding of God's heart of redeeming, transforming love.

The two concepts, or tracks, may seem only parallel, but if you stand at the back of a train as it moves out of a station, you will observe how the two tracks seem to converge on the horizon and become one. My conviction is that the Christian Faith flows out of God, and A.A. flows out of Christian Faith. Both need to be held together—and can be—if we engage the potential of both imagination and creativity.

THE TWELVE STEPS
as expressed by
ALCOHOLICS ANONYMOUS

Step One

We admitted we were powerless over alcohol—that our lives had become unmanageable.

Christian Interpretation: Self-centeredness, the essence of sin, separates us from God and our true selves. Our selfish attitudes and bad habits hold us captive. Our lives go out of control and we need help.

Step Two

Came to believe that a Power greater than ourselves could restore us to sanity.

Christian Interpretation: Our finite selves cannot find God, the infinitely great Power of the universe. God, therefore, takes the initiative to make Himself known on our level through Jesus Christ—the God Man Who once said, "All power is given to Me in heaven and on earth."

Step Three

Made a decision to turn our will and our lives over to the care of God as we understand Him.

Christian Interpretation: As we surrender our right to control ourselves and let Jesus Christ "lord it over us," we can understand God and experience his love and care personally.

Step Four

Made a searching and fearless moral
inventory of ourselves.

Christian Interpretation: The New Testament says, "Examine yourselves whether you be in the faith" (2 Corinthians 13:5). The Psalmist says, "Search me, O God, and know my heart, try me and know my ways, and see if there be any wickedness in me, and lead me in the way everlasting" (Psalm 139:29).

Step Five

Admitted to God, to ourselves and to another human being,
the exact nature of our wrongs.

Christian Interpretation: Christianity teaches, "Confess your faults one to another that you may be healed" (James 5:16). "If we confess our sins, God is faithful and just to forgive our sins and to cleanse us from all unrighteousness" (1 John 1:9).

Step Six

Were ready to have God remove all these
defects of character.

Christian Interpretation: Only God can transform human life. When He releases Himself into our lives He begins to change us from within, giving us power to become new people. If any man is in Christ, old things pass away, yes, all things become new.

Step Seven

Humbly asked God to remove our shortcomings.

Christian Interpretation: God has the power to set us free. Jesus can save, liberate and emancipate to the uttermost all who come to God through Him.

Step Eight

Made a list of all persons we had harmed and became willing to make amends to them all.

Christian Interpretation: Restitution is fundamental to the Christian life. Zacchaeus said, "Whatever I have taken falsely I will return fourfold." Jesus responded, "Today salvation is come to this house" (Luke 19:9).

Step Nine

Made amends to such people wherever possible, except when to do so would injure them or others.

Christian Interpretation: Love and forgiveness lead us to new relationships yet discretion and sensitivity must be employed. Love in all its fullness must motivate our restitution.

Step Ten

Continued to take personal inventory and when we were wrong promptly admitted it.

Christian Interpretation: Life that is truly life yields to the constant assessment of its thoughts and acts. Preoccupied with judging ourselves, we are less inclined to judge others.

Step Eleven

Sought through prayer and meditation to improve our conscious contact with God, praying only for the knowledge of his will for us and the power to carry it out.

Christian Interpretation: Prayer opens the way to encounter God and meditation upon his Word provides the avenue for the Holy Spirit to order our lives according to his will.

Step Twelve

Having had a spiritual awakening as the result of these steps, we tried to carry the message to alcoholics and practice these principles in all our affairs.

Christian Interpretation: Christians reach out to others, seeking to share their victories with humble and loving attitudes. To be valid, Christianity must be openly practiced.

CHAPTER ONE

STEP ONE: We admitted we were powerless over alcohol and that our lives had become unmanageable.
Alcoholics Anonymous

TRACK ONE: No one is ever made better by having someone else tell him how rotten he is, but many are made better by avowing the guilt themselves.
Bishop Fulton Sheen

The Necessity of Confession

As Chaplain of the Maple Cottage Detox in New Westminster, British Columbia, I met a young man in his thirties one evening who seemed desperate to see me. As he entered my office his face reflected complete despair. Without introduction, he simply blurted out a hopeless, "Help me." After he calmed down, he told me the long story of his alcoholic life. His drinking problem had been accelerating for ten years. He lost his home through gambling, and to mask his subsequent self-hate, he consoled himself with alcohol. Yet despite this obvious tragedy, he hadn't admitted that his life was unmanageable, that he was licked. He would describe himself as a drunk, a lush, a problem drinker, but not a helpless alcoholic—it seemed the words wouldn't come. But now, bereft of family, unemployed and penniless, he realized the desperation of his life. He was an alcoholic. Now at the bottom of the rung, he blurted it out, "I need help." It was a tremendous step for him, but he was taking it.

We human beings characteristically refuse to admit defeat because we are so proud. We doggedly resist admitting that we are powerless to overcome particular habits or attitudes, or overcome our alcoholic drinking by willpower alone.

Alcoholism as a Disease

The disease of alcoholism compares easily to bankruptcy, the creditor being alcohol. It robs the alcoholic of self-respect, acceptance, work, money, the ability to function responsively and of the love of his family. Working among alcoholics in a downtown Mission in the city of Ottawa, I have personally known men brought to the very brink of physical, moral and spiritual bankruptcy, experiencing complete ruin and sometimes suicide.

But There Is Hope

When a person afflicted with alcoholism confronts the possibility of regaining his self-respect, strong feelings of humiliation often take over. Many people enter the A.A. Program reluctant to admit the pernicious effects of this all-consuming lifestyle. But the moment a person acknowledges the truth of the First Step, the door of hope opens, with its promise of physical and spiritual freedom. Admitting that life has become unmanageable because of drinking is essentially an act of repentance, a word that indicates the need for change. This confession of need is foundational to Christ's Sermon on the Mount. The famous passage begins with the words "Blessed [or happy] are the poor in spirit for theirs is the kingdom of heaven" (Matthew 5:2). In other words, happy are those who have come to the end of their rope and admitted it. A new door of life can now be opened. To retain self-sufficiency is to forfeit hope for the person who seeks recovery from alcoholism.

Facing the Facts

Every recovering alcoholic will admit the hard cold fact that to confess weakness, failure and impotence is, paradoxically, the beginning of strength, success and power. This truth is basic to Christianity as well as to Alcoholics Anonymous. The Apostle Paul confesses in his letter to the Corinthian Christians, "When I am weak, then am I strong. I will therefore boast about my weaknesses, that the power of Christ may rest upon me" (2 Corinthians 12:9). Dr. Paul Tournier, a leading Swiss psychologist illuminates this point in his book, The Weak and the Strong. He makes it clear that people who try to project the illusion of strength are actually weak, too insecure to risk exposure, and therefore threatened by criticism and correction. But those who admit their weaknesses and their inability to maintain meaningful lifestyles, strip off the facade of superiority and self-delusion. These, he asserts, are the truly strong people.

The many alcoholics I have talked to and listened to in A.A. meetings have openly admitted that acknowledging Step One was their highest hurdle. They had been willing to say they handled their drinking problem poorly, and were unable to cope with life. They acknowledged that they were "phonies, lushes, drunks"—anything but say openly and candidly, "I am an alcoholic." These words seemed to stick in their throats. Facing the reality of defeat went entirely against the grain. Self-confidence had been their intellectual hallmark both at home and in school. To face the fact of its deficiency proved the greatest obstacle to gaining true confidence.

Overcoming Deception

Our educational training has brainwashed many of us into believing we could achieve what we wanted if we simply tried hard enough—the great "American dream." We have been taught to admire the "self-made man," who boasts of his aggressive success in reaching the top by sheer self-effort. The philosophy of those gripped by this humanistic concept is reflected in the poem by William E. Heney, "I am the captain of my fate . . . . I am the master of my soul" (Invictus, Stanza 2).

This kind of self-deception militates against our true happiness and our willingness to accept ourselves for who we actually are. The sponsor's role in A.A. is to help the new person seeking sobriety understand the futility of trying to beat alcoholic addiction by willpower alone. The alcoholic must be encouraged to see the two-fold nature of the problem and its solution: firstly, that the physical symptoms of alcoholism indicate the allergic nature of the addiction; secondly, the fact that alcoholics continue drinking despite its physical consequences indicates a moral and spiritual problem. It falls into the area of pure, self-centered resistance to truth. They refuse to give up, determined to maintain control over their own lives. Their self-will, rooted in pride, refuses to face reality until driven to desperation. This willful splurge into dissipation must be dealt with, relinquished not merely by human willpower that will ultimately fail, but by spiritual power.

Reaching Bottom

In the early years of Alcoholics Anonymous, often only those whose lives had collapsed into shambles listened to what A.A. members proposed. Their desperation couldn't be denied. At the end of themselves, they discovered to their complete amazement that the program worked. They began to get well. Their story is told in Alcoholics Anonymous, affectionately called the Big Book. It chronicles the histories of sick and confused alcoholics, many of whom tried the program, and failed to achieve sobriety because they wouldn't admit their total inability to handle their drinking not even one drink.

As the years passed, the situation changed. Many successful people, comfortable with a few social drinks, crossed over the invisible line between social drinking and problem drinking. Fortunately, they did not have to hit rock bottom before they recognized that they needed to do something about their increasing number of blackouts (becoming unconscious of what was happening). They saw what A.A. had done for other alcoholics and found sobriety through the same avenue. Those who reached rock bottom, however, greatly inspired those who knew they were "hooked," but didn't know what to do about it. People uncertain about the seriousness of their drinking problem have sometimes been encouraged to continue drinking in a controlled way (if this is possible) to discover whether or not they needed to discipline themselves. This positive approach has often helped people look positively at their drinking patterns and become more aware of what they were doing to themselves and to others. As life becomes more and more unmanageable, the need for help hits home. The guilt, uncontrolled fears and broken health have all been used by God to drive the alcoholic to repentance, to change his life. Ultimately, the defeated person admits Step One: "My life has become powerless over alcohol." This confession unleashes a new Power of healing.

STEP ONE: We admitted we were powerless over alcohol, and that our lives had become unmanageable.

Alcoholics Anonymous

TRACK TWO: Open confession is good for the soul. Get it out in the open. *Handbook of Proverbs, H.G. Bohm, p. 471*

Open Confession is Good for the Soul, Get It Out in the Open

Every year when E. Stanley Jones, the famous missionary bishop of the Methodist Church in India, visited North America, he would hold an ashram, an Indian word for a retreat, a coming together of people to share life's experiences. After people arrived and communication barriers had evaporated, Dr. Jones would ask those present, "Why have you come?" People would then open up and explain. "I have come," said one, "because I am a church member, but I don't seem to be getting anything out of my church life." "I'm here," said another, "because I feel so powerless over the temptations constantly overcoming me." "I've come here to commit suicide if something doesn't happen to me," said another.

These ashrams deal with real life. No attempt is made to hide behind the wall of nicety, churchiness, or self-sufficiency. Everyone is encouraged to express what is really happening to them in life.

The same is true of Alcoholics Anonymous. There can be no hiding. Basic problems of unhappiness and disorder are faced openly with a readiness to see the problem and to do something about it.

Alcoholics Anonymous first challenges a person to realize their sickness is a disease, but not just a physical one. It is also a disorder with emotional and spiritual roots. The physical manifestation may only be the "tip of the iceberg."

Many people become alcoholics because of the chemical imbalance immediately created by the entrance of alcohol into the bloodstream. Others become alcoholics gradually as they become increasingly uncertain of themselves and insecure about who they are. They use alcohol to relieve them of life's difficulties.

I have a dear friend who became alcoholic simply because she had so many children close together. She began to drink to help her relax after a hectic day. Before she knew it, she was hooked. Not until another dimension entered her life, did she kick this nine-year addiction.

But alcoholism also has a spiritual side that cannot be ignored. Inferiority drives many people to alcoholism because of its promise of power. It generates a spurious sense of control. No problem is too great to face. They stand ten feet tall, and believe they can take on the world. It enhances their sense of personal worth. It makes them come out of their shell, where they have been hiding, frightened to be themselves.

Chris, an alcoholic woman told me, "I could never get up on the dance floor without a drink." A former secretary said to me one day as she was relating her experiences with alcohol, "After my first taste of wine, I said that I would never be without this again as long as I live." Within two years she grappled with serious alcoholism that ruined two marriages.

This illusion of well being ignores the real facts of life, preparing the way for a total eclipse of self-esteem. Not only can alcohol create a world of make-believe, but it helps people cut themselves off from their true selves, and from meaningful relationships with family and friends. It opens the door, not to heaven, but to hell. As one man said to me in my study, as I was counselling him about alcohol, "Life is hell." The unmanageability of life becomes the pattern of existence. Life becomes increasingly distorted and twisted. In the light of this, we must deal with alcoholism, not just as a physical disease, but as a moral failure that contributes to physical and emotional illness.

A.A. provides us with a challenge to change. It is Track One, truth that proceeds from the mind of God. But another Track also flows from the mind of God. Its truth is expressed in the vocabulary of the Christian faith, the inspiration behind A.A.'s understanding of life.

Life Demands Change—A Repentant Heart

When Jesus sat down one late night to talk with one of the Jewish religious leaders, Nicodemus, He told this devout man that he needed to begin life all over again. Obviously, Nicodemus was confused. He had never heard such talk. "How can a man be born when he is old?" he inquired. "Can he enter his mother's womb for a second time and be born?" Jesus made it clear to him, that He wasn't talking about physical birth. He was talking about the birth of the spirit—the birth of the real person—suppressed under a whole load of spiritual garbage, which the Bible calls "sin." If Nicodemus wanted to enter into life, he had to drop his old lifestyle, his self-sufficiency, and begin a new life, whatever his age. Jesus presented the challenge to change.

This challenge, foundational to the Christian Faith and Alcoholics Anonymous, faces all of us. It is not just the alcoholic who needs to change. Everyone must acknowledge his or her powerlessness to overcome destructive habits. If we fail to recognize life's downward pull, our lives will end up completely divorced from reality—from what they were meant to be. When we become aware of ourselves as we are, we must begin to face some real problems: our self-centeredness, our distortion of the truth about ourselves, the practice of bad habits that have marred our inner lives and our relationships with others. We look into the mirror of reality and see the real person—we don't like what we see. For us, the moment of truth has dawned.

My wife Alice tells how she was brought up with complete disdain for anything that had to do with alcohol. But in her pride and self-righteousness she thought she was much better than the alcoholic. When she came to understand who she was in the sight of God, she had to deal with her unwarranted pride.

Repentance—the Positive Pointing to Change

Christians describe this process, this moment of honest self-awareness, by using two important words—sin and repentance.

These words may initiate a negative reaction in the minds of some people, especially the word "sin." An enormous amount of misunderstanding about the nature of sin must be cleared away before we understand its true significance.

The word "sin" in the Hebrew language comes from the root word meaning "to separate, cut off, alienate, die." Certainly we can see that alcohol creates this kind of situation. It alienates your true self, and cuts off relationships with significant others in our lives. It breaks up friendships. Many alcoholics have lost families and friends simply because their drinking patterns caused problems others could not tolerate. This sense of separation has driven some alcoholics to futility, despair, and in some cases, death.

The moment of truth eventually surfaces with its incumbent havoc of broken relationships. Some alcoholics, however, refuse to face the fact that their day-by-day drinking is creating hurt and tragedy for others. Some have felt it was better to die drunk than to seek a door of hope. But many others, in their desperation, turn to A.A. and find help. In their recovery process, they begin reconciliation with family and friends and a new life takes shape.

Sin Creates Separation

This understanding of sin as separation is basic to the underlying convictions, both in the Twelve-Step Program of A.A. and the Christian Faith.

Old railway tickets had these words printed on the bottom: "Not good if detached." This has basically happened to the human race, not just to the alcoholic. We have become separated from our Creator God, the Source of all life, love and goodness. Because of this separation, we live in a world marked by death, hatred and evil. No honest observer would dare to say that humanity is characterized by consistent goodness, love and moral achievement. The nineteenth century touted the viewpoint that man, with enough education and scientific progress, could annihilate his problems—including war. But the twentieth century ushered in an era of nuclear weapons. It murdered six million Jews in Nazi Germany. These and other atrocities helped prick the balloon of our century's vulgar optimism.

Science, despite its benefits, has helped create a world of dread. What has happened to mankind over the centuries has not eradicated our problem. No amount of optimistic philosophizing about man's need to be "good" has overcome them. There has been a breakdown between God and man, between man and man. This separation is what Christians mean by "sin." It is the severing of a relationship, God's moral laws exchanged for our own relative, false standards.

How Has This All Happened?

We need to ask, how did this dilemma arise? The evolutionists, who adhere to the theory of man's progressive, inevitable development, claim that the moral defects and brutality of human life merely reflect our animal nature. Enough patience, combined with education, will overcome this problem of man's apparent evil. The human race, to a greater or lesser degree, acts like a naughty child who needs help to overcome his temper tantrums of personality, immorality and social evil. This will undoubtedly happen if we countenance the perfectability of man's human nature, the essence of the humanistic approach to man and his problems.

Some people claim that we have already reached this position, relatively speaking. We have on record the reaction of the great eighteenth-century New England philosopher, Thoreau who, when asked by his aunt if he had made his peace with God, replied, "Why Auntie, I didn't know we had quarrelled!" Others make fun of the old-fashioned idea of sin, like Oscar Wilde, the humorist and playwright who once said, "The only way to get rid of temptation is to give in to it." We all know the famous line by the black comedian Flip Wilson: "The devil made me do it." I remember on one occasion seeing a car stuffed with high-schoolers driving at top speed across a bridge with the words "The White Sinners" painted in big black letters on the car door. Sin was just a barrel of fun. Many churches also give the impression that sin is an antiquated theological concept that has to be "scratched" in light of modern psychology and the constant change in our understanding of what is right.

False Solutions

This kind of attitude promotes the naive idea that sin can somehow be eradicated by "good deeds." These people expound a credit and debit system of morality. Their good deeds line up on one side of the ledger, their bad deeds on the other. If the good deeds outbalance the bad ones, everything will turn out well in the end. Many people justify themselves and their actions in this totally unrealistic way.

The Real Solution

The Bible is the only book I know that honestly addresses the problem of man's separation from his Creator and also his fellow man. Only those who accept the realities of biblical thought can truly understand the nature of sin. The Bible insists that we have been created for intimate friendship with God but something has marred this relationship. The account of man's loss of fellowship with God is recorded in Genesis 3, giving us an account of how sin entered the stream of human history and became an integral part of our own personal experience.

Some Christians insist that the story of man's "Fall" must be understood exactly as it is recorded—in a completely historical, literal way. Others want to spiritualize the story, and thus remove it from the historical scene. However, I believe a middle viewpoint can hold both positions together.

Honest observers agree that a broken relationship exists between God and man, evidenced by the brokenness on the human level. This is historical fact. Why, then, should it be difficult to believe that at an initial time in history something happened that alienated man from God?

But if we only view the story of the Fall as recorded in Genesis 3 from an historical perspective, then we lose its meaning in terms of our own personal history. The account of man's Fall is not merely the record of what happened in the primeval past to people called Adam and Eve. It also chronicles my personal Fall. Study the story carefully to see the serious nature of your own broken relationship with God. It will force you to admit with the great English poet, T.S. Eliot, after his conversion to Christianity that the "doctrine of original sin is the most profound teaching on the subject of sin to be found in the religious literature of man."

Bringing the Past into the Present

As we examine this biblical narrative, we discover the inspiration behind the first step in the A.A. program. It articulates our broken relationship with God, our impotence to solve our own sin problem.

What are the first words we read in this story? "Now the serpent was more subtle than any beast which the Lord God had made." This serpent represents the special enemy of man—Satan, the devil, who exists not merely as a vestige of the old-fashioned theory of evil. Someone operates in our universe to militate against our welfare. He is not an impersonal force, but an active being who seeks to undermine and destroy God's purposes for his universe.

What does this identification of evil with a serpent infer? Notice that the serpent is described as "subtle." He does not "bulldoze" his way into our lives, yet he advances like a swift and slithery snake. Before we know it, we are powerfully tempted to say no to God—to do our "own thing." It does not come from God nor from man, but from outside us both.

How does this happen? We read further, "And the serpent said, Yes, has God said, You shall not eat of the tree which is in the midst of the garden?" The tree's location in the center of the garden indicates that temptation lodges at the heart of man's existence, his freedom to make choices. His ability to make moral choices separates him from the animal kingdom. We can decide to make positive or negative responses to God's revealed will. Without this indispensable gift of freedom, we would become mechanical robots. We would be unable to enjoy the satisfactions of fellowship with our Creator God.

Our struggles to respond either positively or negatively to God aren't wrong in themselves. Temptation is not sin. They simply indicate the need to listen to the voice of God, not to the dictates of our own will.

In this contest, the serpent questions Eve. "Yes, has God said, you shall not eat of the fruit of the tree which is in the midst (the center) of the garden?" He subtly suggests an alternative. Perhaps she misunderstood what God has actually said. Is this not the pattern of our inner conflicts? The Tempter does not overtly ask us to do evil—at least, not at first. He simply raises doubts about God's fairness. Does God want me to do this or that? Once the question has been doubtfully posed, temptation's pull strengthens. As the Apostle James writes in one of his letters, "No man's temptation is due to his own desire (which can be enormously attractive). His own desire takes hold of him, and produces sin. And sin in the long run, means death" (James 1:13-14, J.B. Philips Translation).

The leaves, sewn together to provide garments for two guilty people, also illustrate our separation from God. Instead of facing their sin, they used the goodness around them to cover their nakedness. This action points to our own behavior. The good leaves of our good works, our churchianity, our activities in lodges and service clubs often veil our alienation from God, and from the very people we pretend to befriend. Novels are replete with illustrations of our attempts to escape guilt through good works.

In A.J. Cronin's novel, *Beyond This Place,* a man sets out to find a person responsible for his father's unjust imprisonment for murder. As the story proceeds, we meet a fine gentleman who carried on an outstanding humanitarian ministry among the city's poor. He provided them each with a bowl of soup and a half guinea every day. He was widely praised for this generosity. But to the reader's surprise, this benevolent man is the actual murderer, attempting to hide his crime behind the "leaves" of social service.

I am not trying to generalize that all good deeds are a cover-up for sin. However, this story does illustrate how we anxiously evade the consequences of our wrongdoing. We attempt to justify ourselves by diverting attention to the good we do rather than the evil we have committed.

This Genesis story reveals the human tendency to hide from our

Creator and distort the truth about ourselves—one prime reason why the alcoholic falters at confessing his offenses. But what is true of the alcoholic is true of every other person in varying degrees.

Excuses, Excuses

To the question put to her by the serpent, Eve replies, "God has said, you shall not eat of it." We know in our hearts what we are meant to do. It forms part of the general revelation God gave us about right and wrong. The law written in our hearts constitutes our moral fibre. At first the woman accept's God's word for it. We do not always yield to evil immediately. But before the moral decision can be finalized, the tempter thrusts another arrow. "You shall not surely die, for God knows that in the day you eat of the fruit you shall be as gods, knowing good and evil." The Enemy now becomes much more overt. He tries to imply that God is depriving us of power—the power to be as gods, the power to be in the driver's seat of life. We are tempted to imagine that taking life into our own hands without any interference will mean real freedom and real happiness. The outright lie.

In the teaching of Jesus, Satan is described as a "murderer and a liar from the beginning" (John 8:44). Analyzed in the light of man's universal experience, this power is what we all want. We may not want to rule an empire, but we certainly desire control over our own lives, despite the cost. History's dictators are not alone in grasping for power over others. Everyone wants to master his own life to some degree independent of God. Modern liberal theology suggests that this desire for complete freedom represents "man coming of age." In reality, man is asserting his own warped desire for independence from his Creator. Surfacing by degrees, this false promise, "You shall be as gods," is always appealing, whether in the form of manipulating another person to do what we want, being in control of the office, having enough power for economic independence, or dominating some group in the church, community or country. It is the craving to control—a common, universal desire.

The Illusion of Power

This story demonstrates how the desire to control appears to be admirable. The tree in the Garden is described as "being good for food, pleasant to the eyes, and a tree to make one wise." This is how the lust for power strikes at the root of our human nature. It comes in one or all three ways. Some of us yield particularly to the sins of the flesh; others to the self-glorifying sins of the intellect, especially the kind of intellectualism that makes us think we are better than others, and therefore have control over them. Some of us are enticed by the fashions of this world, the sins that encourage us to believe we will have power over others through material possessions. The temptation to "false power" attacks us all—no one escapes. It lurks at the center of the garden of life.

Sin is Social

As the woman gazed at the tree, she became increasingly fascinated. She felt compelled to reach out and take the fruit. Having taken for herself, she gave to her husband and he ate along with her. The more we reflect on what the world promises, the more we listen to the demands of our physical natures and the more our resistance weakens. This process describes what happens when we yield to the power of self-centeredness.

Notice that Eve did not eat alone. She involved her husband in this act of disobedience. Sin always involves others. It is a social act. It affects others beyond ourselves. We do not sin privately, but in relationship to others, to groups, to gangs, to nations. In so doing, we find means to protect ourselves from accusations. Misery likes company, someone has said, and so does sin. Mankind as a whole sins together, making our sins against one another social sins. The race problem, the drinking problem, the horror of war, the selfishness of the rich who refuse to share with the needs of the poor and the outward crimes of man against his neighbor all indicate our common separation from God and from each other.

The Great Cover-Up

As soon as the man and the woman had taken the fruit, we are told, "And they saw that they were naked and hid themselves." Not only being naked bothered them, but also the realization that they were morally and spiritually exposed. It was guilt that made them feel naked, making them anxious to hide. Instead of walking freely in the Garden, we see them hiding in the bushes, seeking to cover their moral nakedness with leaves.

How descriptive of the human heart. We too want to run away from our sin—it's too hard to live with. We do this by hiding from God, by denying his existence, by suppressing our guilt, by pretending that nothing is wrong. We hide behind a multitude of façades. Alcohol certainly provides a formidable hiding place, killing sensitivity to our consciences, at least while we are drunk. Pleasure, endless activity, as well as the inability to sit still and be quiet divert us from searching out the truth in our hearts. People hide in churches trying to create the impression that they are "okay." We participate in many worthy causes and organizations hoping that this will atone for our sin and help cover up the real situation. We hid in religion, one of the most popular ways man chooses to hide his separation from God. We can't face ourselves. We are guilty, but we do not want anyone to know. So we hide behind our own fig leaves.

I can remember as a young child of six, before I ever read the Genesis 3 story, taking a dime from my mother's purse without her knowing and buying some candy. I bought the biggest bag of candy you could get for ten cents in those days. But in my fear of discovery and inner guilt, do you know where I ate the candy? Behind the chesterfield in our front room. I was afraid and I hid. It was Adam and Eve all over again. The story of man's moral fall repeats every day. We seek lifestyles devoid of God's control because we want to control ourselves. We want to be "as gods."

Into this context, God eventually comes to us. The story continues, "And the Lord God went walking in the cool of the garden. And God said, Adam, where are you?" This revelation of God's nature is radically different from what other religious philosophies teach. The biblical God takes the initiative and reaches out to meet us in our sin and separation. He comes to us where we are—hiding from our Creator, full of fear and self-justification.

The Triumph of God's Grace

God's reaching out to us is biblically termed, "grace." Seeing our need He approaches us in love seeking to draw us back into fellowship with Himself. He does this first by speaking a personal word to us, calling our name. "Adam, where are you?" God always comes to us this way—personally. He knows us and draws near us motivated by infinite love. He meets us with forgiveness as we struggle with fear and self-deception.

Because sin has so confused us, we do not know exactly who we are—a tragic human condition. Mystical eastern religions reduce man to an impersonal "It," who will ultimately be absorbed into the sea of nirvana—the sea of nothingness. Pagan philosophies of the West either glorify man, worshiping him as a god—the measure of all things—or they degrade him into a high-class animal or complicated machine.

Do You Know Who You Are?

A young man in a downtown city Mission, who was struggling with drugs and alcohol once said to my wife, "Why are you doing all this? It's only a Mission." Moments before he had said with a ruthless sneer, "I'm just garbage." Here was a young man who didn't know who he was. In his confusion, and because of his guilt about his behavior, he saw himself only as a piece of garbage. Many people share his sentiments about themselves.

Only when the Judeo-Christian Faith is adopted can you possibly begin to know who you are. You are Adam. You are Eve. You are Man-Woman, created in the image of God, capable of fellowship with the Supreme Power of the Universe. You are the man, the woman whom God loves and seeks to restore to Himself as a child—wayward, disobedient, power-hungry, sinful—yes—but still his child.

"I don't know where I've come from, and I don't know who I am." This is the way Brother Joshua felt, a young man who once played in the Indian theatre as "elephant boy." His father, brother and uncle had all died within a year, plunging him into the depths of despair and self-destruction. Attempting to commit suicide, he had a dramatic encounter with God. He discovered that God not only wanted to reveal Himself, but also to teach Joshua who he was as a person. "Who am I?" cries the human heart in this alienated world. From scared politicians, restless adolescents, confused parents, militant racists, jaded sensualists, oppressed minorities and perplexed majorities, the cry rings out for self-discovery. "I want to know who I am."

Self-Knowledge Comes From God

God's cry, however, is loud and distinct. It rebounds down the centuries, through the lips of the prophets, and finally through the lips of Jesus Christ, "You are the one who is loved by me."

The conversation that took place between God and the first man in the garden provides penetrating insight into how we react when confronted by God. The Lord says to Adam, "Who told you that you were naked? Have you eaten of the tree whereof I told you not to eat lest you die?" God fingers the sore spot. He does not ignore what had happened, but seeks to help man face his dilemma. How can we ever know ourselves unless we admit our moral and spiritual bankruptcy?

We become aware of our separation from God and our inability to close the gulf in two basic ways.

The first way is through the Ten Commandments which express God's moral law, and the second is through the personality of Jesus Christ and his moral perfection. When we stand in the light of the Commandments, we can't help but recognize our inability to measure up to them. The Law, good from God's standpoint, becomes an instrument of judgment to us human beings because it exposes our disobedience and separation from Him. As we examine ourselves in this awesome light, we clearly see our failure to keep these commands, literally and spiritually.

I argued on one occasion with a university student battling with his alcoholism and losing ground. "I may be a drunk on the weekends," he said, "but I'm not a bad person. I'm sure not as bad a some characters I know." He sought to justify himself on the basis of his morality. But if you examine his defense closely, you see that it doesn't hold water. If you were trying to jump across a river six feet wide and missed by one inch, you would be just as wet as the person who tried to jump the distance and missed by two feet. If you want to jump a river six feet wide, you must go all the way.

The Bible makes the same claim with its moral law. If you base your acceptance by God on moral perfection, then his whole law must be perfectly kept. The Apostle James writes, "He who keeps the whole law of God, and yet offends in one point, is guilty of all" (James 2:10). We don't need much convincing to acknowledge that humanity has universally broken the Laws of God. The New Testament does not exaggerate the problem when it states unequivocally, "We are dead in trespasses and sins. . . . the wages of sin is death. . . . for all have sinned and come short of the glory of God" (Romans 6:23, 3:21). It is just as true for the queen in her palace as the beggar on skid row. None of us measures up perfectly—our sin and self-centeredness separate us from God.

Coming to Grips with the Truth in Jesus

The Ten Commandments reveal the truth about ourselves in a negative way, but the New Testament approaches the problem from a different perspective. The New Testament confronts us with the person of Jesus Christ. Compared to his untarnished goodness, we immediately perceive our own moral unworthiness. We respond like Peter when he first met Jesus, "Depart from me, Lord, for I am a sinful man" (Luke 5:8). He didn't believe Jesus would want to associate with a person like him. When we face the wholeness of Jesus Christ, we become cognizant of our own brokenness. When we witness his complete harmony with God, we see our own disharmony with Him. In his light, we see our darkness.

In Charles Dickens' famous novel, *Great Expectations*, a scene includes Miss Haverisher, a woman jilted on her wedding day who subsequently withdrew from life. She lived within her great mansion, confined to the banquet hall. It is here that she meets tragedy. One day, she backed too close to the fireplace and the train of her wedding dress caught fire. Her terrified screams were heard by Pip, who came dashing up the stairs into the semi-darkened room. Assessing the situation, he tore down one of the heavy drapes and wrapped Miss Haverisher's body in it. At this point, brilliant sunlight streams into the once-dark room. And then for the first time in twenty years, the accumulated dust, grime and cobwebs are unveiled. No filth escapes the light.

The application to our lives is obvious. In the presence of Christ, our moral failures and our darkened hearts are exposed. His light plunges the depths of our personal darkness. We discover the moral perversion created by our determination to be self-governing.

The Struggle to Accept Responsibility—"Who, me?"

God searched for man in the garden to lead him back into fellowship with Him. But at first Adam and Eve rejected this. When Adam was questioned about eating the fruit from the forbidden tree, he tried to divert the responsibility to his wife, an empty attempt to justify himself. "The woman you gave me she caused me to eat" (Genesis 3:12). Likewise, the woman also passed the buck, and blamed her decision upon the serpent, "The serpent beguiled me, and I did eat" (Genesis 3:13). How powerfully this speaks to us of our attempts to sidestep our own personal guilt.

We often try to cover up our moral failure and powerlessness by rationalizing it in terms of heredity or environmental factors. "If I hadn't had such a father, I don't believe I would have got into drinking," a young man said to me one day, as he grappled with his own need to find sobriety. We are all guilty of blaming our circumstances and explaining our behavior in terms of necessity. "I had to do it. . . . because . . ." We need to face life and what we have done in the spirit of the tax collector Jesus told about. He acknowledged in the spirit of the tax collector Jesus told about. He acknowledged his moral bankruptcy and cried out from the steps of the temple, "God, be merciful to me a sinner" (Luke 18:13). He made no attempt to justify himself. He did not explain away his actions by blaming it on the Romans, or upon his need to make a living. He simply recognized what he was doing and realized he needed to repent. He turned to God to break his false way of living.

As long as we deny our inadequacy, our impotence to achieve moral perfection, our inability to cope with life, our enslavement to the downward drag of our human nature, we will not be able to appropriate God's help. Like the alcoholic, everyone must face his own powerlessness and admit it.

God's Answer To Our Need

In the final stage of the Fall story, Adam and Eve are banished from the garden. Before they go, however, God substitutes their fig leaves for coverings of animal skins. The text does not try to interpret this action, but obviously God knew they would need something more than just the skimpy leaf coverings.

As we study biblical messages, we see God's desire to cover man's moral shame with something He provides. This introduces us to two major themes to be developed in a later chapter.

Let me simply say at this point that our attempts to cover ourselves, to escape from our responsibility with self-justifying excuses and blaming our behavior on circumstances is complete futility. It only leads to dishonesty and false security. Religious activity cannot strengthen a person's relationship with God, if we resist facing our true selves. Good works and ethical behavior, regardless of their forms, may only be attempts to hide the real problem of our powerlessness.

When you look at an iceberg, it may only appear so large. But six-sevenths of it hides below the surface. The outward moral acts of seemingly good people, may only be hiding the unresolved problems of guilt and spiritual failure.

A restored fellowship with God cannot be achieved by our own the initiative to deal with our sin and the separation it causes. In actual fact, when Adam and Eve ate the fruit of the tree in the garden, something radical happened to them. They died. Not physically, of course, but spiritually. Just as death separates us from life, so our sins separate us from God, a form of spiritual death. And only God can bring life from the dead.

Sin is a Matter of Life and Death

God did not mete out the judgment of death in a spirit of revenge or punishment. It was the natural outcome of man's act of rebellion. In his desire for power, he made it impossible to live under divine control. In taking power to himself he actually lost his real power. His self-will weakened his moral and spiritual character and made him powerless over life's realities. Above all, God became remote and distant, no longer the intimate Father of love. This is one reason why the human race can talk about believing in God, and yet not really know Him intimately. We all feel uncertain about Him. He seems vague and unreal. This only serves to create apprehension in our hearts and inner guilt that we try to cover up, either consciously or unconsciously.

God's Provision

The animal coverings provided by God symbolize that sin and separation from Him can only be eradicated through sacrifice. In his book, *The Origin of Religion,* Robert Brow says the farther back we go in studying man's religious life, the more we discover that it was marked by simple sacrifices. These sacrifices emphasize that the way back to fellowship with God is through sacrifice for sin. This does not imply that sacrifice can manipulate God, to get into his "good books" again. The outward act of sacrifice means far more than just burning an animal on the altar. The sacrificial system of the Old Testament pictured God judging human sin—annihilating it—as the animal sacrifice was destroyed by fire. In the process, God offered love and mercy to the person truly sorry for his sin and selfishness. Released from the guilt of wrongdoing, the worshiper could freely rejoice. Thus, the Psalm writer could say, "Happy is the man whose sins the Lord has covered, and the transgressions of whose life are no longer remembered" (Psalm 32:1). Forgiveness comes through God and does what we cannot do for ourselves.

The Sublime Message

The Christian Faith is the only system of belief that takes sin and forgiveness seriously. It cannot be dealt with flippantly. What would happen if our law courts let a criminal off if he simply told the judge he was sorry for what he had done. The whole balance of justice would be threatened and the moral life of a nation would be seriously undermined.

Can this be any the less true of God, described in the Bible as the righteous Judge, the Holy God? Sin must be challenged and defeated. It is not overcome by an act of mere forgiveness. It has to be paid for.

The good news of Christianity proclaims that God has already done for us what we are totally unable to do. He handled the sin problem Himself. He atoned for it. The word "atonement" means "to make one." God has done this for us. He eliminates our separation from Himself. How? He did it through the cross erected nineteen hundred years ago on a hill outside the city of Jerusalem. In that historic moment, the sin of the world was assumed by Jesus Christ. He accepted its guilt and punishment as if He Himself was responsible. He allowed Himself to be judged and condemned in our place. As he hung on the cross his earthly life ebbing away, He prayed a radical prayer, "Father, forgive them, they know not what they do." This prayer not only encompassed the Roman soldiers and Jewish priests responsible for his crucifixion, but all of us. God the Father heard it. That's what the grace of God means. On our behalf through the sacrificial love of Jesus, He frees us from all condemnation. This is what the Apostle Paul meant when he wrote to Roman Christians, "When as yet we were without strength [powerless], Christ died for the ungodly. God commended his love toward us in that while we were yet sinners [separated from God]

Christ died for us" (Romans 5:6,8).

This is Track Two. Like the other Twelve Steps, it proceeds from the heart of God. When the alcoholic admits his or her powerlessness to cope with the disease of alcoholism, God makes it possible for sobriety to become a reality. When we admit our powerlessness over self-centered living, and turn to God's answer in the love and free grace of Jesus Christ, we find our way back to the God Who has already forgiven us, and Who wants to live in intimate fellowship with us.

CHAPTER TWO

STEP TWO: Came to believe that a power greater than ourselves could restore us to sanity.
Alcoholics Anonymous

TRACK ONE: It is much more difficult than one thinks, not to believe in God.
Andre Gide, "Les Nouvelles Nourtures" 1936

From Atheism to Faith

Late one night after an Alcoholics Anonymous meeting, I sat with Bob in his downtown flat, overlooking the dark flowing Fraser River. He was touched by something I said in the A.A. meeting we had just attended and wanted to talk about it. I had quoted the words of Andre Gide in my little talk, "It is much more difficult than one thinks, not to believe in God," and these words "hit" him.

They triggered a memory of how he came to believe in the existence of God. He was brought up in a home where his parents rejected all belief in a Higher Power. They came to Canada from Russia after the 1917 Revolution, and what they suffered led them to turn their backs on all religion. So Bob was brought up an atheist.

"I had never been to church a day in my life, never read the Bible, never prayed," he told me. "Then World War II came along, and I was a navigator flying over Germany one night. The Gerries were out in full force and our bomber got hit in the tail. As the plane swerved recklessly through the dark sky, I cried out, 'O God, help us.' Somehow, we got back to base in southern England, a flight I will never forget."

"After we landed, I was lying in my bunk and began to think

about what I had said when I thought the plane was going to crash. Why did I cry out to God? You don't even believe there is a God, so why would you cry out to Someone you don't even believe exists? It set me thinking in a way I had never thought before. I began to realize that although I had been taught to reject the idea of a Supreme Power, that something inside me reached out to Him almost spontaneously. I began to feel that maybe all of us believe in God in some way or other but, for various reasons, this truth has become repressed in our subconscious minds. I knew I had to start searching for this Being, if I could ever find Him. It began to happen when I came to Alcoholics Anonymous and began hearing how this Power some people in A.A. called God was really helping alcoholics, like myself, find a new way of life by believing in Him. It wasn't long before I started believing in Him, too. It was harder not to believe than to give in and start believing."

The Necessity of Belief

Bob's experience has repeated for untold numbers of people in A.A. They came to believe not because they actually wanted to, but because they couldn't escape "not believing."

The alcoholic who begins to deal honestly with his or her drinking problem and enters Alcoholics Anonymous often experiences a time of self-searching. The bottom has fallen out of life, and they are desperately seeking faith in something.

As they begin to admit that life has become unmanageable because of their alcohol abuse, many alcoholics listen openly to recovering alcoholics who speak about a Power greater than themselves, Who can lead them outside the insanity of destructive drinking. This Power is called God by most A.A. members. In fact, God is named seven times in the Twelve-Step Program of recovery. This shows how seriously A.A. treats this fundamental reality. God is not an option, to be believed in or not. He is a necessity.

The Evolutionary Hypothesis—Does it Disprove God?

People who have accepted the evolution theory sometimes find it difficult to accept the idea of a Divine Creator in the long history of man's development. Unfortunately, many people with this problem have made philosophical deductions that have no basis in fact. Because they believe that man has evolved from lower life forms to higher, they rule out the possibility of God. Everything happened by chance.

Without expounding the veracity of evolution, I want to emphasize that some of its believers, as well as Christians, have no difficulty with this so-called scientific approach. It does not affect their belief in a God Who created all things in orderly process. They simply believe He chose this method of creation. In no way does it undermine his supremacy over the universe. I say this because the evolution theory is often touted to justify a non-belief in God. Evolution neither proves nor disproves the existence of God. It is simply a widespread theory about creation. But God cannot be proved or disproved in this artificial way. Proof of God's existence comes through personal experience, as well as reason. Science limits itself to observable investigation and, therefore, cannot explain the theological side of life. Honest seekers discover it with other dimensions of proof, by "faith, not by sight," as the well-known poet, Lord Tennyson, so aptly says.

Faith Requires Openness

Newcomers to A.A. need not let their uncertainty about who and what God is keep them from discovering the power He wants to release into their lives to help them. The only requirement is a willingness to discover the reality of God as He unfolds Himself. Thousands of people have entered A.A. with many real and imaginary difficulties about accepting the possibility of God as a Supreme Being. But step by step, they have opened their minds to it, and eventually entered into an experiential faith. Even confirmed atheists have found God when they have honestly explored the possibility.

Jane was such a person. She had many disappointments in life and allowed them to embitter her, creating deep resentments. So, when I met her one night after an A.A. meeting, she said to me haughtily, "How can an intelligent person like you believe in a worn-out concept like God? Don't you know that God no longer exists? Even the theologians say that God is dead, so why are you trying to hold on to such an unproveable assumption?" She came on strong!

"It's a big subject," I replied, "but why don't we get together this week and talk about it?" To my surprise, she agreed.

When she arrived, I asked her if she had ever read Eldon Trueblood's outstanding book, The Philosophy of Religion, an ideal book to lead people, especially students, to a living faith in God. Her reply was negative.

I then went on to say, "Jane, if you're going to be a real atheist you should really understand what atheism is all about. It might shock you to learn that the Bible is not the least bit interested in whether or not you believe in God. The question is never raised in the Bible."

She looked puzzled. "I thought the Bible was all about religion and God," she said.

"It is," I replied, "but not in the way most people think. The Bible recognizes that everyone is religious in one way or another, even the atheist. The question in the Bible is not whether or not you believe in a God or whether or not you believe God exists, but rather, Which god do you believe in? The gods of your own making that you allow to control your life, or the true and living God?"

Jane was still perplexed. She had never had anyone speak to her this frankly.

"What do you mean, Everyone is religious? I'm certainly not. I gave up believing that fairytale long ago. Just one course in philosophy took care of that theory. I'm anything but religious."

"Jane," I responded, "the word religion doesn't mean what you think. Religion encompasses that which is central—whatever holds your life together, whatever idea or person or thing—that is your religion. In the Bible the challenge is, 'You shall have no other gods before Me' (Exodus 20:3). Jesus once said, 'You cannot serve God and man'—materialism (Matthew 6:29). Everyone makes gods out of something. It may be our work, our money, our pleasures, our family life—husband, wife, children—and of course, most commonly, yourself. Everyone of us either believes in the living and true God, or in some other power that exercises control over us. In fact, we may even say we believe in God, as many church people do, but show by our lifestyles that something else is central."

Our conversation went on until the wee small hours. I challenged her to take the idea of atheism seriously. "Read the literature of atheists, like Bertrand Russell, Albert Camus or Jean-Paul Sartre, but also read what believers have written. They have also grappled with the idea of whether or not God is real or just a figment of our own imaginations."

Some months later, we met again after an A.A. meeting. She looked at me with a smile and said, "You know one thing I have discovered? If Bertrand Russell and the other atheists are right, then one thing is certain—you can never be happy. They are such pessimists. I had to decide whether I wanted to go through life unhappy and miserable, or whether I was willing to put God to the test, and find out if He was there or not. That's what I have been doing since the last time we met, and somehow I think He is getting through to me."

Everyone who has difficulty believing in God has to get to the place where he is willing to let go and be willing to let Him reveal Himself. As we are willing to search for Him wherever He might be found, something will happen. You might need to start by examining the intellectual arguments for his existence. Down through the centuries, Christian thinkers have wrestled with the reasons for God's existence. Do not ignore what they have to say.

But in the last analysis, God can't be proven, only experienced. The Bible offers God's challenge, "If you seek me with all your heart, you will surely find me, for I am always ready to be found of those who earnestly seek for me" (Jeremiah 29:13). The only way you can prove the truth of that promise is to seek God wherever He claims to make Himself known. If He is not there, you will not find Him. But if He is, you will enter into the knowledge of God.

Experiment Provides Proof

Alcoholics Anonymous does not make dogmatic statements about God. It simply asserts, "These suggestions are there for you to examine, if you are desperate in your desire for sobriety." As a person examines the claims of the Twelve-Step Program, he or she will find them either true or false. A.A. claims that they are true, but encourages people to find out for themselves. It promises, "Rarely does a person fail who follows our path." Millions of people from every walk of life testify to its veracity.

A.A. wisely challenges people to take one step at a time. Begin in square one—with all your doubts—and then move forward. It demands courage. It involves risks. But life would be paralyzed by fear if we did not exercise faith in many ways, every day. Why not experiment by placing faith in God's existence? You don't have to understand everything about Him to believe in it. This precept encompasses much of life. Electricity is something most people don't understand, at least in depth. Correctly harnessed, its energy provides light for millions of people who simply turn on their light switches. Understand it? Maybe, maybe not. But we still use it whether or not we understand how it works.

This also applies to God. If God exists, we can be certain we will never be able to understand Him fully with our puny, limited brainpower. But we can "experience" Him by "plugging in" to the power He offers, the power of his love. God then releases his energy, enabling the alcoholic to resist the driving inclination to drink uncontrollably. A.A. encourages people, initially, to lay aside their doubts and desire for intellectual proof and experiment with the truth or falseness of God's existence. The truth will not be discovered on an intellectual level.

Doubt—Honest or Dishonest

We must decide to be honest or dishonest doubters.

Jim had been an alcoholic for years. He has lost his wife and was now ruining his health and about to lose his job. He turned to a friend for help, and his friend asked me to contact him. Jim and I met in a downtown coffee shop. He didn't want to invite me to his ramshackle room.

"I just can't believe all this God business," Jim said with hostile eyes.

"Tell me," I said, "what kind of father did you have?"

"Oh, the old man was a tartar," he replied. "You couldn't talk to him about anything. If you disagreed with him, or argued, you got a slap across the face. I learned to shut up when I was around him. He wasn't much of a dad. He was away a lot, drank a lot, and treated my mother like dirt."

"It's hard to think of God as a heavenly Father, when you've got such negative memories of your father," I replied. "Is there anyone in A.A. you admire?"

"Yes," he said, "I really like Bob. He's a great guy. But what does all this have to do with believing in God?"

"Well," I answered, "Bob used to have difficulty believing too. But he took a big step and was willing to risk. He prayed one night, 'Oh God, if there is a God, I am willing to have You speak to me, if You can speak.' He then started to read some passages from the Bible I recommended to him, and before he knew it, he found faith had activated his mind in a surprising way. He had never expected this to happen, but it did. Do you think you could be daring enough to do what he did?"

He looked at me quizzically, and then said, rather slowly, "Well, if I didn't, it would sure show how narrow-minded I am. I guess I could take a shot at it."

So I gave him a copy of the New Testament, along with a Twelve-Step book on A.A. I suggested what he might read in his struggle with unbelief and doubt. He was amazed how faith actually started to emerge.

One night he came to see me. "Cal," he said. "I started to read the Bible with a whole lot of doubt, but before I knew it, doubts started to evaporate and although I don't think I could tell you how it all happened, I think I believe in God. I just can't figure it out, but I know it's happened."

"Jim," I said, "you don't have to understand how your body

digests food and transforms it into energy before you can enjoy eating."

"Of course not," he replied.

"Tell me, do you think you have to understand everything about your bones and muscles before you can enjoy playing soccer?"

"Don't be ridiculous," he retorted.

"Well," I replied, "you don't have to understand how great and powerful God is before taking hold of his power to overcome your alcoholism. We all need to risk and, in an act of faith, ask Him to help us."

As Jim surrendered himself to the reality of God, his sobriety became an increasing day-by-day experience, and his whole way of life pointed in a positive direction.

Honest doubt has a place. Often it's faith in the making. Dishonest doubt, a kind of unbelief, won't take an honest look at the claims made by religious faith. Like Gamaliel Bradford, the great man of culture and the arts, this doubter refuses to read the New Testament for fear of changing some of his long-held views. They resemble butterfly or stamp collectors as they bring out their doubts for display with no intention of dealing with them. They really want to harbor them and not search for the truth seriously.

Honest doubt, on the other hand, often precedes real faith. Ask your questions, present your arguments both for and against the existence of God. See what will happen in the process.

The Supremacy of Science—Good or Bad?

Many people have come into A.A. completely accepting science as the ultimate authority.

A young man attending the University of British Columbia said to me one day while we discussed the claims of Christianity, "If science says it, I believe it. It's my highest authority."

Like millions of people in today's society, he had made science a "sacred cow." In India, among the Hindus, the white cow can roam where it wants and do what it pleases. No one obstructs its path. It enjoys special status—it's sacred. Many people treat the claims of science the same way. What science says must be accepted without reservation.

But as much as we appreciate what science and technology have accomplished, some systems cannot be proven scientifically. A certain piece of music. Is it beautiful or not? A breathtaking sunset. How can you prove its beauty in a scientific way? These attributes belong to the world of the subjective and can only be proven inwardly.

Be Scientific, But In The Right Way

The great contribution of Western science has been its method of testing. It challenges every idea and compels us to submit every claim to an examination. Everything must be subjected to the searchlight of experimental truth. We should not resist its precepts, although we often do.

Alcoholics who doubt the validity of their faith in God are challenged to set aside their doubts temporarily and examine the claims of those who have experienced real faith in Him. Both Alcoholics Anonymous and the Christian Faith stand confident that the truth of God's existence will become obvious.

The new member in A.A. needs to approach the possibility of God in an open-minded, unprejudiced way. It would, in my opinion, violate his freedom to insist that he find the reality of the presence of God in some prescribed manner. For example, if a person has difficulty accepting the Christian understanding of God, then he must begin in his own way. After all, Jesus handled his first followers this way. When they met him initially, He seemed nothing more than a teacher with exceptional ability and conviction, proclaiming the arrival of God's Kingdom. He wasn't wearing a sign on his chest, "I am God." They had to be with him a considerable period of time before they realized that God was revealing Himself through Jesus in a unique way. They listened. They observed. They watched Him in action. It didn't happen overnight.

Faith Takes Time

New members in Alcoholics Anonymous must be given the

same privilege. The solution to overcoming alcoholism doesn't demand theological accuracy at first. Furthermore, God isn't hung up on what we think of Him initially. He will increase our understanding as we develop toward spiritual maturity.

Often an alcoholic comes to sobriety by believing in the A.A. Group, first of all. This identification is called Group Consciousness. Before we react negatively to this approach, we need to remember that this happens in our own lives as children. A newborn baby knows nothing about God. He only knows those people who take care of his needs, usually the parents. The feeding, the changing, the cuddling—essential to the baby—are provided by the two parents. They become "God" to the newborn child. But eventually, the distinction between the parents and God takes shape. The parents, if believers themselves, will explain the existence of another One, infinitely more important than they. That person is God. This kind of process happens in the life of the alcoholic, who has not yet found a uniquely personal understanding of God.

Eventually, the alcoholic will need to move beyond this limited, misconceived understanding of God. This happens when the alcoholic realizes that he or she is a separate, distinct personality from the Group Consciousness of the A.A. meeting and begins to realize that the Higher Power shares this distinction. God is a distinct personality just like us. The Christian claim is that the invisible Creator, has revealed his personality through Jesus of Nazareth. The more that personality is examined, the more the reality of God as a Personal Being takes on new meaning.

Secondhand Faith

I have observed, in my long association with A.A. members, that many people in Alcoholics Anonymous, have lost the "faith" they once felt they believed. Others, for some reason or other, believe the Church they were brought up in has let them down. Now they don't care. At least they feel this way on the surface. They may also inherit a "secondhand faith" from their parents, or the Church—taught the doctrines of the Christian faith without ever experiencing their personal reality. It has been purely a "head trip," with no heart appreciation. This situation needs correction, and the only way it can happen sometimes, is for the secondhand faith to be denied and rejected. It needs to go down the "drain."

Many people have also endured deep disappointments in life, and for this reason they believe God has forsaken them. They have turned away from Him in resentment, deeply hurt that He has seemingly deserted them. Many people find it hard to accept that God really does care.

I remember ministering to an alcoholic woman, Mary, who was a battered child and abused sexually by her father. Yet, she was brought up in a religious home where the parents went to church. She even attended a Bible school herself when she was older. But one day, she decided that nothing she had been taught to believe about God was acceptable to her anymore. She threw the whole concept overboard, and lived without God for many years. Only after she came into A.A. did she experience God in a different way.

When a person struggles to regain an acceptable understanding of God's nature, he doesn't deserve the condemnation of the Church and Christian people. The alcoholic simply needs to hear that A.A. works—if they will consider it carefully and not take half measures.

Religion Can Block the Way

The person who has had a "brush" with religion, or what I often call, Churchianity, whatever form it may take, often finds it harder to believe in God, than someone unexposed to a particular religious opinion. People brought up in a pseudo-religious atmosphere with the observance of religious duty and without inner conviction, often "chuck" this hypocrisy and decide to be true to themselves. They rightly disallow its place in their lives. Having put this false religion to the test, they have discovered its bankruptcy. They remain, however, unable to distinguish between true and false religious practice.

May was a very religious person when I first met her. She was full of hostility, however, toward her husband Barry, who had been an alcoholic for most of their married life. Interestingly, he eventually found sobriety through A.A. and later found a living faith in Christ. But sometimes he would "fall off the wagon" because of her nagging in the home. This gave him an excuse to go on a "bender," which only intensified May's self-pity, self-right- eousness and feelings of superiority. Finally, their marriage broke up. When this happened, May felt an urge to start drinking herself. Her nominal Christianity had no power to give her strength for daily living. I found it impossible to convince her that she was no different than Barry. Her religion kept her from seeing God from a perspective of dependence. Tragically, one night she took too much alcohol with her sleeping pills and died in her sleep.

What has to happen for truth to flow freely into our lives? We all know that rivers clogged with debris must be blasted before the water flows freely again. The same is true for the person whose mind has become clogged with prejudice, defiance, self-righteousness, resentment and self-pity. These must be blasted away before the new freedom of God's power can flow. Agnostics need to clear out the debris of uncertainty, and start afresh their search for the seemingly hidden God. A person bewildered as to who is right—the believer, the agnostic, or the atheist—often needs to assess these various points of view.

I have listened to many A.A. people tell me that their childhood faith had to go down the drain before they could discover a faith with some reality to it. Sometimes a person has to undergo what I call a "scorched earth policy" before they can grow green grass. I have known many university students who had to lose the secondhand faith of their childhood and wander in a "no man's land" of unbelief before they were willing to consider the claims of Christ. This also holds true for the alcoholic.

Cut-Flower Faith

We have all seen a beautiful bowl of cut flowers decorating a table. We admire their beauty and fragrance. But we all know that those flowers are actually dead, because they have been cut off from their roots. Soon their color will face, the fragrance will disappear, and they will be thrown into the garbage.

The same deterioration happens when beliefs divorce behavior. Many alcoholics have grown up in homes where Christian ethics were practiced to some degree, yet without a living faith in God. I call it "cut-flower religion. It looks good on the surface because it supports many morally acceptable precepts—love, peace, honesty, tolerance, etc. But this source of morality has no roots in personal faith. The power to love, to be honest and tolerant can't surface from nowhere. It comes from vital faith in God, the Author of all good. All moral virtues originate within Him, and can't be detached from faith and commitment to Him. When this happens, morality and ethics may linger for awhile, but eventually, they will wither and die.

One Saturday night after an A.A. meeting, a bunch of us sat around discussing the talks we had heard from our various members.

"I certainly don't agree with Bob's statement that you have to believe in God if you are going to live the good life," said Mary. "I've known lots of people who have come into A.A. who didn't believe in God, and yet apart from their "alcohol sins," they have lived pretty decent lives." Several others agreed with her.

"I don't think you have to believe in God before you can express the attributes of understanding, kindness and fair play," Mary went on. "I know that these things exist without having to believe in some supreme power. I'll bet all of us sitting around this table practice the Golden Rule, but we don't necessarily have to believe that Jesus is divine or something. Lots of people live by that time-honored principle who don't have much faith in God."

I felt that I was the odd man out, as I listened to the feelings being expressed.

"What do you think about this, Cal?" someone asked.

"Well," I replied, "I know that many people appear to live good lives, and are still agnostics, or even church types who have no living faith. But I look at it this way, Do any of you remember when our railway tickets used to have these words printed on the bottom of each ticket, 'Not good, if detached'? I think that when morality is cut off or detached from God, it may appear to be good, but in fact it has lost the quality of real goodness. I think that is one reason Jesus said to the man who called Him good Master, 'Why do you call me good? There is only One who is good, and that is God' (Matthew 19:17). He wanted us to realize that all goodness comes from God, and if we break fellowship with Him, our own moral goodness becomes a false claim. Completely dependent upon God, Jesus emphasized that any good news from Him originated from God, and no one else."

"You know," Tom piped up, "I think you are right. I was brought up in a home where moral values were pretty important, but when I started drinking, all my moral standards were powerless to keep me from drinking too much. I didn't have any inner strength to help me rise above the downward drag of my alcoholism. Everything went haywire, including my moral values, and I began to sense complete moral bankruptcy. It wasn't until I took Step Three to heart, and turned my will and life over to the care of God, that my sense of right and wrong got sorted out, and I began to have the power to live the so-called 'good life.' "

Alcoholics Anonymous attempts to deal sympathetically with the person whose moral fibre has disintegrated because they have no power to resist the vicious hold of their alcohol addiction. This non-judgmental attitude has helped them discover the possibility that power from God will not only set them free from their alcohol dependency, but also produce a new morality born out of living faith.

The Bankruptcy of Intellectualism

Another problem some alcoholics face is false intellectualism. They come into A.A. believing their intellects sufficient to overcome uncontrolled drinking. Yet, so far, their intelligence hasn't kept them from falling into its quagmire. Actually, it impedes the humility needed to find the help available. Unfortunately, their own intellects—complete with quick-wittedness, astuteness and a critical spirit—have blinded them. They do not necessarily flaunt these characteristics, but inwardly they feel head and shoulders above the ordinary rank and file of those they deem deficient in brain power. Reason reigns supreme. Scientific pursuits can discover the whole truth about mankind's perplexing problems. Difficult hurdles of life can be overcome by the application of good reasoning.

But alcoholism perniciously undermines these assumptions about the ability of reason. The intellectual world of the classroom and the science laboratory have produced as many alcoholics as skid row. In the Mission where I served we had men highly trained as university graduates, professors and scientists, yet totally deficient of power to kick their alcoholic addiction. They knew their drinking was illogical, but they had no power to remedy it. And their drinking, of course, deteriorated their ability to think clearly. It is well documented that alcoholism reduces intellectual capability, creating a treacherous enemy.

The intellectually sustained alcoholic must admit that he or she does not have reasonable answers to help them with some deeper life issues. Their inflated reason exercised with pride throughout their lives, has proven bankrupt in their battle with alcoholism. Those people in A.A. who used to think like them serve as eye-openers. They know the futility of brainpower alone. They discovered that the god of reason had to be dethroned. Overconfident intellectualism could not free them from addiction. The conflict between unchallenged reason and unchanging faith to overcome addiction can only be resolved by realizing the soundness of faith in God.

Humility—The Vital Ingredient

The Alcoholics Anonymous Twelve-Step Program, influenced by the Christian understanding of life, insists that humility dominate a person's life. This virtue predicates the discovery of a new life, freed from the domination of alcohol.

Jesus refers to it in the Sermon on the Mount, that opens with the words, "Blessed [or happy] are the poor in spirit, for theirs is the Kingdom of God" (Matthew 5:2). Another way of saying it was simply, How blessed are those people who are willing to recognize their poverty and spiritual bankruptcy. If in humility they seek help, they will find it. When this happens, the door to self-discovery, as well as God-discovery, will open. Freedom from control by life-destroying habits will also begin. The humility of Jesus was a source of great spiritual power. As He submitted to the Father in all things, He demonstrated the power of God working through Him. For this reason, He could change every aspect of life for good. He acknowledged that the Son, "can do nothing of himself; he can do only what he sees the Father doing" (John 5:19). There was no inflated self-trust, but rather a confidence in God alone to unlock the storehouse of spiritual energy.

People can never rise above the power of alcohol addiction until they have come to the end of their intellectual ropes and called out for help. This act of humility can wed the intelligence to a new awareness that only God can liberate the alcoholic from compulsion to drink.

Robert was my professor of philosophy in my first year at university. He was a brilliant man with innate ability to convey knowledge in the classroom. However, in the process of social drinking, he crossed the invisible line that separates this kind of drinking from problem drinking. He came regularly to classes hardly able to stagger to the lectern. Fellow professors reasoned with him, trying to help him see that he was ruining his career. But nothing changed. Eventually, he was dismissed from his job, and ended up, in due time, on skid row, bereft of money, family and friends.

One winter evening, he wandered into a Rescue Mission, seeking something to eat, and a place to sleep. But he found something more. Someone took a personal interest in him, refusing to reject him because he was an alcoholic. He invited Robert to stay in the Mission for awhile, which he did because there was nowhere else to go.

Over a period of three months, as he talked with counsellors who cared and began to realize his own powerlessness over his drinking problem, he turned his intellectual mind over to God. This act of humility released a power that began to free him from his addiction. "In no way could I have beaten this without God, Whom unfortunately, I had rejected for so many years of my life."

Overcoming Religious Prejudice

Throughout the history of Alcoholics Anonymous, another kind of person has emerged whose false assumptions need to be challenged. This person haughtily sweeps aside the presumption that the Bible, religion in general and Christianity in particular, have any place in the life of the self-sufficient. The Bible is regarded as outdated myths, based upon meaningless past superstitions. The language of the Bible has stifled any understanding of its essential message. Even with new translations in modern idioms, some people still refuse to consider it. Like Gamiliel Bradford, the great man of letters previously mentioned, they have not read the New Testament for fear of changing some of their long-held views. These people, confused by the Bible's morality, believe it impossible of attainment, or so far from practicality that it's not worth considering.

This type of alcoholic regards the institution of the Church and the people who attend church, as hypocrites, whose insincerity signals a religious facade that only impedes living in the real world. The history of religious wars and the brutal treatment to which professing Christians have subjected their enemies point to the "illusion of religion." As such, it has no appeal for those attempting to face life in the modern world.

"You don't mean to tell me that I need to 'get religious' in order to stop this damn drinking," Mary said to me, as I visited her one evening on a Twelve-Step call.

She had been drinking seriously for a month, and her apartment was in total shambles. But she had sobered up enough to phone for help. So I was there to encourage her to take the step that might bring her to Alcoholics Anonymous. Somewhere along the line, she had discovered that A.A. talks about God and this angered her. As we talked about the reason she felt so offended by the concept of God, I discovered that it wasn't just an intellectual problem.

"My old man believed in God, but I've no use for him," she

snarled.

As I discussed her relationship with him, I discovered that she was the victim of incest at a very early age, and the thought of him terrified her. Every time she thought of him, she found herself rejecting everything he stood for, including his religious beliefs.

"Why would God—if there is a God—let that happen to me?" she wailed, as tears filled her eyes.

I could identify with her, because faith in God is communicated to us by our parents. If breakdown occurs at that level, getting from the misdeeds of the earthly father to belief in the heavenly Father proves difficult indeed.

I agreed that her father had obstructed her discovery of God's reality. But I encouraged her to shift her gaze to someone she admired, someone who might possibly have a faith in God that was real and sincere.

Then she remembered a youth leader from her church, whom she deeply admired and loved. This young man had shown her love and lived out his faith consistently. But he was transferred from her parish, just about the time her father began to abuse her. She felt abandoned by God, and began to doubt his existence.

But that night she was desperate, and craved help for her chronic drinking. She felt good about my coming to her apartment in response to her call for help. And so, as I met with her many times later, her mind gradually relinquished the hurt, the resentment and the unbelief she had harbored. The barricades that had separated her from God fell. Faith began to emerge slowly. But it did grow and become a reality for her. Because I believed in God and took time to reach out to her in her time of need, faith was nurtured in her heart.

I believe Jesus was driving at this when He said to his disciples, just before his death, "You believe in God, believe also in me" (John 14:1-2). Sometimes God seems so remote and distant, totally uninvolved in our lives. But Jesus seems to be saying to these men who had been following Him for about three years, You may find it hard to experience God, even though you believe He exists. But if you find it hard to believe in the invisible God of the universe, then look to me, because in so doing, faith in God will become more personal.

People often say, Where is God anyway? Show me where He is and then I'll believe in Him. God knows we need this. He shows us what He is like through Jesus Christ, Who interprets in human terms the reality of God. He gets down to where we live, where we experience the sins, the hurts, the tragedies of life. He demonstrates through loving action that God is not far away or distant, but near and ready to help free us, forgive us, and make us whole.

STEP TWO: Came to believe that a power greater than myself could lead me to sanity. *Alcoholics Anonymous*

TRACK TWO: I doubt, therefore I believe. *Marshall Fishwick*

What Does It Mean To Believe?

"I simply can't believe. It sounds too far-fetched," John said to me, as we talked about the meaning of faith, and how it relates to life.

"What do you think it means to believe?" I replied.

He paused, then blurted out, "Believing something without using your mind."

Many people reflect this thinking when they consider the reality of God. They think that their brains must shift into neutral in order to accept it. Believing, however, penetrates the whole of life and, engaged properly, affects your life and behavior.

Belief can either be a passive acceptance of an impersonal truth or an active acceptance of truth that affects my personal life. For example, if I say I believe in the moon, I mean I accept the fact that a heavenly planet called the moon exists in our solar system. The science of astronomy has discovered interesting facts about the moon. The moon reflects the light of the sun. About 246,000 miles away from the earth, its temperature is 127°C below at noon, and 173°C above at night. I can learn many other facts and admit to their veracity. Yet, I don't incorporate their importance into my day-by-day life.

Likewise, when I say, "I believe in Australia," I acknowledge what geography claims is true. An island continent exists in the southern hemisphere. Although I have never visited there personally, enough evidence enables me to profess belief in such a place. But again, I live my personal life apart from its existence. My belief is impersonal.

However, when I say I believe in my wife, my mother, my father or my friend, I enter a different realm of believing. These people have affected my personal life in significant ways and mean a great deal to me. My belief in them is not impersonal. My relationship with them influences the order of my life, makes me who I am today. This belief radically differs from my believing in the moon or in Australia.

The same principle applies to faith in God. Some people have an impersonal belief in his existence that does not affect their lives. Others have a personal faith that links them to God in a life-changing way. Alcoholics Anonymous and the Christian Faith stress this latter form of belief when they state the importance of believing.

Belief Demands Response

But even personal belief demands a response to God demonstrated through obedience.

One summer I worked in the grocery delivery department of a major department store in Vancouver. I met a young man who became a friend. When he learned I was a Christian believer, he bombarded me with questions about science and religion. A skeptic himself, he said he could never believe in the existence of God unless proven to him as a clear, unmistakably scientific fact. After many attempts to present the reasonableness of belief in God, I made no impression upon him.

One day at lunch, when the subject of religion re-emerged for discussion, I said, "John, if I could prove to you that there is a God—prove it to you without a shadow of doubt—would you be willing to turn your life completely over to God and serve Him the rest of your life?

He sat quietly for a moment, in pensive reflection. Then looking me straight in the eye, he replied, "No, I don't think I could go that far."

"John," I responded, "that is what believing in God is all about. It doesn't mean that you just believe in his existence. He wants to engage a relationship with you. The prerequisite, however, is complete surrender to his directives. Belief in God demands it."

Proofs Not Important

As you read the Bible, you will notice the absence of intellectual proofs for the existence of a Supreme Being. His majestic presence is assumed and undeniable. To those who feel everything must be scientifically proven, this must seem like a ridiculous assumption. Surely there must be some reasonable proofs for his existence. If He exists, He must be discoverable to the reasoned mind. If He is non-existent, that will become obvious too.

Throughout the history of Christianity, leading thinkers and theologians have made many attempts to prove the existence of God. Their logical reasoning "proves" that belief in God as the Supreme Power of the universe does not require blind, unthinking faith. Religious scholars, including Father Schmidt and Dr. Samuel Zwemer, have claimed that the acknowledgement of a god is indigenous to all people, regardless of their culture or their particular era of religious development.

On the other hand, these proofs have been attacked and undermined by leading philosophers, especially since the period in European history known as the Enlightenment. They attempted to prove conclusively that God's existence cannot be sustained by logical argument. The Bible favors this point of view, rather than the former, because, as I have already stated, biblical writers present no case for the existence of God. For them, it is already a basic axiom of life. To them, reasonable people perceive God as Creator, without need of reason to bolster his reality. The Bible challenges us not to discover the reality of God, but to give up the false gods—the idols—we have created as substitutes for the living and true God. Biblical writers knew that people could have many reasons for believing God's existence, yet still be far away from Him personally.

Everyone is Religious

Biblical faith perceives that all mankind is essentially religious. By religion I mean, that encompassing belief, philosophy or point of view in a person's life central to his being. Biblical writers call that "god."

The prophets of Israel knew that a person could harbor logical reasons for God's existence while still worshiping their own all-important "little gods." This constitutes real atheism—the practical rejection of the true and living God for something else. Again, biblical faith doesn't challenge the existence of God but rather, what constitutes the centrality of our lives—your personal god. Everyone, therefore, is religious, including the atheist. A person may not believe in the God Who created the universe, but still have something central to his life. It may be money, business, family, friends, children, goals and ambitions, church, good works, or most commonly, ourselves. These become gods in our lives, what we really believe in more than anything else. When Alcoholics Anonymous asks the alcoholic to believe in a Power greater than himself, he must understand what real belief means.

The Power of God

What power must we believe? What describes this Power that A.A.'s Twelve Steps and the Christian Faith call God? I call it the supreme power of love. What can rival it? Can nuclear power, atomic power, economic power, black power, or Arab power? Granted, each contains some degree of power. But do they actually benefit our lives or confuse and destroy us? Probably the latter. However, wherever the power of love operates, you can be sure that benefits will accrue. The Apostle John writes to a group of first-century Christians and states, "God is love" (1 John 4:8). God's intrinsic nature displays dynamic, self-giving and unconditional love. This certainly means that God is essentially personal, because nothing is more personal than being loved and loving.

This is what I believe Christians mean when they confess, I believe in God, the Father Almighty. God, unlimited in love, wants to set us free from the tyranny that would rule over us and rob us of meaningful life. Beneath his Ten Commandments that help us experience freedom lies a foundation of love. When He gave them to the people of Israel, He prefaced them with the words, "I am the Lord your God which brought you up out of the land of Egypt" (Exodus 20:2). Here God indicates his primary concern that they might be free from four centuries of slavery. He wanted them free.

And so Moses declares to the king, "Let my people go." The Ten Commandments provided them with a basis for freedom. Jesus reinforced it by stressing that loving God and loving our fellow man was the heart of the Law. The Apostle Paul also stressed it. "Love is the fulfillment of the law" (Galatians 5:14). Without love you cannot obey the spirit of the command. And without the Law to govern your life you cannot know real freedom. For example, a train can travel anywhere it wants to, from Halifax to Vancouver, as long as it remains on the two tracks provided. But if it "jumps" the tracks, it relinquishes the ability to move forward. The same principle applies to human life. If we reject the laws of God to live as we determine ourselves, we will be controlled by other influences. This happens when the alcoholic begins to be "hooked" on alcohol. He forfeits freedom and becomes subject to a power beyond his control. But if the alcoholic acknowledges a Power greater than any other power, liberation can begin. Its essence is the love of God.

The more we submit ourselves to God's control and the expression of love—his commandments—the freer and more loving we become. This reflects the true nature of power.

I hadn't seen Bruce for several years when I met him one night in an A.A. meeting. I knew him in university as a very harsh, opinionated person. He loved fraternity party life and somewhere along the way he crossed the invisible line of social, party drinking, to a life of uncontrolled alcoholism. Friends tried to help, but he refused to listen, unwilling to seek help. The last time I saw him was in court when his wife had charged him with assault.

Needless to say, I was astonished to see him at this A.A. meeting. We immediately picked up where we had left off.

"What's happened to you?" I queried.

"Well," he said with a big smile, "I spent six months in jail at Okalla. But they had an A.A. meeting there, so I thought I'd better go. I didn't have much faith that anything would happen. I was so down in the dumps. I knew I'd lost Helen, and I don't blame her. In fact, the best thing that ever happened was her laying charges. It forced me to look at myself. So, I started going to the meetings in jail. I found so much love and acceptance at the meetings that at first I couldn't believe that it was for real. But gradually, the sincerity of the people began to get to me. They were so accepting, and because we were all struggling with the same problem, I felt they understood what I was going through. I felt loved and accepted by them, and I guess that gave me the determination to do something about my drinking. As I attended regularly, listening carefully, I began to feel that I no longer wanted alcohol as part of my life. And that's why I'm here tonight." The power of love had taken human form and its expression through the members of that prison A.A. group, released energy sufficient to help Bruce want to change his destructive patterns of living.

Christianity teaches the same principle about God. It asserts that this almighty Power of love donned human form in Jesus of Nazareth. His life story, contained in four accounts (Gospels) in the New Testament, expressed perfect power and the freedom released by love. He loved, first of all, by giving Himself completely to the Father. On one occasion He said, "I can do nothing by myself" (John 5:17). He then expressed perfect love by giving Himself to others for the sake of their need to be free. Deliverance from disease, hatred, pride and self-righteousness were his prime concerns. He announced his manifesto of freedom to his own people by reading the words of the prophet, Isaiah, applying them to Himself.

The Spirit of the Lord is upon me.
For He has anointed me to preach the gospel
to the poor
To heal the brokenhearted
To proclaim recovering of sight to the blind
To delivery the captives
To proclaim the year of the Lord's Salvation
Luke 4:18

Jesus didn't just talk about love and freedom, He embodied them. As He moved among people, He ever sought to free them from bondage by the power of his great love. He did not come into the world to condemn the world, but to liberate it. All who met Jesus and allowed his power to touch their lives, experienced forgiveness, cleansing and healing—body and mind. They began to accept themselves and experience freedom in the depths of their beings.

When Alcoholics Anonymous calls upon the alcoholic to believe in a Power greater than himself or herself, the Christian faith says that this Power is evidenced through love. Unfortunately, Christians have not always expressed this love in the long history of the Church. But whenever Christians have really believed God, not just given lip service to his existence, they have been set free to love others. People like Mother Theresa of Calcutta, Kagawa of Japan and others like them know that when Divine love is released into the lives of needy people, they begin to experience the love of God for themselves. It changes and transforms human life and society. Fundamental to successful, creative, social action is the power of God's love in Christ. Alcoholics Anonymous, begun by two men controlled and motivated by their love for fellow men and women suffering from destructive drinking, provides ample testimony.

The Fullness of Love

God's ultimate love was revealed at the cross where Jesus forgave his enemies for his unjust crucifixion. In the hour of deepest suffering, when He could easily have been preoccupied by pain, He thought of his crucifiers. "Father, forgive them, they know not what they do" (Luke 24:34) was uttered in deepest agony. In that moment, the love of God in all its fullness was released. Nothing could deter it.

Furthermore, Christians believe that Jesus not only died, but that He was raised to life by the power of God's triumphant love. This illustrates that the power of God brings life from death, and many alcoholics have experienced this personally. The love of God in Christ, displayed in his sacrificial and triumphant love, can set us free from insanity, not only from alcoholism—from any way in which lovelessness controls, manipulates and destroys human relationships. In the resurrection of Jesus from the dead, God makes known that his love cannot be destroyed. It creates the possibility of new life.

The Need for Resurrection Power

We need resurrection power to escape the tombs of death and destruction. John's Gospel, Chapter 11, records a story about a man named Lazarus Jesus raised to life. Coming out of the tomb, he was wrapped in traditional grave clothes. Jesus' first command to those standing near was, "Loose him and let him go." Although he was alive, he still needed to be freed from his restrictive grave clothes. He couldn't do it by himself; he needed the assistance of others.

The same principle applies to us, as we seek freedom from personal bondage. When Christ is accepted into our lives, we begin to experience life—eternal life—as the Bible describes it, a new quality of existence. But we also have to be freed from patterns of behavior that keep us bound. And we need others to help us. Alcoholics Anonymous activates this principle. In its meetings, a power of loving acceptance sets the alcoholic free as he acknowledges the truth about what others experience. During the Twelve-Step Program, the character defects are confronted. As we deal with them, we are set free.

This experience of freedom also happens in that spiritual fellowship called the Church. In relationship with other believers, Christians can experience day-by-day deliverance from those "grave clothes" that rob us of liberty. In the context of the cross and resurrection, truths take hold of our hearts, and we discover the reality of the words, "Divine love always has and always will meet every human need" (words over the chancel of a church in Vancouver).

Love Overcomes

Lack of love marred and twisted Jane's life. She grew up in an alcoholic home where both parents drank seriously. Her parents deprived her of food and clothing in order to finance their drinking habits. At age four, she was taken from these parents and given to foster parents. Unfortunately, they remained detached from her, although she had more to eat and wear. When Jane reached high school she began to drink, not because she enjoyed it, but because it helped ease the pain of her love-starved life.

One night after an A.A. meeting, Jane and I sat talking. I had provided her with transportation to and from the meeting. As we talked about her six months of sobriety she said, "I can't get over it. I've only been in A.A. six months, and I feel like a new person."

"How's that?" I asked.

"In one way it's hard for me to put my finger on it, and yet I know that two things are happening. I'm being freed from hatred of my parents and foster parents on the one hand, and experiencing a new kind of acceptance I've never known on the other. It's wonderful to be loved for who you are. I've never known anything like this before."

"If you are discovering the power of love so deeply on this human level, Jane," I responded, "how do you think God thinks of you?"

"I've not given that much thought," she said, "even though I believe there is a God. But then, I've never really known whether He loved me or not."

"Well," I said, "that is what Jesus Christ is all about. He is God getting down to our level and helping us see in a concrete, human way, that God's love is for real. When you see Jesus loving and accepting others, He claimed that God was working through Him. You've already begun to experience something of that through the people who have become your friends in A.A. But they are only human and will make mistakes. They may even fail you sometimes, because they're not perfect. But the perfect love of God, revealed so beautifully in Christ, will never fail you, will never let you down."

Jane could hardly believe it, and yet she let it happen without trying to explain it. She simply accepted that she was worth the sacrifice and let it heal her wounded heart. After all, if Christ was willing to die for her, she was worth everything. And his love for her was unconditional—no strings attached.

When we accept the fullness of God's love in Jesus Christ, we can overcome every problem, every degradation that tries to rob us of freedom. Nothing can impede us when the power of God's love becomes our central focus. This is how the early Christians made such an impact upon their generation. "By this shall all men know that you are my disciples if you have love one for another" (John 13:35). Even their enemies could see their love that overcame hatred and won the day against the evil that sought to destroy them. This kind of love works like yeast placed into dough. It makes the dough rise and become a loaf of bread, able to feed and strengthen the body. So the love of Christ incorporated into our lives begins to change us—our attitudes, our prejudices, our lifestyles. It revolutionizes man's inhumanity to man. It elevates those degraded by others. People discover their worth as sons and daughters of God under its liberating power. This has typically happened down the centuries to this present day.

Alcoholics Anonymous exists for this reason. The founders, moved by the love of God in Christ, became concerned for those suffering from alcoholic addiction. The Twelve Steps outline the way to experience the freedom of God's love. Not only alcoholics, however, need to be set free from the bondage of negative, unproductive living. The more everyone yields to this Power, fully revealed in Christ, the more alive they become. We all can discover what it means to say with the Apostle Paul, "For me to live is Christ" (Philippians 1:21). The less we yield to this love, on the other hand, the more we live lives characterized by death, separation and alienation. The Good News of Jesus Christ seeks to invade our lives with his radical love. The more we yield to its claims, the more power we have to live free from the encumbrances of life.

CHAPTER THREE

STEP THREE: Made a decision to turn my will and my life over to the care of God, as we understood Him.

Alcoholics Anonymous

TRACK ONE: My wise and faithful maid said in response to the question of what keeps people from believing, "Too stiff to bend, I guess." *Theodore P. Ferris*

The Key that Opens the Door

When M. Pierre François Boussard, one of Napoleon's military engineers, discovered the Rosetta Stone in the desert sands of northern Egypt, he enabled archaeologists to unlock the secret writings of the ancient pyramids. The hieroglyphics had baffled men for centuries, but now they could be interpreted through the code this stone contained.

We also need a key to discover the reality of the God Who is there. The Third Step in Alcoholics Anonymous clarifies how God can become a present reality to us and not just an abstract religious idea. He provides the key that opens the door to knowing Him—faith. But even before we can use this key we must be willing to seek God wherever He may be found. This involves surrendering our wills to his to discover the power of his caring love.

The Need to Experiment

Tom Reiss, an English evangelist, once professed agnosticism. His Anglican brother, a Christian minister, challenged him one day.

"So you are an agnostic. Do you know what that really means?"

"Well, I think I do," said Tom. "It's a person who doesn't believe."

"Not exactly," replied his brother. "It's a person who does not know whether there's a God or not. He's completely unsure, but he's willing to experiment. If you say you're not sure whether there is a God or not, why don't you put it to the test? For six months live as an unbeliever. But then for the next six months live like a believer and see what happens."

"Sounds like a fair deal," Tom replied. "What you're saying is, that if there is no God, I won't find Him and if there is one, He'll probably show Himself."

"That's right," replied his brother. "Put it to the test. Like Hamlet . . . to believe or not to believe, that is the question."

So Tom experimented. He lived like an atheist for six months, with total disregard for anything religious. Then he began to live like a believer. He went to church, began to read Christian literature, including the Bible; he began to pray and to talk to God as if He was there. And as he did this, committing himself to doing it wholeheartedly, the very thing his brother hoped would happen, did. He came into a living faith. But he had to be willing to experiment. He had to be willing to take that step of faith.

Now faith and surrender are two things greatly misunderstood. Some people imagine that faith believes something contrary to reason, but accepts it blindly, despite the evidence. In this age of science, many people demand proofs for the existence of God before they decide to believe in Him.

But God is not like the pot of gold at the end of the rainbow. The knowledge of God comes as we willingly experiment by seeking Him and allowing Him to reveal Himself. In this process, you must be willing to believe his Word. Otherwise, He will remain just a philosophical or theological principle, and not a present reality.

One evening I was leading a study group of people who had found sobriety through A.A., but wanted to understand more about the Twelve Steps. So we were going through the steps methodically and reached Step Three.

"I don't know what you mean by faith," Brian said with a puzzled look on his face.

I had anticipated this question before we began the study group, so I had taken a dollar out of my pocket and hid it in the palm of my closed hand.

"I have a dollar here," I said. "The first person who comes over to me may have it."

They all looked at me quizzically. Then John got up from his chair and came over to me. I opened my hand and he took the dollar bill.

"How many of you actually believed I had the dollar?" I asked. Everyone put up their hand. "No, you didn't," I said. "The only one who believed was John. He was the only one who was prepared to take me at my word and come over here and get the dollar." Everyone laughed heartily. They realized they had only had an intellectual belief, but weren't willing to experiment. They weren't willing to put my word to the test. That takes faith. It's not just believing in an abstract God. It takes Him at his word and discovers the truth personally.

Words Call for Action

Step Three in Alcoholics Anonymous comes to us in hope, challenging us to risk ourselves in the adventure of faith. Then we can discover for ourselves, the God Who is ready to be found.

Each of the Twelve Steps of A.A. demands action. Step Three calls us to the action of faith and surrender. What often keeps us, however, from entering into the knowledge of God and the reality of his power, are our fears, stubbornness and self-will, which demand that we continue controlling our own lives. The Higher Power, God, cannot be known as long as we insist on "being in the driver's seat of life." If He actually wields greater power than we do, then reason demands that we yield. We must obviously submit to any power or authority that stands over us, such as government, police, school principals, managers and bosses. The tragedy of societal disorder lies in its resistance to legitimate authority, and its right to exercise measured control over our behavior. Because we so often resist these controls, our lives become miserable, undisciplined and destructive. To acknowledge God as the ultimate Power of the universe is to yield to the importance of knowing Him.

Choosing the Legitimate Power

In Alcoholics Anonymous, God is often described as the Higher Power. I have already touched on the meaning of that Power, seen in the unfolding of the reality of love. We have already noted the many expressions of power—be it racial, political, nationalistic, democratic, socialistic, communistic, financial or physical. These various forms of power bear upon our daily activity and the order of our lives in many ways. We all live under some kind of power or authority. We cannot escape it. Even the hermit who imagines that his withdrawing from society frees him from power struggles still needs power. He needs the protection of the state even to continue living in this isolated, detached way. All of us are influenced by the power of friends, family, and fashion. We must also live by the laws of nature, learned through disciplined studies. These forms of power influence our lives continuously.

A.A. directs us to the greatest Source of power—God. He personifies the power of love. No power supercedes it as it undergirds our spiritual understanding of God. Mercifully He makes this power available whenever we acknowledge its reality.

Live Through Love

During World War Two in Britain, many mothers served behind the lines to support the men on the front. Their children were placed in nursing homes designed to care for them. But even though these homes were completely sanitary, children began to die by the dozens. No one seemed to know why, and it took a long time to figure out. Eventually, the reason surfaced. These children died from lack of physical contact with their mothers. They withered up inside, longing for love. To remedy the situation, doctors prescribed a half hour, or three-quarters of an hour for these children to be hugged and cuddled each day. They couldn't live without love.

Deprivation of love lies behind our feelings of insecurity and warps our emotional relationships with people. This tragedy mars the lives of so many not accepted unconditionally in their childhood. They find it difficult to believe that Supreme Being called God really cares for them. They have known only little tangible love from family or friends. This is why divine love must first be translated into human terms, so that they can begin to experience it on this level.

I met Nancy through Alcoholics Anonymous, and when she discovered that I was a Christian Minister she blurted out, "How can there be a God when there is so much suffering and pain in this world? I simply can't believe that there's anyone 'Up there' who cares a fig." This lashing out against God revealed her deep resentment toward her cruel, unthinking father. I helped her come to grips with the probability that her father was undoubtedly victimized by his own family background, and that he didn't know how to love her because he had not been loved by his family. This gradually sank in. She began to release her hostility and finally, she forgave him.

As she received my loving acceptance, she opened up to what I said about God. One night after A.A., she and I were sitting with a few of her friends in a restaurant having coffee. One of the fellows spoke up.

"You know," Guy said, "believing in God isn't so difficult once you've begun to feel that someone on this earth loves you too. You say to yourself, 'If someone on this earth can love me without any strings attached, I suppose the Supreme Being probably could accept you, warts and all.' "

Nancy was listening carefully, not only to Guy, but to the others who shared their experiences of seeing God's love translated into action through other people.

When I drove Nancy home, she was quiet, and then she said, "You know, I guess I've always wanted to believe that there was Someone out there who cared, but it was so hard to get beyond my Dad, and the way he treated me. But now that I've forgiven him, and worked out my feelings about him, I find that believing in a heavenly Daddy isn't so difficult. In fact, I want to believe."

In Step Three, the alcoholic is invited to take a step of faith, and yield his or her will over to the care of the God Who loves us. This may seem frightening at first because we all like to control our own lives. But if we listen to our deep heart need, we will not let this fear hinder our discovery of the God Who reaches out to us in love—often through another person. This is the love everyone needs, because all forms of human love are inadequate, or will ultimately fail. His love never fails.

Everyone needs this love, including the alcoholic, for inner healing and restoration of broken relationships. Alcoholics Anonymous stresses that how seriously we take the Third Step will determine how soon we find healing love to free us from the grip of alcoholism.

The Destructive Power of Alcohol—Overcome by Faith

Many people who come to A.A. have experienced life at its hardest. Their drinking led them into destructive personal relationships. Believing that a Personality cares and is waiting to help them often seems unfathomable at first. After years of self-centered living with its incumbent marriage collapse, child desertion, loss of work, and other side effects, it almost seems unreasonable to believe someone could actually care. Some people refuse to believe it and carry on with destructive living. But some take a step of faith and discover an Invisible Power intimately concerned. When people have given up on the alcoholic and regard him or her as a lost cause, this Power loves, cares and is willing to receive.

Bob found this true after twenty-five years of destructive drinking. He was living in a downtown fifth-class boarding house when I visited him on a Twelve-Step call. He had been a banker years before, got drinking and lost control. He lost his job, his wife and his children were scattered all over the continent. Lost and lonely, he had nothing but a huge pile of regrets to occupy his mind. The only solution, he felt, was the bottle. And over the years it took a vicious toll. Only in his early fifties, he looked like a seventy-year-old. But one night in desperation he phoned the A.A. office for help. When I entered his room, he was bent over his table, crying his heart out. His sobs were heart-rending. I touched his shoulder and sat down beside him. Eventually he looked up.

"There's no hope for me," he moaned. "I'm lost. I might as well pack it in. But I haven't got the courage. Do you think there's any hope for me? I've tried everything. . . . Well maybe not everything. But I'm desperate."

What do you say to a man in this tragic state? At first I could say nothing. I just stroked his arm. Then I said, "Bob, if I didn't believe there was hope, I wouldn't be here. There is hope, but you have to reach out and take it. As long as you grovel in self-pity and mull over the past, you will sink deeper into the bog of your own despair. But if you'll look away from yourself to God and turn your will over to his care, you'll find the miracle that many alcoholics have found taking place for you."

I knew I was throwing him a curve. I didn't know how he would react to turning his will over to the care of God. But he was ready. I got him to his first A.A. meeting and he began to hear testimonies from people grappling with the same lifestyle that ruined him. But he also heard words of hope, that if the will is turned over to the care of God, new possibilities of life unfold. This message of hope came alive for him and he soon made that commitment. As he accepted the God Who cares and empowers us in crises, his whole life changed.

"I don't know how I ever lived so long and was so blind," Bob said to me, as we relaxed over a cup of coffee. "It seems so difficult at first, but when you begin doing it, it seems to be the only reasonable thing to do. After all, if there is a God, He surely must care. The trouble is we are so darned self-sufficient, that we think we can go it alone, and that's where we really 'bung up.' "

The Power of Testimony

The witness of those who make this great discovery of faith helps us open the door of hope. Hearing from those who have proven the reality of this Third Step provides a great encouragement. At first, it may seem too good to be true. But the enthusiasm of those who witness so positively proves difficult to denounce. The testimonies of A.A. members at the regular weekly meetings, nurtures the faith to take a chance. Perhaps God, Whoever He is, will meet me too. The key of faith opens the door to the knowledge of God, however hesitantly turned in the right direction. God will honor that step of faith and will open the door on the other side. The door to the knowledge of God's love and power may be only slightly ajar at first, but as Christ said, "If you have faith as a grain of mustard seed, you can say to this mountain [in this case, the mountain is unbelief], be removed, and it shall be removed and nothing shall be impossible for you" (Matthew 17:20). With increased exposure to truth, spoken by healing alcoholics, the door of faith will open and more steps toward God will be made. In the process we may sometimes close the door and step back because of fear. But eventually, we will learn that this is a step backwards. We will begin again, but with less fear overshadowing us.

The Necessity to Experiment

Because so many people in the twentieth century have been overwhelmed by the claims of false science, the concept that a Supreme Being cares for us seems unreasonable. But this doubt can be overcome.

One night after the Good Samaritan A.A. meeting in my Church, I invited Joe to join us for the Wednesday night supper held in our church basement. After the meal, we featured a particular film series known as God and Science. He came willingly and after the meal, we saw a marvellous film entitled "The God of Creation." In beautiful color, the wonders of the galaxies unfolded. The immensity made you feel at first like little more than a speck of sand upon all the seashores of the world. But then the film changed gears and showed the marvel of infinitesimal creation. We saw intricately designed flowers in so much variety that it boggled the mind. Then the commentator described some places in the Sahara desert where flowers were too small to be seen with the natural eye. They were visible only through a microscope. They displayed a beautiful range of colors, and in some mysterious way that even the scientists had not yet discovered, they received moisture from the desert sands to keep them alive.

Joe was really impressed. "I can't believe it," he exclaimed. "Flowers so small you can't see them. Wow, that's small."

"Yes," I replied, "it sure shows you that God, even though He's so great that He holds the whole universe together, still cares for the smallest of little things—even invisible flowers." I then said, "Joe, doesn't that make you realize that God isn't ignoring you either? He'd like you to experience his caring, and not have you go through life thinking that you are all on your own."

Joe didn't respond much to that, but later on he said, "You know, I just haven't been able to forget the fact that there are flowers so small that you can't see them. Me, you can see, so I guess God might care a little bit for me."

"He cares more than a little," I replied, "and you can know that for a fact, if you will simply turn your will and your life over to Him." One night, within the privacy of his own room, Joe did that, and the miracle of new life took place. He now knew that God cared, that God loved, not because he had figured it out intellectually but because he was impressed by the reality of God's creative activity in nature. It spoke to his heart about his own worth. That enabled him to step out in faith, and commit his life to God and to his care.

The challenge of the Twelve-Step Program is simply, Try it, and find out for yourself. All the Steps function as a unit, and each one addresses the caring power of God that makes life worth living. When you begin to acknowledge your need of help to solve your alcoholism, you are approaching the Power available. When you admit Step One, accepting the truth of Step Three will follow with less difficulty. You will begin to realize that the stronghold of your will must be surrendered.

The Program Versus the Power of God

Many people who enter A.A. begin by letting the Program itself serve as God, as mentioned in Chapter Two. Although this falls short of a full understanding of God, at least from a Christian standpoint, God allows this to happen—it happened when we were children. At first, the only God we know of is expressed through the actions of our parents. For awhile they are one and the same. But as we begin to grow, we realize that Someone is greater than mere earthly parents. We learn this from our mothers or fathers, especially if they believe in God. They will point us, as children, beyond ourselves to the One greater than them. The One Who reigns Supreme. The same principle needs to be remembered when we consider the alcoholic who can only begin with the Group and the Program.

Bill grew up in a home where a lot of fear was associated with the concept of God. He was warned from childhood that if God disapproved of what he did, God would judge and condemn him. When he joined the air force and engaged in fighter-plane bombing, he constantly faced the reality and possibility of death. He could only handle his fear of God by denial. He subconsciously rejected his childhood concept of a God Who was angry with him and eager to judge him and began to hate God.

When I met Bill during a marital struggle he was having with his wife Marie, he viewed me with suspicion. I was a "priest" in his eyes, and "priests" reinforced the idea that God was to be feared. But when I began to show some love and understanding, and insisted that God was full of loving compassion, caring for us and wanting us to live life in all its fullness, he could hardly believe it. We would often argue about what God was like. But as I showed him verses in the Bible that stressed the loving nature of God, his fears began to subside.

It wasn't a matter of me proving that God was love in a purely intellectual way. He had to watch that love in action. And amazingly he saw that love working through me, in the time that I spent with him, and in the marriage counseling I gave. In some way, I was "God" to him, because I was expressing love and care. But eventually, because I insisted that I wasn't "God," but simply privileged to reveal his love through my humanity, he began to understand that God cares. Reason didn't prove it to him, but love in action did.

If a person begins by treating the A.A. program or the A.A. meeting where he or she finds the expression of love, acceptance and forgiveness as the Higher Power, then we may say, "Great [for now]." But authentic A.A. encourages an alcoholic not to limit his or her thinking there. We know, and A.A. knows, that God doesn't equal the Twelve-Step Program or the Group Consciousness. We must be willing to discover as much of God as is possible. With that attitude, we will not be content with anything less than the full knowledge available. The secret is willingness. This must also include an openness to having our own misconceptions about God readjusted, especially if they have been perverted. Bill needed his heavy dose of fear of God counterbalanced by the dominant message of love in the Bible. In fact, when A.A. first began, the founders did not have any other Book to guide the new, seeking alcoholics. The Big Book had not yet been written, and so the Bible provided the basis for their study. Through the insights of the Bible, the A.A. program of twelve-step recovery originated. Each Step reflects a biblical grasp of human need, and God's ability to meet that need. The Bible confronts us with the truth about God and ourselves in order to transform our own ideas often out of tune with the truth.

Sometimes when people come into A.A., they resemble a drowning man, in danger of going under for the third time. They don't need a textbook of theology, but a lifebelt of truth to save them from perishing in the guilt and shame of their alcoholism. The Bible provides that lifebelt. After they have been rescued from the destructive power of alcoholism, they can carry on to discover the fullness of God—the Higher Power.

Surrender—the Pathway to Salvation

The word "salvation" is a religious term not often used today, except in a religious context. But the word comes from secular roots indicating the need for liberation. Slaves in the ancient world often talked about being "saved." By this they meant being released from their master's power and domination.

You can easily understand why the word took on a spiritual

connotation. If ever a person needed liberation—or salvation—the alcoholic does. Life has become so totally bound by the effects of alcohol, hardly an ounce of freedom remains. But how do we experience that liberation, that salvation?

We come now to the importance of surrender, or yielding our lives to the power of God through faith. As the new A.A. person faces the possibility of surrendering his or her life over to the care of God, a severe struggle of the will may emerge. Our desire to live independently wields powerful influence. We want to control our lives. We want to grasp the "steering wheel" of life. But where did that get us? For the alcoholic, this same spirit of independence thrust him into his present pattern of destructive behavior. Its promise to enhance life shattered on the rocky shores of destitution.

But even in blatant need, we stubbornly resist relinquishing control. We falsely presume that surrender to God robs us of personal uniqueness and the freedom to choose.

Alex and Sandi had just gone through a marital breakup, and both were suffering from the subsequent pain. One night I was visiting Alex, listening to him dump his resentment on Sandi for their marital breakdown.

"You can't blame Sandi for all that happened," I said. "After all, you were a pretty independent cuss, always wanting it your way, and treating her as if you were still single. It seems to me, that you still wanted to live your independent life, especially when it came to drinking. I guess Sandi just couldn't take your independence any longer."

Alex, who had begun to confront his alcoholism through the help of A.A., looked at me with a scowl. He knew I was right, but he didn't like hearing it. We enjoyed good rapport so I felt comfortable sharing my perspective. He had also come to a new belief in God and was trying to yield his life to the care of God, as he understood Him.

"God doesn't want you to be a mechanical robot," he retorted, "He wants us to use our own willpower."

"That's true," I said, "once you've surrendered your will to his. It's only when our wills are united to his will, that our decisions begin to work for our best, our highest good. That may seem like a paradox, or maybe even a contradiction.

"How can your will be exercised freely, if God's will is in control at the same time?" he questioned.

"It's a case of priority," I replied. "If we yield to God's will first, then He will begin to remold our wills so that we will want to do his will and not our own—if we give Him the green light. The more we become dominated by his loving power, the more we will want to blend together with his will. We will discover that God has nothing in mind but good for us, especially if we are growing in our love for Him."

"I can hear what you're saying," Alex replied, "but I don't see how all your problems, difficulties and disappointments work together for good, as you claim."

"Well," I said, "don't you think that your divorce from Sandi has forced you to take a look at your alcoholism and to come to A.A. for help? Your divorce isn't good in itself, but God has certainly begun to work some good out of it, don't you think?"

He sat quietly for a few moments, reflecting on what I had said. "I guess you're right," he breathed with a sigh, "but it sure is a tough way to find that you can't go it alone. I've just begun to discover what a lot of healed alcoholics have known for a long time—that the more we yield our wills to God, the freer we become within ourselves. I never thought I'd ever say a thing like that, but I guess I'm a slow learner."

"Oh, you're not such a slow learner," I smiled. "It takes most of us a long time to realize that dependency upon God leads to inner dependence, and then a sense of interdependence with others. Many people are totally unaware that independence in any absolute sense is totally unrealistic and unattainable. That's why we have so many people falling apart at the seams or making a mess of their relationships."

"That's perfectly right when you stop to think of it," reasoned Alex. "The gas we put in our cars, the food on our tables, the clothes we wear, the house we live in—they all point to our need for others."

"Yes," I said to Alex, "the most deceptive illusion is the delusion of independence. We all need one another, and the sooner we realize and accept it, the quicker our self-centered human pride finds its place."

I was encouraged to see Alex learning how the independent spirit fatally deters real living. Many of us understand this truth theoretically, but when applying it to our decision-making processes we are still prone to assert our wills over others. We demand the right to do what we want when we want to. The popular song, "I Did It My Way," reflects this thinking that only results in conflict and dissatisfaction. We won't tolerate interference in our personal lives. We presume to have the intelligence and the willpower to steer our own lives in the right direction.

But can this be true, especially in light of what alcohol has done to us? This philosophy of independence makes every one into "little gods," each asserting his own will over life's circumstances. Some of these "little gods" rise above others and they become the dictators of nations. We resent this happening, but in reality it only reflects our lifestyles on a larger scale. Everyone wants to play God. If we reflect on what our lifestyles have become because of alcohol, it becomes obvious enough that we have neither the intelligence nor the willpower to redirect our lives positively. Many people, incapacitated by pride and self-righteousness, can recognize their plight only with great difficulty.

The Dead-End Street of Self-Centered Living

As we attempt to keep the "rules" of correct conduct, we stumble at confessing our shortfalls and turning our wills and lives over to the care of God. This happens to anyone, as much as the person mastered by an addiction. If we analyze our society, problems arise when groups of people juxtapose their wills against the wills of others. This applies to the international and national scene, as much as to the personal scene. How can human problems be solved when everyone insists that his way is best? It is a dead-end street. Unyielding human pride makes compromise impossible.

No peace or brotherhood in our troubled world can exist as long as the human will resists the call to yield to God.

Man's Extremity is God's Opportunity

In many ways, alcoholics are fortunate people. Through their own misguided decisions, they have discovered that willpower alone cannot overcome difficulty. Alcoholics realize that self-centered living results in despair. But in despair, the door of hope has opened.

The door opened for Rita after years of struggling with alcoholism and its negative effects. In her mid-fifties, she had gone through two husbands and was separated from the third. She was brought up in wealth and indulged by her parents, who both had high expectations for her. Failing to meet these expectations, she found that alcohol helped her cope. Eventually, however, its dividends enslaved her. She forfeited the ability to develop good relationships with anyone.

I met her one night at a dinner party, in the home of people who had just become believers. They were reaching out to Rita because they knew she was desperate but wouldn't admit it. As we talked about God and what He had done for us, Rita grew irritated.

"You people blow my mind," she sneered. "You're educated, and yet you still believe in all this 'God stuff.' I can't understand it."

Bob, the host, replied, "Well, Rita, when you've reached a dead-end street, like I did, you discover that reason and all the knowledge you picked up at university doesn't help much. It wasn't easy for me to admit to my need, but eventually I had to. It wasn't a great flash of light or anything like that, but there was a moment of truth, when I realized that I didn't, have the inner resources to find meaning in life. At coffee one day, in the staff lunch room, one of the fellows I'd grown to respect suggested I might find some intellectual stimulation from reading C.S. Lewis' book, *Mere Christianity*. He brought a copy of it the next day, and I started to read it. He presented logical arguments communicated in such a way that I couldn't put the book down. As I read and thought about all my prejudices, I began to realize that if C.S. Lewis, who was at one time a confirmed atheist, could find reality in yielding to God, what would stop me? But pride is a big thing Rita, and I didn't respond right away. I had to go through a few big crises in my life before I was 'shook-up' enough to look beyond myself to God."

Rita didn't say very much from that point on in the dinner conversation, but knowing that I was a Christian minister, she phoned me later that week and made an appointment to see me.

"I need help," she blurted out when she dropped into a chair in my study. "I'm just not making it and haven't been for thirty years. Here I am at fifty-two, and I'm sick, I'm depressed, I don't know why I'm here or why I'm living." She held back her tears, but her face was drawn, reflecting inner despair.

"What do you think the problem is?" I asked.

"Well, I've begun to realize that I've been too damned independent. I've tried to make good decisions, but it's obvious that I haven't known how. I've been to psychiatrists and psychologists but somehow they haven't helped. I feel so disoriented. I think that part of my problem relates to my domineering father who set out to control me, and I made up my mind I wasn't going to let it happen. But my attempt to be independent and rely on no one has only ended in disaster. My relationship to him and with many others has been so distorted and unfulfilling because I thought some of them were trying to control my life. And I wasn't going to let it happen."

"That's very true Rita," I replied to her open confession of struggling to be free, "and yet it is sometimes necessary to break away from the controls others have tried to have over us and find ourselves. The important thing is how we do it. But when we talk about turning our wills over to the care of God, as Step Three encourages us to do, we have a different concept altogether. If a person is dominated by others he does need to be freed, but this freedom doesn't give a green light to resist all dependency, both upon God and one another."

Rita nodded her head silently. I could see that she was discovering some new principles that would transform her life.

God Never Robs You of Freedom

A.A. testifies that the more you turn your will over to the care of God, the freer your spirit becomes. Even when members left a home A.A. group, as so many did during World War II—separated from many people who meant so much to them—they did not "fall off the wagon." They still maintained their freedom from drinking because they daily yielded their wills over to the care of God. They found that the Higher Power of God's love still fortified them, even when surrounded by drinking buddies.

Yielding Is Not Slavery

What does it mean to live a yielded life? Soon after a person enters Alcoholics Anonymous and has agreed to turn his will and life over to the care of God, he realizes other problems need to be tackled. Other areas of your life also need to be examined.

Jean's eyes opened to the realities of her lifestyle after she had been sober for three months through the A.A. message. She began to realize her lack of discipline in spending money. She also began to examine the bitterness she had piled up against others she was determined not to forgive. She began to understand why she still felt emotionally and sometimes physically ill, even though she was dry.

She came over to my office one afternoon and burst into tears, "Oh, I'm desperate. When I look at the pile of problems in my basket, I think I'm about to go under. But I'm determined not to drink, even though I feel like it. How are my problems going to get solved? I don't think I have the energy to solve them. Who can I turn to? Well, here I am turning to you. Have you got any answers?"

I looked at her quietly for a few moments. I didn't want to blurt out pat answers. I knew she was struggling but could win the battle, if she took Step Three seriously.

Eventually I said, "You know, Jean, I'm not wanting to sound 'holier-than-thou,' or pious when I say this, but you've got to turn these struggles over to God."

She replied, "You make it sound as if God's a bellhop and all I've got to do is hand over my problems to Him like suitcases."

"Well," I said, "it's pretty much like that. The more we relinquish our right to control our lives and bring our problems to Him, the more help and the more freedom we discover. But that may not only require yielding everything to God in prayer, it may also involve some A.A. friends who can help you sort through your behavior patterns. After all, the A.A. member can't live alone, but in relationship to others, especially those farther along the road of sobriety than you. It's called 'discipleship' in Christian terminology."

Jean responded to what I was saying. She knew she needed help, and it began to make sense that God, working through others, could help her add more discipline to her life.

"What do you think I should do?" she asked. "I haven't been in A.A. long enough to make too many close friends, and I don't know whether they would want me to unload all my problems on them."

"You'd be surprised how many people in A.A. know you right now and would be willing to help. They probably know the exact struggle you're going through, because they've been through it themselves. You'd find them ready to listen. Don't let negative thoughts about yourself or the size of your problems keep you from reaching out to someone," I replied.

And so Jean looked around and found Gert, a few years older and a healed alcoholic of ten years. She had endured much but had become known in A.A. for her helpfulness.

As Gert and Jean met together regularly, their friendship deepened, and Jean opened up about her struggle to achieve discipline. Gert gave her helpful direction without robbing her of the decision-making process. They both realized that grappling with their personal struggles made them partners together with God in creating new life.

One Day at a Time

This pet A.A. slogan cogently expresses the practical truth of Step Three. The decision to turn your will and life over to the care of God must be made on a day-by-day basis. Friendship needs constant commitment to be real and lasting. The more time we spend with God, turning our lives increasingly over to Him, the more his friendship kindles power for living. His promises provide the assurance that nothing in life need conquer us. In fact, the early Christians expressed their confidence in this possibility when they said, "We are more than conquerors through Him who loved us" (Romans 8:37).

The alcoholic may sometimes feel that he or she is struggling alone without God. But that feeling often comes because we want quick answers to our problems, and don't want to work them out patiently. The harmony of living in God's will happens when we handle life's difficulties without yielding to despondency. Here the yielding of our wills to God takes on great significance. Our wills need to be fortified daily with positive thinking, life-giving meditation and prayer, just like our bodies need vitamins. We will consider these aspects of the A.A. lifestyle in Step Eleven. No growth in the knowledge of God's power can occur without daily reflection upon his truth and drawing upon his resources.

Chris was one of those guys always on the go. He boasted that he never took the time to brush his teeth—he just licked them with his tongue! He was Mr. Active. But this also made him prone to depression.

We ran into each other on Columbia Street one evening. "How about a coffee?" I asked.

"Sounds like a great idea," he replied.

As we sat talking, I could tell that he was struggling with something. He looked down and I knew something was bothering him.

"I feel like having more than this coffee," he eventually said. "I've been sober three months now, but I've sure had to struggle with the blues. I don't know why I get so depressed."

"Do you use the 24-Hour Day Book?" I asked.

"Oh, once in a while I turn to it, but you know me, I'm so itchy to get going that I just can't take the time to get into this meditation bit," Chris confessed.

"Why don't you try to discipline yourself just a little each day?" I suggested. "You know, you'd be surprised how the habit of meditation will grow gradually, if you just set aside a few moments each day. Take your 24-Hour Book and maybe a reading from one of the Psalms or Gospels and just allow it to speak to you. You may not even remember what you read a few hours later, but that doesn't matter—the truth will release power in your mind to help you deal with depression. You know, it's like eating your dinner. Once you've eaten it, you don't sit around all evening thinking about what your digestive system is doing. You're not asking, What part of this food is becoming blood, tissue, or cell? That would be foolish. You just let the body break down the food and create energy. But that food creates the energy you need for your daily work. It works the same way with reading and reflecting upon truth in the 24-Hour Book, or the Bible. The truth released inside you gives you the inner strength you need for daily life. Why don't you try doing it? Start with five minutes a day and see what happens."

I didn't see Chris after that evening for another six months. But we met one night in late summer and I asked, "How's it going?"

"You wouldn't believe it," he smiled, "but I'm now up to reading thirty minutes on a daily basis. It's hard to believe that I could ever settle down to do it. But I started out, as you said, five minutes a day, and I increased it by a minute or two every week. Before I knew it, I was feeling much less depressed, and much less prone to wanting a drink than ever before. I can't thank you enough for showing me a new way to deal with depression."

"Well, it's not me who discovered it," I replied. "It was Jesus Who said, 'the truth will set you free' (John 8:32). The more you meditate on the truth, the more inner freedom you have. The sword of truth can beat down the old enemy of depression. Keep at it."

Overcoming the Misuse of Power

The Third Step in the A.A. Program reveals how distorted our lives become by the misuse of Power. We took the power of choice into our own hands, without any reference to the laws of health, temperance and self-control. We thought *we* could deal with life. But the power of alcohol trumped our cards. As the Big Book says so clearly, "Alcohol is cunning, baffling and powerful." Our trouble stems from Adam in the garden. Like us, he ignored God's directive because he believed that by eating the forbidden fruit he would be as "god," knowing good and evil. He yielded to that powerful temptation. Unfortunately, it alienated him from God and from creation. He felt afraid. The self-will always creates fear and suspicion.

The misuse of power undergirds human problems and crises. If we try to solve our problems—especially alcoholic drinking—with willpower alone, we will eventually encounter an impasse that we can overcome only by an about-face.

That about-face proves indispensable to creative living. As we line up our lives with God's will, life will form new patterns of meaning. The key is to pray, "Not my will, but yours be done." This was germaine to Jesus' life. It must be to ours.

STEP THREE: Made a decision to turn our will and our lives over to the care of God, as we understand Him.
Alcoholics Anonymous

TRACK TWO: God as we understood Him. *Alcoholics Anonymous*

Getting to Know You

"I don't know whether I'm ready for all the God bit in A.A.," John said to me rather wistfully, "but I sure know I need A.A."

"You don't need to be worried about God," I replied, "because He won't force Himself on you. In fact, Alcoholics Anonymous purposely makes no attempt to define what is meant by God. Their chief concern is to help you find sobriety. It does not want to muddy the issue of your recovery by derailing on a potentially confusing theological sidetrack. A.A. realizes that many people have had a negative religious background and have been 'turned off' by what they were taught. Many of them believe that God is angry with them and condemns them. Therefore, they have recoiled from relationship with Him."

"Yes," interjected John. "I don't know who told me, but I think I remember someone saying that the founders of A.A. tried to minimize the theological controversy. They felt that sobriety was their chief concern, achieved through the One called God. But understanding Who He was wasn't emphasized.

"That's true," I responded, "but that does not mean the founding fathers of A.A. didn't care about God or understanding his identity. Their A.A. Big Book stresses in the chapter to the agnostic that God must be sought after and that He can be found by the honest seeker. Step Eleven also encourages A.A. members to consciously improve their contact with God through prayer and meditation. This obviously infers that God can be known. He can be experienced and our relationship with Him can be improved, as we approach Him. Right now, John, you may feel a little reluctant to move at all, but I'm convinced that feeling will lift. I'm sure that God's power will help you overcome your reluctance at this point."

Getting to know God challenges the human heart, because its

innermost being desires to know Him. Naturally, the question must be asked, Where do you seek for God? How does God make Himself known to the honest seeker? How can you improve your conscious contact with Him?

As previously stated, both the Christian Faith and Alcoholics Anonymous have been fathered by God. A.A. arose from a Christian context, because all Twelve Steps relate to a Christian understanding of life and God's relationship to us. That being true, A.A. people must be challenged to examine the Christian beliefs or doctrines to discover Who God is.

God is Too Big For Us

The moment you ponder the existence of God, you realize you need help finding Him. When we consider the immensity of this universe and the seemingly insignificant little planet we call earth, "hunting for God" seems insuperably difficult. Furthermore, God may not want to make Himself known to us, and therefore remain hidden. We might decide to search for Him, but if He doesn't want to be found, then no effort on our part will locate his whereabouts. God can only be known if He allows us to discover Him. God, therefore, must initiate steps toward us, rather than directing us on a "wild goose chase" into outer space to find Him. Called his revelation, the unveiling of God, He discloses our ignorance and the knowledge of Himself.

How to Know God

What does Christianity profess about the possibility of knowing God?

This question was thrown at me one night when I shared in a "bull session" at a fraternity house on the University of British Columbia campus. Dick, a member of this fraternity, had invited me to assist him in a free-for-all debate. Since he had become a Christian, some fraternity brothers were giving him a hard time. New in his faith, he didn't feel confident taking them on. So he invited me.

Circling the common room of the Frat House, the fifteen or so fellows sat well stocked with beer. The occasion seemed to demand fortification on their part. Although I normally feel relaxed with inquiring students, I could sense resistance in the room.

As soon as we got seated, the president of the fraternity welcomed everyone and then introduced me. "We're here, as you remember," he said, "because we got into a big free-for-all debate or argument the other night about God. Dick thought it might be good to discuss the subject with someone who's been in the 'theological business' for some time. So, let's go."

"Thanks fellows," I replied in response to the introduction. "It's a great delight to be here, and to talk about my favorite subject. However, I don't want to come across as an authority, because I'm still learning and I'm always open to new understanding. I know that Dick felt reluctant to discuss the subject by himself with some of you guys and I don't know whether I'll be that much better. But I think if we rap with each other with an open mind and heart, we'll be surprised what we come up with."

Dick started off the "bull session." "Cal," he said, "why do Christians, who seem to have a fair number of intellectuals in their ranks, feel that believing in God is reasonable?"

"That's a good place to begin," I replied. "Certainly, one reason is the created order itself. When you look at creation, the writers of the Bible felt the logical inference was that Someone made it, and that Someone was God."

"What are some of those statements in the Bible?" asked Bob, one of Dick's close friends.

"Two come to mind, Bob," I replied. "One from the Old Testament where the psalmist states, 'The heavens declare the glory of God, and the whole earth proclaims the glory of his hands' (Psalm 19:1). Then the Apostle Paul, writing to the Christians in Rome in the first century after Christ, wrote, 'What is true about God may be known, since God has made it plain to them. For since the creation of the world, God's invisible qualities, his eternal power and divine nature, have been clearly seen being understood from what has been made, so that men are without excuse' (Romans 1:20ff)."

"Well, does that really offer proof?" Don piped up. "After all, those statements you just quoted were made by people who were believers themselves. I personally find a lot of things in nature that confuse me and make me wonder if there is a creative power behind everything. Things like earthquakes, tidal waves and other natural disasters don't seem to point to an orderly mind. What do you make of such things?"

"There's no doubt, Don," I replied, "that there's a mysterious side of nature. Some theologians call it 'the blood and tooth' aspect of the natural order. But even this side to nature doesn't rule out the fact that most of nature seems quite orderly."

"Yes," Dick added, "nature isn't very personal either. I once heard you compare nature to a beautiful woman. You might see her walking down the street and be attracted to her. She might be fashionably dressed, have a lovely smile, and be a knockout in every way, but that wouldn't tell you anything about her personality. You wouldn't know whether she was cruel or kind, generous or stingy, educated or uneducated. Her external beauty would only reveal some outward facts, but they would say nothing about her character. Nature's a lot like that, isn't it?"

"You're absolutely right, Dick," I responded. "Nature certainly points to order in the universe, but it doesn't let you in on what kind of God created it. You'll never discover from nature whether God loves you or not or whether He's interested in your daily life. To me, this only points to the existence of God as a Creator, but does not reveal his own personality.

"You mean, you think God has a personality? I've always thought of God as an impersonal force, an unknowable that no one can quite figure out," Fred, a bright, young fellow piped up.

"That's a common idea that many people have about the Creative Power of the universe. But that isn't satisfying to the human mind. For one thing, we know that we are individuals with personalities, so why should we think it strange that the highest force or power in this universe is also intensely personal?" I replied.

"That's what I found God to be," answered Dick, glad for an opportunity to express his own personal faith. "I always thought of

God as some cosmic 'It,' if there was a God, but when my faith in God came into existence, I found Him personal to me."

"That characteristic is unique to the Hebrew-Christian faith, compared to other religious systems," I replied. "When you read mankind's religious literature, the human heart is crying, Show us the Father and we will be satisfied. In other words, Tell us Who God is, and what He is like. It seems to me that when we are honest with our innermost feelings, embedded within our human nature lies a longing for something that reaches out for more understanding. We all experience impulses stirred by an inner yearning for more than just the physical universe. The struggle is as old as man himself. One of the richest men who lived in the ancient Greek world was Crocius. He once asked the great philosopher Thales, 'What is God?' This wise man asked for a day to think about the answer, and then for another, and then another. At length he confessed he was unable to answer the question. He said that the more he deliberated, the more difficult he found the question. He demonstrated that God can't be discovered through thinking and reasoning processes. Something deeper must confront us. Reasoning about the question, Is there a God? does not always result in inner satisfaction. Many of man's philosophical systems insist that the more you think about the possibility of God's existence, the more difficult it becomes."

"If that's the case," John inquired, "why is man so religious? Everywhere you look in history you find him worshiping some deity or other, and accomplishing fantastic feats in the name of religion. How come?"

"You're absolutely right, John," I answered. "Someone has said, and I think rightly so, that man is incurably religious. But it isn't just people in other cultures who are like this. You see it everywhere, even in our society. Just think how many people, who call themselves agnostics, still have sentimental feelings at Christmas or Easter, or when they watch a sunset, or see a sunrise. Something in each of us reaches out for something! We don't know exactly how to describe it, but Christians believe that it is an inner longing for God."

"Yeah," interjected Brian, "even reading the Bible, or praying, or attending religious services, doesn't seem to bring you closer to whatever God is."

"That may be true," I replied. "Those things might even be used as a substitute for reality. Many people, unfortunately, equate their religious devotions with a knowledge of God. There may come a time, however, when they realize that all this outward devotion hasn't brought them to God. Some may 'chuck' religion entirely, but on the other hand, some may be driven to search more earnestly. It all depends on how deeply conscious you are of your inner need."

"That sounds 'way out' to me," replied Brian. "It sounds unsettling to people who identify God with those kinds of religious activity. How can you know God, if those activities don't lead to Him? I sometimes wonder if knowledge of God can be acquired."

"I know how you feel," I responded, "especially when you think of yourself living on this little planet called earth. We seem nothing more than just a speck of dust surrounded by vast galaxies of untold universes that exist beyond us in outer space. You ask yourself, How can I know Him? He seems too far beyond us."

This "bull session" eventually boiled down to analyzing the Christian claim that God made Himself known in terms we can understand. The Christian doesn't profess to know everything about God, but he does believe that he has discovered the reality of God, revealed in human form. Instead of reaching up to God in hopes of finding Him somewhere, the Christian Faith witnesses to God's breakthrough to us. The concept of God stretches so far beyond us that if we are ever to learn of Him, He has to reveal Himself to us. The New Testament teaches this. Now we can confront the claims the four gospel writers make about Jesus of Nazareth, along with those of the Apostle Paul, once an enemy of Christianity.

The New Testament—Meet the God Revealed in Human Flesh

The writings of the New Testament reveal that God eagerly unveiled Himself in the person of Jesus Christ. He entered into our unveiled Himself in the person of Jesus Christ. He entered into our common birth, childhood and adulthood, displaying through action and teaching that God was truly among us. Christ claimed that to understand Him was to experience a personal knowledge of God. When you think of what Jesus said about Himself and God, you have to form one of three conclusions. Anyone who could say, "He who has seen me, has seen the Father," or, "I and my Father are One," was either a megalomaniac, a lunatic or what He claimed to be—God revealed in the flesh.

Bruce, a psychologist, dealt with the problem this way: "I began to realize that the way to inner happiness was learning to accept yourself for what you are. If you are an average student imagining you are a genius, you certainly haven't faced reality. If you think yourself a talented singer when you only have a mediocre voice, your personal evaluation is flawed. Many people in mental institutes believe they are famous people—like Napoleon or Queen Elizabeth. Mentally ill, they live in a dream world. Well, apply the same principle to Jesus. If he, mere man—even the best man—imagined that He was God in the flesh, it would be obvious that He hadn't learned to accept himself for what He was—a man, and nothing more than a man. He should display the characteristics of imbalance, a neurotic out of touch with himself. But the opposite comes through when you read the New Testament. The writers portray Him as completely aware of Who He is, and what his mission was all about. He accepted Himself for what He was, the man through whom God was revealing Himself. And everyone close to Him realized that this was true. Through the personality of Jesus, God became real, knowable and above all, loving."

But you might ask, Wasn't the New Testament written by men biased about Jesus? Weren't they writing from the standpoint of faith in Him? Could they be objective in their evaluation of Him?

Yes, the Gospel writers did share their faith in Jesus, after becoming convinced He was what He claimed to be. But they didn't invent this story of Jesus to be popular. They paid heavily for believing as they did about Jesus (most of them were martyred for their faith). But the truth aflame in their hearts could not be

Testament simply presents the reality of what Jesus was, said and did and, in the process, challenges us to make it our own.

And God was never so real as at the crucifixion and the resurrection. Undoubtedly, Jesus was executed as a common criminal by the Roman government in 33 A.D. He was convicted for his claims about Himself that alienated Him from the Jewish leaders. But despite the cruel treatment He endured, the cross pictures God's love and forgiveness in all their fullness. While hanging on the cross, Jesus prayed for his enemies in those inimitable words, "Father forgive them for they know not what they do" (Luke 23:34). This event displays the forgiveness of God to those who so unjustly crucified Him. It infers that nothing in your life or mine is unforgivable. By receiving this forgiveness, God will become real to us. We experience his grace, his unmerited love.

The resurrection pictures something else. God shows that even death cannot conquer Jesus. All who come to Him in faith, accepting his love and forgiveness, welcoming Him into their lives and committing themselves to his teaching enter into a new beginning. Many alcoholics have experienced the power of God in resurrection.

"I was as good as dead," John said to me one afternoon as he took his initial Fifth Step. "I was physically destroyed, emotionally shattered and spiritually lost. But with the power of God released into my life through A.A., I felt resurrected from the dead. I began to live again. So I don't have difficulty believing that God could raise Jesus back to life. If He could give me life again, He can do it for anyone."

Christians claim that believing in Christ and trusting your life to Him will introduce a lifestyle with love as its primary focus. God becomes real. His forgiveness becomes a daily exercise in acceptance. No longer does He seem distant, but nearby and real.

Accepting or Rejecting

We must keep in mind, as we try to appreciate Who Jesus is and what his claims actually mean, that religious people often resisted Him strongly. He threatened their authority over the people. Christ challenged many of their presuppositions and made them consider the essence of what believing in God means. This angered them. And when He claimed that God could be fully known through Him, it rang as blasphemy in their religious ears. They wouldn't tolerate Him and plotted to destroy his influence.

The same process happens today. I remember when Sandi became a Christian. She was an alcoholic for many years and experienced much tragedy. When she started coming to our church, she told me about an experience she had one afternoon. She had dropped in to a local restaurant for a cup of coffee and met Mrs. McDonald (not her real name), a lifetime member of the church. Prim and proper in her mid-sixties, she led a well-off, educated and relatively boring life.

Sandi recognized her and went over to her table. "Hello, Mrs. McDonald," she said cheerily. "Mind if I sit down and join you for a cup of tea?"

"Certainly not," replied Mrs. McDonald. "I would be delighted to have you join me." Tea was ordered and they began to talk.

"I'm just thrilled with my life since I've joined the church," Sandi started. "I used to be so angry at the church. I thought everyone who went was a hypocrite. But when I found sobriety through A.A., and after a few talks with Cal, I knew a new door was opening up for me. Sometimes, I get a little nervous about meeting all you fine people in First Church, but I usually get over it."

"It must have been quite a change for you," Mrs. McDonald replied. "I've been in the church all my life and I have always been a Christian."

"Isn't that wonderful?" Sandi enthused. "Could you tell me how God became real for you?"

A slight tinge of pink emerged on Mrs. McDonald's cheek. She had never been asked such a question in her life, and certainly not by someone she regarded as somewhat inferior to her.

"Oh, I find talking about God much too personal. My religion is very much a private thing," explained Mrs. McDonald.

"You mean it is hard for you to put into words?" Sandi questioned.

"I suppose you might put it that way," replied Mrs. McDonald. "I really haven't much patience with those people who think they know the exact hour when they believed. I've always believed."

"What is the most important thing you believe?" asked Sandi.

"Well, I think the most important thing in life is doing good for others. The Golden Rule is what my religion's all about," replied Mrs. McDonald, with an air of self-sufficiency.

"Oh," responded Sandi, "I used to feel that way too, until I began to realize that you can never measure up to the high standards of Christ's teachings. In fact, the more I tried, the more desperate I became. It wasn't until I recognized my need for forgiveness and that God was willing to give it to me that my spiritual life came alive. I'd hate to have to measure up to God's standards before He would accept me."

Mrs. McDonald's face revealed her bewilderment. All her life she thought acceptance by God meant being good and, because she never doubted her own goodness, she had never experienced the reality of forgiveness. Even though she had always attended church, the message of personal sin and God's incumbent forgiveness had never registered. But Sandi's words cracked that self-righteousness, and made her realize she needed something more. Her own moral goodness had masked her deficiency. She needed God's forgiveness just as much as anyone—just as much as Sandi.

Humility Leads to Self-Awareness

The proud and the self-righteous rarely see their need. Centered on themselves, they fail to recognize their own spiritual poverty—foundational to a right relationship with God. Jesus said in the Sermon on the Mount, "Happy are the poor in spirit" (Matthew 5:3). Only when we recognize our own spiritual poverty do we begin to reach out for the spiritual riches that only come from God. To the humble-minded, the words of Jesus formed a bridge to cross over into a life free from self-centeredness and full of gratitude for the love and grace of God. Christians all down the centuries to this present day cite its reality. Humility of mind opens the door to truth.

I have personally known a considerable number of A.A. people who have progressed in their faith from acknowledging the Higher Power, to believing the God fully known through the Christ of the cross and the resurrection. When you confront the God fully revealed there, your human pride collapses, and you know acceptance by God does not emerge on the basis of your own morality, hopelessly depraved compared with Christ's. Acceptance comes on the basis of his love and your repentance. Every alcoholic anxious to improve his or her conscious contact with God can personally discover the reality of the Higher Power through Jesus Christ, Who became human that we might share his likeness.

The radical message of New Testament Christianity declares that God stooped to our level, to lift us up to his. He did not become human merely to heal diseases of the body and mind. He came primarily to heal our souls by reconciling us to God and restoring an intimate relationship with Him. Jesus as God in the flesh injected new meaning into our warped and twisted lives. He freed us from sin and self-centeredness. When we humbly respond to this Christ, we rise out of the old life into the new.

In a little book entitled, *The Changed Life*, Henry Drummond, a famous naturalist and theologian of the nineteenth century, recounts a remark once made by the famous scientist and theist, Julius Huxley. This great man once acknowledged, "I confess, that if one great power could make me agree to think always what is true, and do what is right on the condition of being turned into a sort of clock and wound me up every morning I should instantly close with the offer."

At this point, Drummond writes, "I now offer, in all seriousness to make such an offer without being turned into a clock." He then tells his readers about the power revealed in the life of Jesus that enabled people from every walk of life to find a new relationship to God and others, by responding to his will.

Creative Change

Christ has constantly changed human lives down the centuries. The New Testament witnesses this claim in numerous ways. But in every generation, from every stratum of society, people have been lifted into newness of life, through personal faith and commitment to Him. Not only the famous names of history have responded to the power of his love, but millions of unnamed persons have yielded to his claims and discovered a release of spiritual power that completely transforms them.

I could relate many stories to support this claim, but one is particularly significant to me. In the Fall of 1949, I was in Chicago on my way to seminary in Toronto. Several of my friends were studying in the "windy city" and invited me one Sunday afternoon to attend the seventy-fifth anniversary of the founding of the famous Pacific Garden Mission. This downtown Mission had so presented the message of Christ's love and grace through the years, that the lives of thousands of men and women crippled by alcoholic addiction were restored to usefulness.

A choir of men, ranging in ages from sixteen to sixty, sang the praises of God and inspired the audience. These men, I was told, had been lying about in the flop houses and gutters of Chicago three months previously, the victims of alcoholic indulgence. Now new men in Christ because the power of God's love and forgiveness had entered their lives, they faced life with a new sense of self-worth and purpose.

This witness to Jesus Christ, as the unfolding of God in human terms to set people free from the power of sin and self-centeredness, has inspired Christians to say, "If you want to understand God in all his fullness, look to Jesus Christ, and you will come to know Him, as you can know Him in no other way."

CHAPTER FOUR

STEP FOUR: Made a searching and fearless moral inventory of ourselves.   *Alcoholics Anonymous*

TRACK ONE : Let nothing stand between you and the light.
Henry David Thoreau—Letter March 7, 1848

The great nineteenth-century Russian novelist, Dostoievsky, says that we tell the world about some things, we tell a small number of friends other things, we tell still other things only to a personal confidant. But certain things we tell only ourselves.

However, we are afraid to face some things about ourselves and therefore we bury them in our subconscious. Few people accept the challenge of Step Four. We naturally pull back from making a searching and fearless inventory. None of us eagerly diagnoses himself to come to grips with what he actually is. And yet self-diagnosis leads to freedom.

About five months after Fred had entered Alcoholics Anonymous and had stopped drinking, he sat one evening having a coffee. Our friendship had strengthened enough that I felt free to inquire about his making the Fourth Step. He grimaced and said, "Man, I don't know whether I'm ready for that plunge into reality. Yet I know I've got to do it if I'm really going to get well."

"What do you think is standing in the way?" I questioned.

He paused for a moment and then he said, "You know, one part of me says, You'll go back drinking if you start digging into your past to see what went wrong, and yet, the other part of me says, You've got to get rid of that garbage or you'll never make it."

"It takes courage to do the Fourth Step, Fred," I said, "but you've already come a long way in five months and I think you *can* make it. After all, A.A. wouldn't ask you to take such a step, if it didn't feel it was crucial to sobriety."

And then I remembered a scene in Charles Dickens' famous novel, *A Tale of Two Cities*. Sidney Carton, the hero of the story, looks into the mirror one morning, facing for the first time his drink-sodden features and exclaims, as he shatters his wine glass on the floor, "Sydney, my boy, you're an old fool." This for him, was the moment of truth, the beginning of self-examination.

When I told Fred this story, he looked at me and said, "Maybe that's what I am, an old fool, for not being willing to take a good look at myself." The next day he got hold of the Twelve-Step Book and began preparing himself for the exciting adventure of self-discovery.

When we have the honesty to face ourselves, we begin to walk out of every shadow into the sunshine. But we must be willing to be specific about ourselves and not deal in generalities. As Philip Brooks the great Bostonian preacher once said, "Men should not be content to call themselves miserable sinners and leave it at that. Call yourself a coward, a liar, a cad, a thief, a drunk, if you like, but never by such a general term as 'sinner.' "

Facing the Fear

We probably all recognize easily that nothing can trigger off fear more quickly than the prospect of searching our hearts fearlessly, looking at ourselves from a moral point of view. It can cause so much nervous anxiety that we feel better off not doing it. But if we are going to "find ourselves," we must come to grips with the moral foundation of our lives—where we have succeeded and where we have failed. It's scary, but it leads to liberty.

Cecil Osbourne, in his book *The Art of Understanding Yourself*, states that we all deal with anxieties in one of four negative ways. Because of inner fear, we either suppress our anxiety or ignore it. We either rationalize it by explaining it away or numb it, usually with the help of drugs or alcohol. Each option increases anxiety. Only by confrontation can it be constructively modified as Step Four in the Alcoholics Anonymous program of recovery encourages. It compels us to face the reason behind our reluctance to face ourselves fearlessly. Why are we reluctant to deal with the real truth about our attitudes and behavior produced by an alcoholic lifestyle? Is it because in our heart of hearts we know we won't like what we see? This, understandably, creates fear. We imagine it too great an undertaking, and opt out of this encounter with self.

I've known a considerable number of alcoholics who have achieved sobriety without taking the Fourth Step. Some boast about it, but most recognize they have missed the full meaning of true sobriety. If an alcoholic's peer, however, has taken the Fourth Step, usually he will as well. Fear can be overcome by a positive example.

Dr. Victor Frankl, the great Jewish psychiatrist, tells us in his book, *Man's Search for Meaning*, that during the war when he was in the Nazi concentration camps, only those people with something to live for survived. If a person gave up hope, they simply turned their faces to the wall, and died. We must have purpose.

Don't Minimize the Struggle

The Fourth Step doesn't deny its difficulty. It requires a fearless spirit to undergo thorough investigation. But even though we approach this step with trepidation, we can follow some helpful guidelines. One is to recognize the need for a life of purpose. Without a sense of meaning, life simply doesn't compute—it goes nowhere.

Bob was dry, but not sober. True, he hadn't had a drink for five years, but he had character defects he had never faced, making it hard for his family to get along with him. "Sometimes, I don't know if I'd rather see him drunk again, or living the way he is right now," his wife Eileen sighed. She was grateful that he was not drinking, yet his refusal to modify his character stymied their married life.

But when Bob took the challenge offered by an A.A. brother one night to examine his life, a new sense of purpose began to grip him. "I never thought I'd feel so good," Bob exclaimed, almost bewildered by what was happening. But the more he looked at his past and recognized his need for its honest exposure, the healthier he became.

We should also recognize that this inner need for meaning intertwines with our craving for security. This powerful instinct reduces to one of our most basic needs. Minus our securities, we can potentially fall apart at the seams. Food preserves us physically. Our sexual relationships reflect that we need good friendships with other men and women—to care for others as well as ourselves. These fundamental, innate drives help us realize our full humanity. But because we so often succumb to anxiety, we exaggerate their importance. They can take over and control our behavior.

The power of appetite, sex, money and pleasure can enslave us. Characteristic of unfulfilled humanity, they are experienced universally regardless of race, color, culture, education or sex. Psychologists agree that most of our emotional problems stem from uncontrolled, unfulfilled, instinctual desires. These God-given gifts, rather than blessing our lives, often hinder our maturity and satisfaction.

Being Set Free From the Powers

The Fourth Step challenges us to face these controlling powers, so we can find freedom from their grasp.

How have these natural instincts come to wield such power over us? We need to stop running and examine the dynamics of unhappiness that have warped and twisted our lives. If we shrink in fear refusing to face ourselves, we will have little hope of inner peace or lasting sobriety. This new way of life will elude us if we fail to examine our hearts with their pernicious character defects.

The Daily Fourth Step

While Alcoholics Anonymous encourages the Fourth Step for lasting sobriety, it does not preclude the need for daily self-examination like an unknown poet who writes:

Let not sleep come upon thy languid eyes
Ere thou has scanned the action of the day
Where have I sinned? What done or left undone

From first to last, examine all, and thus
Blame what is wrong and in what is right, rejoice.

In T.R. Glover's book, *The Conflict of Religions in the Roman Empire*, along with asking the question many Christians ask themselves at day's end, he records one believer as saying, "I hide nothing from myself. I pass over nothing." Both Roman Stoics and Christians were admonished by their spiritual leaders to "Look within."

Of course, the character formed by the Christian understanding of morality is going to undertake this process with greater assurance of forgiveness than anyone else. Already the Christian experiences the joy of being forgiven past sins and, therefore, he or she can undertake this daily examination with courage—especially in the light of the words of Jesus from the cross, "Father forgive them, for they know not what they do" (Luke 23:34).

If we want our lives set free from the disturbing effects of a bad conscience, we must honestly examine our daily behavior in the presence of God. We will find that sleeplessness (a common problem among alcoholics) evaporates and the need for sleeping medication disappears gradually. A calmness and peace of mind will begin to develop in our hearts and minds when we honestly assess our actions, words and attitudes.

Allowing the Holy Spirit to Illuminate

As we ask the Holy Spirit of God, called the Spirit of Truth by Jesus, to examine us and report to our conscious minds our previous actions forgotten or repressed, we will be set free from the guilt piled up in our hearts. Jesus taught that one liberating ministry of the Holy Spirit was to convict our consciences of sin. This process is not negative or designed to make us feel miserable and hopeless, but rather, to draw our sin out into God's light for healing. Called "catharsis" by psychological therapists, it recalls from the sub-conscious all that needs disposal. Just as the body alerts us to the danger of a sore or cut by creating pain, so guilt stirs to seek relief from the poisonous effects of personal sin and misbehavior.

The Key to Spiritual Growth

Throughout Christian history, self-examination has been necessary for maturity in Christ. The Puritan Christians of England in the seventeenth century stressed its practice. They worked hard taking honest inventory of their words and actions. Although they dispensed with the confessional used by Roman Catholics, Anglicans and Lutherans, which required a priest intermediary, they devoted themselves to the personal, sometimes grueling, task of daily assessment in God's presence only. Ruthlessly honest, they depended upon the Holy Spirit to search out their hearts in rigorous self-revelation. Some of their later critics believed they resorted to unhealthy self-crucifixion that degraded their personalities, rather than uplifting them. But credit must be given for the fervor of an inventory that sought only right relationship with God and their fellow man. The Quakers also indulged in this practice. From their calm and self-possessed behavior, we can surmise they achieved this inner peace because they diligently engaged in self-examination.

Some people, influenced by modern psychology, warn us that excessive introspection can only produce a somber approach to life. I readily admit that the possibility exists, because searching the depths of the subconscious and unconscious to dredge up the past resembles digging in a Irish bog—there is no end to it. That is the reason why the psalmist prayed, "Search me, O God." He asked God to investigate his conscience, because He alone knew what needed surfacing and when. To enter complete understanding prematurely may only result in depression. Unless we can cope with it, it could cause despair or suicide.

God deals with us so tenderly. In releasing the subconscious, He only permits measured amounts to emerge, so we can deal with it effectively at a particular point in our spiritual journey. For this reason the Fourth Step is an on-going process, never completed once and for all.

I know many A.A. members who undergo self-inventory

regularly. On an annual basis, they also undertake the Fifth Step of sharing with another person about the exact nature of their faults (dealt with in the next chapter). In this way, they can live with a clear conscience free from relentless guilt.

Our Reluctance to Face Ourselves

Today, however, we seem in little danger of excessive self-scrutiny. Few people, even professing Christians, willingly examine their behavior. Many of us are remiss in daily stock-taking, to say nothing about dealing with our past. We need the light of God's Word to reflect our behavioral defects.

A story is told about a Portuguese nun in the Middle Ages who escaped from her convent because she could not adhere to the strict discipline of her Order. At the house she fled to for safety, the first thing she asked for was a mirror. For years she had not been allowed to see her reflection and she had forgotten what she looked like.

Our lives need this reflection too. The mirror of God's Word enables us to discover what we really look like inside, enabling us to attain true self-knowledge. The ugly witch in *Snow White and The Seven Dwarfs* couldn't countenance the magic mirror because it only revealed the beauty of Snow White. Many of us are afraid to take up this task of self-examination for the same reason. We are afraid of what we will see. Yet we needn't be because the Christian Faith assures us that confessing our shortcomings to God results not only in forgiveness, but also cleansing. The past is removed as if it never happened. The Apostle John writes a most reassuring truth about biblical Christianity, "If we confess our sins, God is faithful and just and will forgive our sins, and cleanse us from all unrighteousness" (1 John 1:9). The Apostle Paul also reaches the same principle. We do not merely receive forgiveness when we are open-hearted about our need. God clothes us, as it were, with the spiritual righteousness of Christ Himself. God looks at us, not just as his children whom He has freely forgiven, but as his children whom He has dressed in the moral perfection of his own Son. That is why Charles Wesley could write so happily:

Jesus, Thy blood and righteousness
My beauty are, my glorious dress
Mid flaming worlds, with these arrayed
With joy shall I lift up my head.

The Need to Be Fearless

When we begin to work out Step Four, we can do it fearlessly because we have already taken Step Three to heart. We have begun to commit our lives to the care of God, as we understand Him. With no need to fear, we can remember that God is love and that perfect love casts out fear. For this reason nothing is more spiritually satisfying than discovering the reality of God in Jesus Christ. No one ever revealed the mercy, love and forgiveness of God—as well as his restoring power—more than He.

Perhaps the problem many alcoholics and others struggle with today is knowing how to take a fearless inventory. We all need help following good procedure and utilizing hints on how to make it successful. As an ancient writer states, "There are many hiding places and recesses in the mind." Alcoholics Anonymous provides members with helpful guidelines on how to take a good inventory in the book, *The Twelve Steps of Alcoholics Anonymous.* But other ways may also be utilized. If a person comes from a Roman Catholic or Anglican background, they can be helped by seeking a spiritual director to assist them in their pilgrimage. Reading some of the great literature of famous Christian people can also be helpful. For example, in *Works of John Wesley*, chapter eleven (p.521-23), he recalled how he and his friends at Oxford formed a fellowship they called by the rather severe name, "The Holy Club." He reported how, after attending Church, they met together to examine themselves in the light of God's Word, using five particular subjects to assist them: (1) awakening - moral or ethical; (2) purgation - purging the flesh through self-denial; (3) illumination - the witness of God's Spirit; (4) the dark night of the soul - compelling or forcing the mystic to come to him by naked faith; (5) union with God - involving a constant awareness of God's presence (*John Wesley -*

His Life and Ideology, Robert Tuttle, Zondervan, p.116). Then beginning Monday, they devoted themselves to a consideration of how they treated their fellow man. This occupied their attention for the rest of the week.

This may sound excessively introspective for the average person today, for we know that the Christian life is more than just analyzing what we have done and what we haven't done. However, we all need some effective method of self-examination. The Twelve-Step book in Alcoholics Anonymous suggests that you begin with the art of meditating. The Eleventh Step, considered at the end of this book, suggests that the Holy Spirit uses this medium to put us in touch with ourselves and our past. He helps us recall the sins we need to confess. If we use the Bible as a means of meditation, He will direct us to the appropriate promises of God. Self-examination primarily challenges us to appreciate the love and grace of God, alone able to lift our hearts with the hope that He hasn't given up on us and never will. He rescues us from the downward drag of past failures, be they with God, significant people in our lives or with ourselves.

The Secrets of Self-Assessment

The uplifting, liberating secrets of self-assessment are twofold. In the concluding verses of Psalm 39, the writer reveals this primary principle no one can ever discover apart from the illuminating work of God's Spirit. He invites the Lord to "try our reins and our hearts." In other words, to put our lives to the test. For this to happen, we must give Him the "green light" to proceed searching our hearts. God will never work against our wills. Hardness of heart will develop only as we reject the ministry of his Spirit, ever-seeking to confront us with the truth about ourselves. Often, confession of sin, and the willingness to let God search our hearts first happens when we come to the "end of our rope"—when we tire of basking in the false light of our own moral achievements, no longer given to self-congratulatory righteousness, no longer justifying ourselves and our actions. Then we are ready for honest confession.

Mary D. was a moral, upright person, comfortably conscious of her stature in the community. Suddenly, her husband died. As she grappled with her loneliness after thirty years of married life, she relied more and more on the crutch of alcohol. Before long, she was lost in dissipation.

"I don't know what do do," she wailed one night, as she sat in my study. "I've always tried to do the right thing, but here I am, hooked on alcohol."

"Have you ever thought you might need what A.A. offers?"

She looked at me with raised eyebrows. "That's for drunks," she replied with disgust.

"No," I answered, "it's not for drunks on skid row alone, but for everyone trying to escape alcohol addiction, no matter what side of the tracks they come from. I know people in A.A. from every walk of life, and most of them are achieving sobriety. I think you need to take a look at it too."

Some weeks later, I took her to her first A.A. meeting and she began to discover that she didn't need to resort to self-destruction in dealing with her grief. She began to take the A.A. program seriously, and eventually got to Step Four.

"I don't know what I can say about myself," she said to me. "I've always lived such a respectable life before alcohol took over."

"Why don't you just sit quietly in your room," I suggested, "and ask God to show you what He wants you to know about yourself." She was a little dubious, but, not willing to give way to fear, she started the process.

"I never thought I was as rotten as I've been discovering," she told me one evening. "I've been so snobbish, so self-righteous, so proud of my accomplishments. I could never have discovered what kind of person I am unless God had showed it to me. It sure works, when you give Him a chance. But the great thing is that I'm feeling free for the first time. I sure had a lot of garbage to get rid of, the kind that most people don't think is too awful, but I certainly needed to discover what I have done to others and to myself through my pride."

Jesus illustrates this principle of self-discovery by telling of two men who went to pray at the temple at the appointed hour of prayer (Luke 18:9-14). One of them was a Pharisee, part of the religious establishment. Impressed with his own moral character, he didn't hesitate to boast about it. "Lord," he prayed, "I thank you that I am not like other people. I pray, I fast, I tithe of all that I possess." Our Lord, with veiled humor, comments, "This man prayed with himself." His admiration society had one member. He would never ask the Lord to search his heart. All he expected from God was, "Congratulations."

The other man was a publican, a despised tax collector who exploited his own countrymen through embezzled taxes. Wealthy, no doubt, from his liaison with the Romans, he eventually repents of sin. He knew he was guilty of breaking the Seventh Commandment, "Thou shalt not steal." Now he was ready to renounce his self-righteousness and admit that his life was shot through with the holes of disobedient behavior, selfishness, and materialism. In honest desperation, he hardly dared look heavenward when he cried, "God, be merciful to me a sinner." It was this man, and not the other who returned home in right relationship with God.

This always happens when we are freed from misconceptions about ourselves. As we give God authority to search our hearts, the freer we feel within ourselves. "Letting it all hang out" is not easy. If we ask for God's help as the Psalmist did, however, we will find his help beyond imagining. "If God is for us," asks the Apostle Paul, "who can be against us?" This rings particularly true in the business of daily inventory.

Where There Is a Will, There Is a Way

This willingness to let God search us implies that both God and man cooperate in the process of self-examination. He wants us to be free, but He will free us only when we give Him the privilege. We must cooperate by giving Him the right of way.

God always prevails upon us in our life experiences to expose our inner selves. As we sit in a bar, for example, trying to fill our lives with happiness and listen to what is happening in our hearts, we will become conscious of Someone trying to reach us. As we note what is happening, we will sense that He wants to make us realize the futility of seeking true satisfaction from something not designed for it. Most bars swell with people looking for friendship. But almost all healed alcoholics I have met say that the bar is perhaps one of the most lonely places. Alcohol only creates the illusion of contentment, of meeting friends, of being accepted. Little wonder so many today are duped into searching there. But this chemically based illusion cannot touch the deeper dimensions of a person's life. Education, the arts, sport activity, science and even daily work cannot provide lasting fulfillment. God's Spirit constantly warns us about them by creating emptiness in our hearts, if only we would acknowledge it. The more we get, the more we want. The more activity we generate, the more we seek, often to the point of exhaustion. The more we travel, the less we are impressed by what we see. The more we learn, the greater our ignorance.

Being Put to the Test

God ever seeks to search us, by challenging our philosophies, leading us beyond them to truth about real life and satisfaction. He will never introduce this truth, however, without our permission. When we realize the futility of life without Him, when we ask Him to test our moral standards, true self-discovery can begin and lead us to happiness. First comes the pain of discovering our perversions, but second comes the pleasure of permanent satisfaction. This puts divine order into our lives.

This happened to Eileen, a woman seemingly incapable of shaking her false basis of happiness. She grew up wealthy, with alcohol an integral part of her existence. When she crossed the line between social drinking and problem drinking, I don't know. As her drinking degenerated into dissipation, even her family distanced themselves from her. They couldn't tolerate her bizarre behavior. In her misery, she turned to A.A. for help. Its precepts led her into self-awareness and released her from dependency on alcohol. But she balked at the Fourth Step that challenged her to make an honest inventory. Pride had blinded her. She admitted she was alcoholic, but she feared facing her life of rejection.

One night we were talking about her need to "let it all hang out" to understand why she still felt empty inside, despite sobriety.

"I can't understand why I feel so miserable at times. Oh, at the A.A. meetings I get a real lift. It is great being with people who accept you—at least they seem to. But, when I'm alone with myself, I go through hell trying to get my life together. What's wrong?" she asked.

I sensed she was at the threshold of discovery because she was asking questions about herself. That often signals that God is about to break through.

"Eileen," I replied, "one of the most important things I've learned in life is the importance of measuring lives by an adequate standard. Most of us live as a law unto ourselves. Right and wrong has become subjective. With our permissive lifestyles, little wonder chaos undermines our peace of mind."

"Maybe that's why I'm feeling so miserable," Eileen responded. "When I was growing up, no one seemed to place any restraints on my life. I got what I wanted and did pretty much what I wanted to do. I don't think I've ever given thought as to right or wrong. I've just done what I wanted to do. No wonder I'm still depressed, in spite of being sober."

"I'm sure that's behind much of your unhappiness, Eileen." I replied. "One of the most important discoveries that we can make is that when we violate the laws of God, we really don't break them—they break us. Broken, they render us bruised and bleeding. The Ten Commandments help us come to grips with the disharmony in our lives. The teachings of Jesus in the Sermon on the Mount also provide us with a standard to evaluate how we are living. Judging ourselves by these standards, we realize how much we have separated ourselves from others, and particularly from God. Then we can recognize our need for Someone Who alone can set us free to obey these precepts from the heart."

I had given Eileen a New Testament that she had been reading. "Is that why Paul says, 'The Law is a schoolmaster to bring us to

Christ?' I was reading that the other day and it triggered off the realization that I needed something more than rules and regulations to guide my life."

"That's perfectly true," I answered. "As the Spirit of Christ takes possession of our hearts, his power enables us to discover the new way—the way of love between ourselves and God and between ourselves and others. He also helps us realize that He constantly forgives us, because none of us ever reaches the high standards outlined in the Law. Knowing we are forgiven for falling short liberates the mind."

Measuring Our Actions

A psychological error, commonly committed today—even by those enlightened by biblical truth—is to measure our actions by current standards of morality. But this subjective approach changes with every new generation. Behavior frowned upon as immoral a generation ago has become integral to our way of life. This only contributes insecurity and instability, a great part of emotional illness today. Reports from therapists working in mental institutions indicate that many people suffer nervous breakdowns because they built their lives upon the false suppositions others have thrust upon them. Also, many have developed false guilt and inferiority complexes because they have governed their lives by devotional Christian literature that depreciates the self.

Concentrating on the Good

When you approach the Scriptures with an open mind, you will realize that the Gospel writers did not take this position. When the Apostle Paul encouraged the Corinthians to make sure they were living out their faith, he reminded them of a fundamental Christian truth: "Do you not know that Jesus Christ is in you? (2 Corinthians 13:5). Christians are admonished toward positive concentration. If we only focused on the wrong we have done to ourselves and others, we would find ourselves dragged down with depression. We also need to consider the good at work in our lives. The A.A. program also encourages this approach when one begins to take seriously the Fourth Step. Someone has insightfully suggested that we take a miner's viewpoint. He does not concentrate on the dirt and dust in the gold mine but rather searches for the streak of gold.

We too, must examine our lives, not only for the evil, but also to affirm the good. God has produced much in us that is "lovely and pure and of good report." The presence of Christ in us assures us that his presence is creating new life in us. We may not be perfect, as the preamble to the *Big Book of Alcoholics Anonymous* states, but we are not altogether evil. Unfortunately, the doctrine of original sin, or what has been called "total depravity," has been greatly misunderstood, even within the Church. This doctrine does not teach that we can do nothing good, but rather, that we can do nothing good enough to win the love and acceptance of God. He gives it freely, not on the basis of our goodness, or lack of it, but because He wants to be gracious, willing to forgive our sins for Christ's sake. Liberation comes independently of any human achievement. This not only frees us from pride, but helps us humbly rejoice in the love of God. Wonder and liberation come from knowing that He has accepted us as we are, despite our sin and failure. The old black preacher's words reflect these thoughts appropriately: "I ain't what I ought-er be, and I ain't what I'm gon-er be, but thank God, I ain't what I use-ter be."

The Old Has Gone, The New Has Come

Committing your life to the care of God in terms of Jesus Christ, you can live a life of faith. It enables you to adopt a fresh approach to life. Salvation is not just a matter of deliverance from sin's consequences, but it is the process by which Christ living in me—in you—creates a brand new person. Gert Bahanna, the famous converted alcoholic, entitled her autobiography, *The Late Liz,* for this reason. She could look back on the old person she used to be and realize that person no longer existed. The Apostle Paul affirms this when he wrote to the Corinthians, "If anyone is in Christ, he is a new creation, the old things are passing away, and all things are becoming new" (2 Corinthians 5:17). As we close each day, we should ask, "Have I been living out the new life Jesus Christ gives me freely?" This will make your honest inventory a positive, nurturing experience, not a negative, self-depreciating one.

STEP FOUR: **Made a searching and fearless inventory of ourselves.** *Alcoholics Anonymous*

TRACK TWO: **Search me, O God, and know my heart, try my anxious thoughts and see if there be any offensive way in me, and lead me in the way of everlasting [a new quality] life.** *Psalm 139:23,24*

The Challenge of Self-Analysis

The need for self-analysis to improve our behavior originated far before the Christian Church. The psalmist David, who lived a thousand years before the birth of Christ, knew the importance of making an honest search of his innermost being that he called "the heart." He also knew his powerlessness to undertake such a search without divine assistance. Therefore he called upon God to help him scrutinize every part of his life. He knew that only God could give him grace to be completely open to the truth about himself. He knew that we human beings naturally defend ourselves and resist the searchlight of truth. Self-examination, in a thoroughly ruthless and honest way rarely proceeds unless God empowers us to undertake this "scary" process.

"I don't think I'll ever get around to taking Step Four," sighed Bob, as we sat talking in his car after an A.A. meeting. "I'm afraid if I ever honestly get down to the bottom of things, I'd 'chicken out.' I'll just be glad to stay sober—forget about everything else."

"Would you like to take the Fourth Step if you could?" I asked.

"Well, sure. I think I might try it, if I could find someone who would help me," he answered.

"Who did you ask to help you with your sobriety?" I quizzed.

He looked at me quietly for a moment and then said, "Why, God. He's the only one Who could have done it. It's sure not something I did for myself."

"Don't you think He could give you the power to do the Fourth Step, especially if you asked Him to?" I inquired.

"I don't suppose He'd turn me down, if I really asked Him to help and really meant it," he replied.

"Bob, that's what many people have discovered, when they were willing to ask." Not only did King David have the courage to ask God to help him search his heart, but you find the same attitude in many of the famous Greek and Roman philosophers. Senecca, for example, a contemporary of the Apostle Paul, tells us of a certain friend of his who engaged in daily self-searching. "If I remember correctly," he wrote, "when the day is over, Sextus used to ask in his mind, What habit of yours have you cured today? What vice have you resisted? In what respect are you better?"

"I suppose that's a good way to begin," Bob responded, "just dealing with your life one day at a time. I guess if I started that way, I'd find God helping me dig back a little farther, until I had dealt with everything in my life."

"That's a great thing to realize, Bob," I replied. "That's what the early Christians did and they weren't any different from us. In fact, the people from Corinth lived in one of the most morally degenerate cities in the Roman world. Probably most of the Christians had a past that would startle you. But Paul carefully encouraged them to examine their behavior and attitudes, especially before taking communion, a weekly if not daily observance. He wrote them and said, 'But let a person examine himself, and so let him eat and drink of the bread and cup' (1 Corinthians 11:12). In this second letter to these people he reiterates the same principle. 'Examine yourselves daily whether you be in the faith. Test yourselves' (2 Corinthians 3:5).

"So you can see that the Fourth Step of A.A. didn't just begin with the founders, it has had a long history. In fact the men who initiated A.A. were inspired by the Bible as well as other writings and encouraged this practice which significantly marks the spiritual life of those serious about their relationship with God."

This little "pep talk" of mine got Bob moving toward the Fourth Step and within the week, he had not only made an honest, fearless inventory, but he had made contact with a friend to work on the Fifth Step.

When we are willing to examine ourselves this way, we notice that our attitudes toward ourselves and others modify considerably. There will be increasing self-acceptance that develops into more understanding, patience and empathy toward others.

Robert Burns once said, "Gently scan your fellow man." We can do this if we heed the words of Chaucer, "Examine your own thoughts well," or the words of Roger Bacon, "He that questions himself much shall learn much."

Dealing With the Powers

Many kinds of power seek to control us and steal our freedom—not only alcohol, which the *Big Book* describes as cunning, baffling and powerful.

One of the most powerful is sexual satisfaction. This natural need often takes such strong hold of people that they can hardly think of anything else. This is true, not only in our sex-dominated age, but in all preceding periods of history. It dogs us continually, particularly through the power of modern advertising sales—from automobiles to toothpaste. And with sexual fulfillment so often divorced from love, we often forfeit meaningful love relationships with opposite sex partners. The indiscriminate use of our sexual drives will never fulfill us. Young people discover this after living promiscuously in their teenage years. By the time they reach their early and late twenties, they are almost "burned out." The possibility of sexual fulfillment almost escapes them. E. Stanley Jones, in his book *Abundant Living,* tells of a young man who left a suicidal note which read, "Died, an old man at twenty-one."

Money Won't Buy It

Another powerful force that seeks to dominate us is the mania for money—an incessant driver. Many people seek the happiness they believe money can buy. They fail to recognize that, although we all need some money, what we need even more are the things we cannot buy.

It often happens that the more we acquire, the deeper our emptiness, because material things alone cannot buy happiness.

Otherwise, the happiest people in the world would be the rich. But studies show that wealth makes people genuinely more miserable than anything else. Billy Graham once said that the most unhappy man he had ever met was the richest man in Texas. When the Duchess of Windsor died, a leading weekly periodical described the fear-ridden life she lived because of her enormous wealth. Living in a huge chateau in Paris behind high walls, with electronic gates for safety, a night watchman patrolling the grounds with trained dogs and with a revolver by her bedside table, she lived in constant dread of being robbed. Today, millions of people enter government-sponsored lotteries in the false hope of winning a ticket to happiness.

Searching for Security

Another form of power that dominates us is our search for personal security through personal relationships. Instead of entering into marital relationships for love, many people chose a partner to meet personal needs. They substitute "I love you, therefore I need you," for "I need you, therefore I love you." Of course, most people don't consciously marry for this reason—they don't yet recognize their real needs. They haven't matured sufficiently to discern what they are. They have been shielded so often by over-protective parents, never learning to shoulder legitimate responsibilities of life. They always expect their parents to rescue them from tight spots. This situation often accompanies the unhealed alcoholic who seeks their financial assistance whenever he gets into an alcoholic "jam." Many women in Alanon make this painful discovery when they begin to confront their neurotic relationship with their drinking husband.

This kind of insecurity often surfaces from widowed parents who expect their children to care for them both emotionally and economically, with the incumbent pressure of guilt if their expectations are not fulfilled. Their insecurity precludes any effort to fulfill their own needs.

The longing for security often expresses itself in the desire to use and manipulate people for our own ends. False power often goes to our heads, be it in business, government, the money or the church. People will try to control the activities and beliefs of others, threatening repercussions if not received. Many people fear what others might do to them if they resist control. Often this power mania explodes in some bizarre way and those so enslaved seek their own happiness apart from those who sought to dominate them. We have all heard about the husband who walks out on his wife after thirty years of marriage to find his freedom.

Missing Out on Happiness

Wrong use of these instinctual energies results in inner conflict and robs a person of true happiness. People have not discovered how to control these drives and therefore feelings of anger, jealousy and resentment dominate them. Their wishes and dreams are not fulfilled according to their narrow perceptions.

This, in turn, makes the people experiencing the brunt of their outbursts of anger, jealousy and resentment, feel rejected, cut-off and alienated. Those who suffer from alcoholic addiction often invite the rejection of others. Their own self-centeredness contributes to rejection by those they victimize. The circle is vicious. Many alcoholics in A.A. admit they often continued to drink, even after they realized its devastation, just to control their depression, stimulated by their own behavior patterns. Their negative actions and reactions toward others made their lives miserable so they kept turning to alcohol to forget it.

Satisfying sobriety cannot be achieved without a willingness to face these facts, in honest assessment. We must come to grips with all those instinctual, God-given drives, somehow now out of control and frustrated by alcohol.

The Need for Affirmation

Alcoholics must also face the fact that they may have been brought up in homes with little or no positive affirmation. They never received recognition for their accomplishments or abilities.

I have met and talked with many alcoholics who have never had a single word of congratulations for anything they have done. Mary, a qualified secretary, whose drinking brought her life down to poverty and ruin, told me that whenever she brought home her report card with B's her parents would say, "Don't you think you could have done better and got a few A's?" When she got a few A's, instead of recognizing this, they would say, "Well, you sure need to work harder to get your Math mark up." Never a word of encouragement, no matter how hard she tried. Of course, the tragedy is that her parents probably did not receive affirmation in their childhood, so they have no idea how to give it to others. This root problem lies beneath much repressed anger in most people's lives.

Common depression is simply repressed anger that erupts in bad temper and a determination to get the attention of our parents or family in negative ways.

A young man who had been adopted by his parents after thirteen years of marriage lived in my home for several years. He had never been encouraged in anything he ever did. If he excelled in anything, he was always told he could have done better. Never a word of affirmation to acknowledge his ability. Little wonder that he became a hippie, with the long hair, the beard and the sloppy clothes to signal his cry, "Listen, here I am. Look at me. I'm me, and I can do something. I can make you get upset with me."

Negative Behavior Backfires

The lack of positive affirmation triggers negative behavior to get attention. But it always backfires, because it doesn't achieve what it really needs. Bad behavior always produces guilt and self-hate. The discovery of alcohol to remedy these wounded feelings comes as welcome relief. In a depressed state, recovering alcoholics often undertake the Fourth Step with an attitude of morbid self-depreciation. They often search for every character defect, hoping to free themselves from inferiority. On the surface it appears as humility, but actually it expresses hidden pride. When the Fourth

Step encourages us to take an honest inventory, we must not dwell upon the negative aspects of our behavior. We must not embark on a depressing rehearsal of our moral weakness, ignoring the good. This can trigger a desire to return to drinking to overcome the pain accompanying this morbid self-examination.

Facing Up

On the other hand, some alcoholics have been brought up in homes where pride and the spirit of self-righteous accomplishment has been encouraged. When they eventually confront the problems created by uncontrolled drinking, alcoholics are often encouraged by the A.A. sponsor to take the Fourth Step. This may somehow be interpreted as a "put down," and they may take offense that they really need to go that far. Instead of wanting to face their weaknesses and expose them to the light, they attempt to cover up these defects by pointing to the positive elements in their lives—good moral conduct, acts of love and kindness. They imagine this "goodness" atones for the wrongs done to others due to their drinking. They hesitate to give up drinking until it becomes worse. Thus, many alcoholics continue their destructive habits. When they stop drinking, they foolishly imagine that all moral weakness will almost instantly disappear.

However, as an alcoholic seriously tackles the painful, but revealing experience of self-examination, he must be willing to do so with complete dedication to thoroughness. Halfway measures will yield minimal improvements in character. If he remembers God loves him unconditionally, despite all he has done or all he has been, he will be helped immeasurably. God understands perfectly what led to his alcoholism and in his love and mercy readily forgives him. But He knows that the alcoholic cannot experience the reality of his forgiveness, unless he honestly faces the need for self-assessment and repentance. This alone will bring him freedom from the tyranny of self-inflicted rejection, that often stimulates the alcoholic's misconduct. If a person will claim God's love and courageously step forward into a fearless moral inventory, he (or she) will discover

God's presence with all its encouragement and loving acceptance. As he progresses one step at a time through the sometimes dark and gloomy tunnel of moral inventory, God's light will lead him on to the other end. Then he will discover real freedom with its promise of hope-filled new beginnings.

CHAPTER FIVE

STEP FIVE: Admitted to God, to ourselves, and to another human being, the exact nature of our faults.
Alcoholics Anonymous

TRACK ONE: They believed liberty to be the secret of happiness and courage to be the secret to liberty.
Louis Brandeis
U.S. Supreme Court Justice 1856-1941

The Courage to Confess

Confessing moral and spiritual failure takes courage and inner resolution. To do so in the presence of God and then another person only heightens the challenge. Our self-centered ego resists humbling even though we may have an inferiority complex (and most of us do). We still hesitate to expose our innermost beings, because we all share the fear of rejection. We have more than enough of that.

But despite the difficulty, Alcoholics Anonymous knows that the path to full and satisfying recovery from alcoholism requires a Fifth Step. Their experiences have hammered this home. Taking this step will not only launch spiritual freedom, but an unprecedented ability to accept ourselves for who we are.

Opening the Skeleton's Closet

In one of his books, George MacDonald (the man who strongly influenced C.S. Lewis) tells how his wife entered into a new experience of joy and a deepening relationship with him because she exposed her heart to him. He wrote down what she said:

> We sat in the library, where the boxes were being packed and books were lying around the

room, before our departure . . . . and then I opened up my heart to him, as I had never opened it to anyone before. Doubts and fears—sore burdens just then—were bluntly put before him and he sat and listened with utmost patience. It was strange, and yet not so strange, to find myself talking so freely to him. I saw, I felt, his holiness and nearness to God, and yet I should not have been afraid to confess to him my most secret sins. There was a humanity about him, a searching honesty, which along with his sympathy, made me feel that he would understand me. He would not cast me out. Just before I left, he said to me, and I can hear him now, "But after all, whatever help or comfort one may try to give you, it is to follow the advice of Jesus, and to enter your closet and shut the door and pray to your Father, pour out your heart to Him. He will help you as no one else can, and give you the answer of peace.

George MacDonald and His Wife, p. 537

Both dimensions of the Fifth Step converge. She openly confesses to another person and receives the forgiveness only God can give. She opened her heart to George, and he, in turn, encouraged her to seek the full forgiveness that only comes from God through prayer. Both must function together—the human and the divine.

Open confession of our faults (which, interestingly enough, the subconscious mind eagerly unfolds), purges our thinking about ourselves. It will, of course, exercise our wills because God will not force it upon us. Even though we struggle with some particular aspect of our past, confession will create a new power to begin dealing with the faults that have nurtured our carnal nature and marred our past. We need to do this because hidden faults can insidiously infect our whole personality. When we begin to pray, another voice seems to mock our feeble efforts to deal with this particular incident or defect. But when we share them with God and also with another person those feelings begin to lift, allowing a new sense of freedom to surge through our minds.

When Freda took her Fifth Step with me, she acknowledged that trying to be a private person locked away from others was endangering her mental well being. It had only nurtured the drinking problems and character defects she wanted to overcome. Eventually, however, she resolved to face herself. By working on the Fourth Step, she discovered she had offended others and broken the laws of God. To confess her moral deficiencies in a face-to-face encounter with me would be a scary and humiliating process. But somehow she found the strength to begin.

"If I had my 'drothers,' " she said to me, "I'd 'drother' not be here. I'd rather be out fishing, but I can't go on hiding anymore, and so here I am, ready to 'tell all.' "

I encouraged her by reassuring her that what she was about to do would help her round the bend toward a new and exciting road in her pathway to sobriety.

"It is important for you to do this, Freda," I said warmly, "because it will reduce the power of alcoholism and its negative effects. Skeletons in our closets tend to hide there permanently even though our subconscious minds want to shed them. They need to be exposed and faced fearlessly. The only way you can do this is to talk to another person, whom you respect and trust."

I personally felt honored—and humbled—that she chose me to share the deepest secrets of her life. I certainly wanted to be worthy of that trust and respect her right to confidentially.

Fear Leads to Failure

Failure to take this all-important step can only confine us to lifestyles filled with pride. Refusal to be open about the past only strengthens the spirit of dishonesty, a significant defect of alcoholics.

"I could never face the fact that I was more than a weekend drunk," Bob told me, as we began to lay the groundwork for his Fifth Step.

"The Fourth Step forced me to take a good look at myself. Then I began to look around A.A. to find someone who had taken the Fifth Step, and nearly everyone I thought had good sobriety had taken it. By now, I wanted to remain sober so badly, that I knew there was no side-stepping this challenge. All that kept me back was fear. But I knew that if I gave way to fear, I'd be a total failure. I couldn't hack the thought of that, and so here I am—ready to go."

"I'm glad you've recognized the importance of this Step, Bob," I replied, "because this is undoubtedly the reason why a good number of people in A.A. for years have never achieved permanent sobriety. Oh, they've been dry, but there is a difference between being dry and being sober. Slipping off the wagon from time to time happens because they are unwilling and reluctant to confess the exact nature of their faults. For this reason, many alcoholics have never grown spiritually and find it hard to stop taking other people's inventories and criticizing people who have hurt them."

"Right," said Bob, "I've just begun to realize that if we don't come to grips with our past life, our sins and mistakes, our hurts and resentments, then we go right on blaming others for the exact things we haven't dealt with in our own lives."

Here we see that fear—and only fear—keeps a person from progressing toward the kind of sobriety worth having.

Confession Has Been Around a Long Time

Confession to another person as an indispensable feature of inner well being has been around a long time. It was not invented by A.A. It has a significant and honored tradition, particularly in the Christian Church. In fact, A.A. derived it from there. From the beginning, Christians were encouraged to confess their faults one to another. Roman Catholics, Orthodox, and some Anglicans are familiar with this biblical teaching a little more than most Protestants. But in recent years, through the insights of modern psychology, they have become more cognizant of its importance. A.A. seeks to emphasize this critical aspect of spiritual growth in its Fifth Step.

The need to uncover our past to a trustworthy counsellor precedes our growth in spiritual maturity. Many ministers and priests report that they spend much of their time in pastoral counseling, which often involves confession of either true guilt or false guilt. People everywhere, inside and outside the life of the Church, seek release from the disturbing consequences of their past behavior. The founders of Alcoholics Anonymous realized that confession frees a person from the tyranny of the past. The biblical precept that God's grace comes through the medium of a sympathetic, understanding and non-judgmental person builds strong character and develops spiritual maturity.

Discover For Yourself

"What happens when you take your Fifth Step?" Marjorie asked me one evening following our A.A. discussion meeting. "I think I'd like to take it, but what happens?"

"The first thing that happens," I responded, "is to become aware of the inner loneliness brought about by our repression of the past. This unwillingness to open up and confide in another person isolates us. It cuts us off from meaningful relationships with other people, especially in our childhood. You know from your own experience, Marjorie, how much drinking stems from loneliness. Each of us, drinking or not, longs to be known and accepted as we are, yet we fear rejection if we 'tell it like it is.' This fear only insulates us from others. As this sense of loneliness grows unchecked, our lives become increasingly destructive."

"You can say that again," Marjorie replied. "Even when I was supposedly the life of the party, I felt empty and detached from everyone. When I got home and sobered up the next day, I was depressed and desperate with loneliness. All I wanted to do was get drunk again. I didn't want to see anyone, even though I longed for friends and needed them so much. But now, you're telling me, if I hear you, that if I take the Fifth Step, I won't be lonely anymore."

"Well, Marjorie, it will be the beginning," I replied. "Many alcoholics will tell you that even before their drinking affected their relationships with family, friends and co-workers, loneliness was an increasing problem. They couldn't shake that mysterious feeling no matter how hard they tried. They still battled their hurtful past, buried deep in their subconscious minds, yet still affecting their present."

"Right on," Marjorie nodded, "I don't know where I read it, but someone has said that 'life is like a drama in which the major lines are often forgotten.'"

"That's so often true," I responded, "and alcohol helped you play out that artificial part of your life that you couldn't play when you were sober. After every drinking bout, you probably thought that your loneliness would disappear, but the very opposite happened. You were still haunted by the realization that you were still alone—very much alone."

"Yes, there's no question about that," and then she added with a twinkle in her eye, "but since entering Alcoholics Anonymous, I have begun to experience a new sense of belonging. And furthermore, since I've started back to Church again and got involved in one of the discussion groups, this sense of loneliness has begun to lift."

"This was bound to happen," I said, "because A.A. opens the eyes of many alcoholics through the stories told by other sufferers. They begin to realize other people have found sobriety and they bond together. They say to themselves, Could it be that there're other people who feel the way I do about myself? In the realization that others shared their suffering, a door of hope began to open."

"I couldn't agree with you more," Marjorie said enthusiastically. "I have found that being in A.A. has opened up a whole new door of promise for me. I'm not completely free from my loneliness yet, but I feel sure that if I take the Fifth Step and go all the way, I'll start to shake this cloud that has shadowed most of my life since I was in my teens. But I've also discovered that even though I've made many new friends and I'm grateful that they realize where I've come from, I still have a lot of garbage that influences my life and attitudes. I'm beginning to see the need for taking this Step. I need to pour it all out. I need to get rid of everything from my drinking past to be free from the leftovers of my loneliness."

Forgiveness—Freedom from the Past

Taking the Fifth Step not only mitigates loneliness but creates a new sense of peace and forgiveness. Almost every alcoholic I know who takes the Fifth Step, confessing the exact nature of their faults, has discovered this. Many alcoholics have been told that they would never be forgiven for what they have done. But as an open, genuine, thorough confession was made to A.A. friends, or a sponsor, they not only began to feel forgiven themselves, but they had new ability to seek for and accept the forgiveness of others terribly wounded by what they had done.

Robert's long life of drinking alienated him from practically everyone he knew. He had lost his family many years before. His children had faded into the background, and he didn't know where any of them lived. He had lost his job and had been on welfare for many years. His drinking had become more and more destructive, filling his mind with suicidal thoughts.

I met Robert at a mid-week Wednesday dinner I used to have in my church in New Westminster. Through the friendship offered by those who worked with me, and through the message of the films we showed after the dinner, he began to soften up. Instead of leaving immediately after the meal, he began to hang around and talk. One evening we sat down together in the lounge off the dining room and began to share. It had taken four months of bridge-building to make him feel at home. Now he began to open up and talk about his life. He told me all about his drinking years, and how he felt he would probably go right on drinking till he died. "After all, I don't think there's very much to live for," he replied sullenly.

I listened to him as carefully as I could, and then I asked him if he had ever tried A.A.

He replied, "Oh, lots of people have tried to get me to go, but I don't think it would do much good."

"Oh, you might be surprised," I replied. "I know lots of people who felt the same way you do, but they took a chance and went to one of the evening meetings. They met people there whose lives were completely turned around and their alcoholism began to dissipate. They now enjoy a whole new way of life that they might have missed out on, if they had not risked attending. Why don't you try?"

He was thoughtful for a few moments and then to my great surprise and delight he said, "Well, I might go, if you'd go along with me."

We made immediate plans to attend the next meeting. When we entered the meeting hall, we sat at the back and listened to the various speakers describe their alcoholic behavior, as well as what it had done to their lives and the lives of others. Many of the stories described Bob's own life.

After the meeting was over, while we were drinking coffee back at his room, he said, "Well, it does kinda give you hope, doesn't it?"

"Yes," I replied, "it certainly does. And if you keep coming back, you'll not only find sobriety, but new friends who will help you get free from the loneliness eating away at you."

"I sure do need something," Robert answered, "so, if you're game to come with me next week, I'll be back."

Robert not only found sobriety, but the loneliness and despair of his life began to lift. New friends came into his life who became increasingly close to him. Even though family members suspected him at first (when they discovered that he had started to attend A.A.) and kept their distance for some time, they eventually realized that something undeniable had happened to him.

He soon shared with me some deep secrets of his life. After completing the Fourth Step, he took another giant leap and determined to tell God, himself and another person the nature of his faults and failures. In this momentous experience of self-exposure, he discovered a dimension of forgiveness he had never anticipated. A strong sense of his past being blotted out began to take place. As he honestly confessed, he not only discovered that God had forgiven him, but he also began to forgive himself. He then went further and forgave all the people who had hurt him. It wasn't easy, but through the power of God, he forgave others, as God had been forgiving him.

Getting Off Our High Horse

Most alcoholics suffer from a deep inferiority complex, and seek to suppress it. They boast about their drinking bouts, act arrogantly and are filled with pride. They need to "get off their high horse," and discover humility, one of life's most endearing virtues. Realizing the need for humility helps you face yourself as you really are, not as you think you are. Most alcoholics have misconceptions about themselves. Because they tend to denigrate their lives from within, they compensate by acting boastful, macho and opinionated. They need to discover that humility is fundamental to their spiritual renewal.

The virtue of humility, however, is greatly misunderstood. Dickens, in his famous novel, *David Copperfield*, describes a character named Uriah Heep. This man always wrings his hands in an affected way, saying slyly, "I'm just an 'umble man,' Master Copperfield." He is, however, anything but humble. Full of pride and schemes, he feigns humility to cover up his crafty machinations.

"I think humility is just downgrading yourself," Mary admitted to me, when I suggested that this characteristic was vital to alcoholic recovery.

"Do you really think so?" I replied. "I think the opposite myself. I think humility happens when you begin to realize how good God has been to you. When we begin to think about how we have lived our lives and how He puts up with us, we begin to experience humility. Actually, confession helps make us authentic people, not 'make-believe' hypocrites."

"I used to be so deluded about myself," said Dale, another friend of mine in A.A. The Fifth Step helped me face myself and stop hiding from myself and from others."

"I'm sure it has," I responded. "My experience has been that humility makes us willing to honestly examine ourselves. But, have you noticed that this self-discovery needs assistance? By that, I mean that we need to share the discovery of ourselves with another person. Knowing who you are and facing yourself alone is one thing, but sharing yourself with another person makes all the difference. We need the help of another person who has been set free from the slavery of personal guilt."

"I guess that is why I chose you," said Dale. "I sensed in you someone who has experienced God's forgiveness. It makes you seem humble—at least to me."

"There's nothing like knowing God's love and grace," I replied, "so much greater than all our faults and sins. God graciously sets us free from our phoniness, our misconceptions about ourselves, and our oh, so bad misinterpretation of what has happened to us. I can tell you frankly that every person I've ever taken through the Fifth Step has left with a sense of joy and a deeper humility. But they needed someone to act as a channel for his all-accepting love. This helps release healing into every part of our troubled conscience."

STEP FIVE: Admitted to God, to ourselves, and to another human being the exact nature of our faults.
Alcoholics Anonymous

TRACK TWO: Confess your faults one to another, that you may be healed. *James 5:16*

We Belong to One Another

Although the Christian Faith calls a person into personal relationship with God, he cannot mature alone. He must attempt to share his private religious ethic with others at various levels of daily life and behavior.

The words of the Apostle James, "Confess your faults one to the other, that you may be healed," indicate that spiritual life cannot be isolated or detached from fellow believers. We form part of a spiritual relationship described in the New Testament as "the Body of Christ." Just as every part of the body links to some other member, so do Christians. This passage admonishes us to confess sin not only to God but to other Christians. Every person—Christians included—is affected by the sins of others, just as disease in one part of the body affects the other organs and physical parts. True, the individual believer must first get right with God through confession of sin, but this also applies to the believer's relationship with other people. Even though some of our sins have been against ourselves, they are not to be hidden from others in the Body of Christ, any more than hitting our thumb with a hammer can be kept a secret from the rest of the body. But many of our sins have affected others and we must ask their forgiveness. Although we cannot demand repentance from another person, we must seek reconciliation in order to restore healthy spiritual lives.

Despite this clear biblical teaching, most Protestant Churches neglect the need to confess our sins to another person besides God. Some circles roundly resist and condemn as a Roman Catholic practice the "evil" of the confessional. True, in some instances, the Roman Catholic confessional has been abused by the clergy, but overall, I believe that those confessors receive more of a sense of forgiveness, release from guilt and acceptance by God, than most Christians of the Protestant Church. I believe the practice of spoken confession is better than no confession at all.

Vertical and Horizontal Christianity

Confession is good for the soul, not only in our relationship to God, but also in our relationship with each other. It must be vertical and horizontal. The Apostle Paul encourages us as he writes of God's grace shown by his willingness to forgive because of the sacrifice of Jesus Christ. But often we stop there in understanding the full range of divine forgiveness. We ignore, or sidestep the words of the Apostle James. In his letter to the early Christians, he insists that spiritual healing must be experienced on the human level as well. "Confess your faults one to the other, that you may be healed." Much emotional, physical and spiritual illness in the Church can be traced to this neglect. Many Christians, who boast of the grace of God and sincerely believe they are forgiven, still labor under the weight of personal guilt with no real assurance of God's unconditional acceptance. Undoubtedly, a number of reasons abound, but one reason I know about personally is an insistence upon secrecy.

I was brought up in a devout Presbyterian home, where my parents believed they were training us adequately about Christian truths, as they understood them. One concept they hammered home to my brother and I was the importance of not telling anything about our personal lives outside the family. As a consequence, I developed a secretive spirit, and found it almost impossible to be open about my feelings. In fact, I became so out of touch with how I felt, that I became almost totally cerebral in my approach to life. My inner conflicts, doubts, fears and sins were suppressed and often denied. This pattern, that began in my childhood and early teens, intensified in my life as a minister, especially after reading the book, *The Power of Positive Thinking,* by Norman Vincent Peale. If he intended this reaction, I'm obviously not sure. But I do know that I hated to deal with anything negative in my life. If you had asked me how I was feeling, I would have responded by telling you how I thought I should feel—and not my actual feelings at that moment. The suppression of my feelings made me aggressive in my own views about life and Christianity in particular. Often manipulative in what I wanted to achieve in my ministry, I needed emotional freedom and healing from this false way of life. Yet it can only come when you honestly and openly express your struggles.

Change came after two events. In 1956, I was introduced to the Faith at Work Movement through its monthly publication by the same name. This movement encouraged Christians to openly confess their weaknesses, their struggles and their sins. It took seriously the words of Paul in his second letter to the Corinthians, "I will therefore boast about my weaknesses, that the power of Christ may rest upon me" (2 Corinthians 12:9). As I attended Faith at Work Conferences and became involved in small group dynamics, I began to open up somewhat, letting some of my struggles with life, "hang out"—but not entirely.

It was not until 1968 that I opened up more deeply. During a three-month sabbatical study leave at Earlham College, Richmond, Indiana, I studied under Dr. Elton Trueblood.

In my first week at the college, I learned of a discussion group organized by one of the professors and held in his home. Because I was lonely, I felt the impulse to join the group. It enfolded a wide swath of people—some old, some young, some students, some ministers and lay people from various churches. It varied not only in age and occupation, but also in theology. Some were liberal in their understanding of Christianity, others more conservative. Some came from mainline churches, and others from more evangelical congregations. Many points of view were represented, as you can imagine.

In many ways, I could have dropped out after the first night. But as I said, I was lonely and needed friendship. I also liked to meet in groups where I could share what I believed because my faith mattered so much to me. Some people in the group said things I emphatically disagreed with and in my aggressiveness, I tried to get them to think my way.

One young man had recently returned from Laos where he had been serving in the military. Of Lutheran background, he had decided to enter the ministry. But he was trying to assess what he really believed. One evening he confessed his difficulty even in believing in God. I saw him as a person who needed help, so I launched into setting him right theologically. He responded in anger but did not express it openly at first. One night, however, as we engaged in energetic discussion, he lashed at me verbally. He denounced me for my apparent self-righteousness and my inability to hear his heart. I was so stunned by his verbal attack, that I felt the blood rushing out of my head. Everyone reacted. Some thought I needed this put down, others rebuffed him for speaking to me in this way—"After all," they said, "I was older, a Minister and should receive more respect."

How did I react? At first I felt like writing him off as just a young, ignorant student with a lot to learn and who probably needed to be converted. But as I walked home, the Holy Spirit brought to my mind the words of a book I had been reading. The book, *The Release of the Spirit,* by the great, modern Chinese martyr, Watchman Nee, developed the theme of taking seriously the words of the Psalmist, "a broken and contrite heart, O Lord, you will not despise." I began to face my pride, my hiddenness, my egoism, my unwillingness to let people know the real Cal Chambers. As I struggled with my feelings, I was prompted to write Joe a letter. Not only did I apologize for the way I insensitively dealt with his struggles of faith, but I opened up for the first time in my life, and let him know something of my own theological pilgrimage, my honest doubts, my unresolved questions and my need for the courage to be more transparent.

During the remaining three months, I built a relationship with Joe that enabled me to confess my faults, failures and sins. It began a profound inner healing for me that increased steadily. I began to be more honest about my struggles and feelings, and also more accepting of those of others—especially my wife Alice and our two daughters. This healing took time, however, because it's hard to unlearn bad habits and false ways of dealing with life. But that night when I was faced starkly and passionately by a young man unafraid to encounter me, my inner freedom germinated.

Not everyone shares that experience. Still, Alcoholics Anonymous and the Christian Faith encourages us to be open before God, ourselves and others so that divine healing can flow into our often warped and misdirected lives.

Now, why should we confess our faults to some responsible, mature person—especially in the family of God? The primary benefit is to release our minds from the pressure of guilt and strengthen our willingness to reveal our humanity. Once we open up to another person and share various faults and sins, as well as what they have done to us and others, God enables us to overcome their effects in our own personal lives and often, in the lives of others.

"Why do you think I need to take the Fifth Step?" Roger, a two-year sober member of A.A. asked one evening, as we shared coffee in his flat. We had just come from a class where he was preparing to be confirmed into the membership of our congregation.

In my talk that evening, I spoke about the divine and human aspect of the forgiveness we all need to accept. I made reference to this truth not only being in the Bible, but also in the A.A. Twelve Steps. (I knew that Roger had begun to find sobriety, but had never taken the Fifth Step.)

To his question I replied, "Well, Roger, I've personally discovered that when we do this, we begin to be free from the downward pull of our faults, which often bind us. You know," I went on, "a concealed sin can infect our whole character and how we live. The unconfessed sin permeates every part of our daily lives. When we go to God in prayer, this unconfessed secret sin makes fun of us. 'So you're a Christian, are you?' it seems to say, 'well, would a real Christian really act like that?' Unconfessed sin, on the horizontal level, keeps us from the full peace of mind God wants us to experience, not only with Him, but also with others."

Roger heaved a big sigh at this point, and then exclaimed, "Perhaps that's the reason why, even though I've become a Christian, I go about my work at the office, and even here at the church, without much heart. I don't even seem to have any real enjoyment in anything I do because my conscience always attacks me saying, You're not much of a Christian, are you?"

"You are so right, Roger," I responded. "Our faults and failures may sometimes not be as bad as we imagine—even exaggerated. But because they are unconfessed, they attack our inner desire to do what is right, and even keep us from an intimate relationship with God. These sins, because they are concealed, can as you suggest become monkeys on our backs."

"But does this end when we open up and let it all hang out?" Roger queried.

"Well, you may have your doubts at this moment," I replied, "but I can assure you from my own experience, as well as what so many others have told me, that all these feelings evaporate once we tell another person, as well as God. The act of confession seems to put a wall around these sins and they can go no farther. You see the wrong, but that is the end of it. The infection causing so much guilt in other areas of our lives begins to dry up. We have cut ourselves off from it and its deleterious effects. This doesn't mean, of course, that we're not sorry for what we've done, but we're set free from its stranglehold. Before we admit them, we feel like hypocrites, insincere and phoney. But with confession, this feeling of hypocrisy lifts. We complete the process of repentance which the Bible encourages."

The more I deal with people, either in A.A. or in the life of the Church, the more I realize the vital role full confession plays. By that I mean the vertical and horizontal factors—to God and to one another. I don't believe I'm exaggerating when I say that until this kind of confession is made to another person, we can never be spiritually free. I know scores of people who seem to be good Christians, sincerely committed to their faith, yet they still struggle with guilty consciences. They always downplay themselves because they have not accepted the full gospel truth. Confession must not only be to God, but also to one another. All our knowledge of the early Church confirms this. In fact, this confession was not made in the secrecy of a confessional booth, such as in the Roman Catholic church, but it was made face to face. But if we've never confessed to another person the exact nature of our faults, we will find it almost impossible to help others so tormented. And this means the fullness of redemption is only partially experienced.

Harold Begbie, in his book *Life Changers*, tells about counseling a young man eager to help a friend involved in sexual trouble with his girlfriend. He tried again and again, but in vain. He asked Begbie why he couldn't seem to help his friend. He had plenty of sympathy and was anxious to help, but somehow he couldn't. Begbie got him to review his past life, and before long they discovered he had unconfessed sin on his conscience. As a young boy he had stolen money from his father's wallet. It was tough, but he went to his father, told him what he had done and asked him to forgive him. He was not only pardoned by his dad, but he was also able to counsel his friend in a positive, helpful way. As Begbie concludes, he writes, "The boy had real pentecostal joy in his own heart." He now had the strength to go all the way in assisting his friend. It was another step toward being fully sanctified (set apart for God's purposes). Confession to God and another person adds new dimension to spiritual freedom.

Another question arises. In our desire to be fully honest with God and others, to whom shall we confess these faults? I was confronted with this question shortly after beginning my involvement with A.A. people considering the Fifth Step.

I remember Bob, who was particularly burdened about who he should ask. I could only reply, "You must trust your own judgment. Do you have an intimate friend who could assist you in your desire to come 'fully clean'?" Most people have at least one person who they feel accepts them, warts and all. Of course, some aspect of our past lives may require the expertise of a qualified counselor. But each of us must ultimately choose one for ourselves.

Fundamentally, this confession must be sincere. You must have a real desire for deliverance from the power of the past. Embarking on this Step with an inner desire for personal gratification can be perniciously deceptive. Sometimes personal testimonies given by Christians in public services leave the impression that the person was boasting about their sinfulness, glad to call themselves "the chief of sinners." Egoism can motivate us this insidiously. But when we analyze our characters, open up and confess our acts or our words, we must not hide our shame and remorse. Neither, however, should we engage in a picayune confession without depth. Remember what Luther's father confessor told him when he kept coming to him with the most trivial offenses, "Don't return until you've something worth confessing."

The joyful truths of evangelical Christianity, based upon Christ's dealing with sinners, his words of forgiveness and his attitude toward the penitent comprise the hope of all who take Him seriously. To experience his forgiveness firsthand, come to God, Who has revealed Himself in the Christ of the cross. Because we can come to the One whose highest expression of love and grace is shown by granting forgiveness to all who seek Him, we can approach him confidently, without fear of condemnation. The second step toward complete forgiveness is to open our hearts to another who can verbally assure us that, "If we confess our sins, God is faithful and just to forgive all our sin, and will cleanse us from all that is unrighteous" (1 John 1:9).

CHAPTER SIX

STEP SIX: **Were entirely willing and ready to have God remove any defects of character.**
Alcoholics Anonymous

TRACK ONE: **We would rather be ruined than change**
We would rather die in our dread
Than climb the cross of the moment,
And let our illusions die
The Age of Anxiety
Wystan Hugh Auden, 1948

The Old for the New

The development of a new way of life depends upon our willingness to change and root out our negative behavior patterns. Many alcoholics want freedom from alcohol dependency, but they often balk at ridding themselves of character defects that have contributed to their alcoholism.

I remember having a long session one night with John, who had taken his Fifth Step and eagerly wanted to make the right choices as far as his lifestyle was concerned.

"How do you change those aspects of your character that always get in the way of your sobriety?" His sincere question revealed a longing to fully recover his sobriety.

In reply, I said, "We can only develop spiritually when we make an honest effort to seek God's help with the seemingly uncontrollable weaknesses that constantly trip us up. I believe that true maturity only comes when we are willing to confront those obstacles that helped create our immaturity."

I then remembered a statement I had underlined in Scott Peck's book, *The Road Less Travelled,* and I went to my bookshelf and pulled it out. I read John those words that had gripped me when I first encountered them.

> Life is a series of problems. Do we want to moan about them or solve them? Discipline is the basic set of tools we require to solve life's problems. Without discipline we can solve nothing. With some discipline we can solve only some problems. With total discipline we can solve all problems (pp. 12, 13).

John scrunched up his face and blurted out, "Discipline. I hate that word." He then went on to explain how he had been forced to tow the line at home and how his father constantly nagged everyone to get up at the right time, not be late for anything and study at the right time. He endured an incessant barrage of "Do this," or "Do that."

"I simply couldn't stand it. When I got to university I was determined to do what I wanted, when I wanted. Discipline, I have had enough of it. I guess that's why I'm such a free spirit today. But then that is what helped make me the alcoholic I am."

"Well, John," I replied, "there certainly is a right way and a wrong way to go about discipline. Sounds like you had a negative dose of it. But real discipline helps us grow up and become responsible. I think that's what the Apostle Paul was driving at when we wrote to the Corinthians, and shared with them his own personal life. In his great poem or treatise—call it what you like—he was honest enough to say, 'When I was a child, I understood as a child, I thought as a child, I acted as a child, but when I became a man, I put away childish things' (1 Corinthians 12:11)."

"I see. That's what Step Six is all about, isn't it?" John said.

"Oh yes," I replied, feeling happy that John had already begun to grasp the significance of this follow-up to Step Five.

"You're so right. That's what this Step tries to emphasize. The only way we can put childish things out of our lives is by practicing the laws inherent in discipline. It's not trying to put a 'heavy' on us, but rather helping us come to grips with erratic behavior. This Step separates the men from the boys, the girls from the women."

I'm Willing, If You're Willing

A disciplined life cannot be forced upon us. Every active A.A. member can tell you from experience that God will help free us from any defect of character, as long as we desire it. He will not force his will upon ours. He will not overstep or violate our wills, his priceless gift. But we can only discover this through personal experience.

"I used to think that people were being theatrical when they made claims about overcoming some of their character defects," Molly shared with me, as a bunch of us had coffee after a late A.A. meeting. "They were just overly enthusiastic, the way some people are about things. Isn't that the way you've felt when you've heard some of their testimonies at A.A. discussion groups?"

I had to admit that I didn't know any alcoholics who made progress in their spiritual growth without experiencing difficulty. I remember Shannon telling me, "My life was in a shambles. My willpower was reduced to zero, but something wonderful happened to turn that all around." I listened to her at first with real scepticism, because she was badly mixed up, and I didn't think anything would change, at least not for a long time. But when I saw her changing in a rather radical way, I approached her with an honest question, "Shannon, how have you done it?"

She smiled, and then told me, "When I came to the end of myself, and was ready to move forward to new levels of responsible behavior, I found that God was there, willing to fortify my will. In some amazing way, He released energy into me to help me work at those defects that had dragged me down for so long."

Shannon wasn't a Christian yet at this point in her life, but I knew that in some beautiful way, she was experiencing what we Christians often call by the theological word, "sanctification," referred to in the previous chapter. This was spiritual growth, strengthened and empowered by God's Spirit of love.

Drinking Undermines Maturity

"Why do I go on drinking like this?" Don asked me, as he was coming off a drunk, and had phoned me to come over and help him sober up. Something inside him rebelled against this kind of irrational behavior, even though he did allow himself to be talked into going into a bar, for just "one drink."

"My body doesn't like the abuse I'm giving it. My mind is telling me that I'm stupid to go on like this. But alcoholism has produced in me a compulsion I just can't overcome."

I reminded him of Step One in A.A. It insists the alcoholic confess that he is powerless, and that even with the best of intentions, he will never make it. But even when the alcoholic recognizes this, as Don was doing, he still has no power to change the downward drag of his self-destructive drinking. This moral and spiritual disease works against the highest and best concepts of life. It beats a person to the ground, trampling upon him body, mind and spirit.

When the alcoholic reaches out for help, the grace of God begins to empower the will to reject these life-destroying patterns. The natural inclinations of the body, as well as the God-informed intelligence, begin to reject alcohol as a continuing norm. As the alcoholic cooperates with God in complete surrender, he can release God's power to transform every part of his life.

The same principle must be applied when we deal with character defects. The secret is surrender. Most of us realize that many of our daily problems are not as serious as alcoholism. Our natural impulses can be distorted into something else. The desire to eat is legitimate, but it can become uncontrolled gluttony. God-given sexual desires, if not disciplined by moral principles and divine control can become an all-consuming, powerful taskmaster. The longing for acceptance is natural, but it can create a spineless craving for acceptance at any price. God has given us the inner desire to be free, not only from alcoholism, but also from every distortion of our natural desires. These instinctual drives are meant to be nurtured in wholesome directions and this can happen through the discipline of surrender. As we yield daily to his divine control, He bestows gifts of strength to be used in harmony with our human natures. These natural desires, however, if not surrendered to Him, can gain totalitarian domination over us. At this point, when we feel conquered, we have to ask, Who is going to be in the driver's seat?

Step Six says that victory over this spiraling struggle can be achieved only if we are willing—willing to surrender.

"How long am I going to have to struggle with my character defects?" Mazie sighed, as she began to unload her spiritual battles on me.

I think she believed that somewhere along the line you reach a plateau of perfection, and from then on it is clear sailing, onward and upward forever.

"This process goes on to the end of life," I said, with a smile. "Step Six challenges us to keep dealing with every negative, destructive practice or weakness. The impulse to stop drinking may disappear instantly in some cases, I know. But this does not necessarily happen with habitual, negative behavior patterns. Their grip upon us will determine our progress in eliminating them. Initially, however, we must want to either control or limit them."

"Yes, I know that," Mazie blurted out, "but how long do we have to go on struggling? Forever?"

"Your problem, Mazie, is that you project your life too far into the future. You're not meant to live any more than one day at a time. If you look at the long struggle down the road, you'll be beaten before you get started. All Step Six asks you to do is yield yourself to God and his dynamic power for today. And when tomorrow comes, He will be there to continue assisting you.

I said this to her, knowing how much I, too, needed to be reminded of these truths. No victory is permanent. But it can come daily.

Brief, day-by-day victories give us hope. I need only surrender my will to God for today and He will generate the power to reshape my character. Knowing I can cope just for today gives me the dynamic to change. Many of us refuse to make the effort because we are instinctively lazy. However, with even the slightest desire to break free of an enslaving defect, God will respond and work that change. Catherine Marshall, in her book *Beyond Ourselves,* calls it,"setting the rudder of your will." When you go sailing, you first set the rudder in the direction you want to go. Otherwise, the sailboat will simply circle around. But with the rudder set, the wind can catch the sail and blow the boat in the desired direction. So it is when dealing with defects of character. Even the most meager desire on our part to change enables God to fill our sails with the winds of freedom from old habits and behavior.

Relinquishment—Not "Give-up-ism"

When we look at our defects initially, we may feel like "throwing in the towel," and giving up the struggle to change. But if we take a closer look, we realize that basically, we don't really want to give our habits up. Despite their negative effects, they may still be enjoyable. Somehow we feel at home with them. Some things we can never give up, no matter what havoc they create in our lives. God's available grace may often be shunned. That's the way Bob felt, as we sat outside his home after a Twelve-Step Discussion Group.

"There are so many things in my life that have got to go," he complained. "I don't know where to begin. And on top of that, there are some things I would like to hang on to, even though I know they aren't good for me. Do we really have to get so radical?"

Well, I know how you feel, Bob," I responded, "because in my own life I had some defects dragging me down, and yet I hung on to them. But it depends, I suppose, on how much you want to grow up and be in charge of your life, instead of being constantly overpowered by habits you know are no good for you and, in fact, are ruining your life."

"I suppose the big thing is our pride and stubbornness," he sighed. "That may be the first thing I've got to deal with before I can do anything else about the other defects."

"You've hit the nail right on the head, Bob," I replied. "If we're unwilling to surrender at this point I don't think we will ever make it. It isn't a matter of 'give-up-ism,' but of positive relinquishment in the spirit of humility. One approach is negative, the other is positive. But it makes all the difference."

Undermined by the Success Story

Another problem faces the alcoholic when he or she reckons with character defects. People who have been very successful in overcoming some of their defects often brag about it. This makes the person considering Step Six feel discouraged before they get started. Often the "success-story" person lacks patience with those struggling with life-destroying problems. The spirit of condemnation emanating from the person who thinks he has made it may hold us back from launching out ourselves.

Consequently, A.A. members of long-standing, or other family members need to be patient with those beginning to seek change. No one, by and large, intrinsically wants to go through life handicapped by a certain debilitating habit. Inside, we know we were made for freedom. But people who boast about the changes they have made need to recognize the damage they can incur. It can be a major stumbling block to others.

I remember Bill, who wanted to overcome some of his defects, but whose wife, oblivious to her husband's struggle, talked about her own success.

"I feel like a total failure," he complained to me. "Mary's so far ahead of me, it isn't even funny. I don't think I'll ever catch up to her."

"Listen, Bill," I replied, trying not to downgrade Mary's success, "you have to get your eyes off her and zero in on yourself. That's the only way to deal with your defects. Do you want to be free, or not? That is the question."

"Yes," Bill said emphatically. "I guess people who are proud of their success will just have to discover some humility. I mustn't evaluate myself by them. It's my own inventory I've got to cope with, not someone else's."

STEP SIX: **Were entirely willing and ready to have God remove any defects of character.**

Alcoholics Anonymous

TRACK TWO: **"This is the will of God, even your sanctification."**

*The Apostle Paul in his letter to the
Christians in Thessalonica
(1 Thessalonians 4:3)*

A Special Purpose to Life

Another way to describe our willingness to change and be free from our character defects is found in the New Testament writings. We have already referred to the word "sanctification," which means "to be holy, to be set apart for a special purpose, to be special or unique in the way you live."

In the coffee hour after one of our A.A. discussion groups, Mary approached me with a question. "What does 'sanctification' mean, Cal?" she asked, with a puzzled look on her face. "Last Sunday, our minister used the word and I had never heard it before. I don't know why he didn't explain it. I suppose he thinks we are all 'boned-up' on theology. Anyway I thought I'd ask you. What does it mean?"

Mary had been sober for some time and was making good progress in her new life. She had begun to attend a good church where an A.A. Group met every Wednesday night. She also got into one of my discussion groups and that is how we met.

"The word is a biggy, isn't it?" I replied. "But its meaning is very easy to grasp. In Old Testament times, whenever an object was described as 'sanctified,' it was not to be used in any mundane or common way. It fulfilled a unique function. For example, the altar was a piece of furniture in the temple with the unique purpose of burning the daily sacrifices. God Himself was called 'Holy,' which meant He was altogether different from any of the other so-called 'gods' of other peoples. In the Christian Church, we sometimes describe the Bible as 'Holy Bible,' meaning it has a unique message. The Communion Table is often described as the 'Holy Table,' and again we know it functions as no other table does. Baptism is sometimes called 'holy' because it symbolizes a person's entrance into a new way of life. It reflects what the Apostle Paul said to the Corinthians, 'If anyone is in Christ, the old things are passing away, and everything is becoming new' (2 Corinthians 5:17)."

"Now I get it," Mary replied, with an enlightened look on her face. "Being free from alcohol addiction isn't the end of the game. It's just the beginning. I guess that's what Step Six tries to get across. You have to start dealing with everything in your life that 'gums it up.' "

"Absolutely right on," I responded. "It's the beginning of a new lifestyle committed to forsaking all the old ways. To be 'special' or 'sanctified' doesn't mean 'holier than thou.' Rather, it means you're moving toward eliminating all the obstacles that keep you from a full, free and God-pleasing life."

"That sounds like it takes a lot of humility," Mary responded.

"You couldn't describe it better," I responded. "It's undertaking a clean-up program where you are willing to improve every area of life, without thinking you're better than anyone else. It keeps you from taking other people's inventory, as Step Four insists. You have to concentrate on yourself and no one else."

Step Six and Sanctification

In Track One of Step Six, I emphasized the Step's truth from Alcoholics Anonymous' point of view. But now, in Track Two, I want to establish the Christian base for this understanding of life, foundational to A.A. Both Tracks move deftly in the same direction, one complementing the other. In Step Six, I briefly outlined what it means to "grow in grace." It means directing your life toward a noble and lofty goal—that of freeing your life from sin, from anything that creates a break or separation between you and other people, or you and God. Without this specific goal in life, you will end up on a dead-end street, going nowhere. The words of the great

New England philosopher, Henry Thoreau, are apropos: "In the long run, we hit only what we aim at."

What Are You Aiming For in Life?

"I think Alcoholics Anonymous asks too much when it tells us to get rid of our character defects," complained Bob, as we talked about the objectives of A.A.

"It might seem so on the surface," I replied, "but actually, it only expresses what Christianity calls us all to do, and that is to free ourselves from what robs our lives of peace and well-being. Do you recall those words Paul wrote to the Christians in the old ancient city of Thessalonica in northern Greece? 'For this is the will of God, even your sanctification' (1 Thessalonians 4:3)."

"I guess it's obvious that our lives have some guiding principles to help us toward moral achievement, but is it really possible? We're such slow learners. It might take a whole lifetime to discard some hang-ups," Bob sighed, as despair cast threatening shadows on his face.

"I can only tell you how I have tackled the challenge," I replied. "I try to think of myself as a ship's captain, who depends on his compass for right directions. That's the only way he's going to reach the port safely. Or think of people who enjoy archery. If they want to hit the bull's eye, they must aim the bow and arrow in the right direction. The same applies to our moral journey in life. What are you aiming at? What do you want for yourself?"

"How can Christianity help you in this?" Bob questioned. "I hear a lot about what you're to do and not to do, but I don't hear much on how you can do it."

"Well, I think that the New Testament writings provide us with much encouragement, because they describe God's purpose for us in life, called 'his will.' And what is his will? Well, it's discovering a distinct way of life, the antithesis of our previous lifestyles which proved so counterproductive."

"In the New Testament, especially Paul's letters, the early Christians were continually challenged to live differently than they once did as pagans. Is that right?" Bob asked.

"You've got the message," I responded. "Take a look at the people Paul was writing to in Thessalonica. They evidently expected the soon return of Jesus Christ to establish his kingdom. Because of this confidence, some of them, so to speak, had thrown down the shovel and the hoe, and were just waiting for Him to appear. They no longer struggled to live a life of holiness. They didn't seem concerned about obeying God's law of love. Instead, they were just 'lazing around,' not doing much to improve their lifestyles. The result of their behavior was moral and spiritual disorder."

"I suppose Paul often got discouraged with some of those Christians—at least I sense he did. How did he get over that problem?" Bob questioned.

"Yes, there's no doubt that sometimes he was tempted to become discouraged, yet he always seemed to overcome such feelings. I believe he did it by lifting their minds to new levels of creative action. He pointed them toward what God wants for human life, as they waited expectantly for Christ's return. That event was entirely in the future and, therefore, in God's hands. Their immediate and supreme concern was not to be stargazing into the future, but concentrating on the present and what they could do with it," I replied.

"I suppose that's where Step Six comes in," Bob suggested. "If you start working on character defects, you haven't got time for speculation about the future."

"I couldn't agree more," I replied. "We have to deal now with how we can develop a mature, productive and loving life, in relationship with others and with God. This understanding comes as we immerse our lives in the teachings of the Scriptures. The more we reflect on what the Bible teaches, the more we see God actively work in our lives to free us from the downward pull of our sinful, self-centered nature. As we live in the light of his truths and strive by God's grace to make the right choices, we will discover how satisfying life can be," I responded.

I then compared life to a train travelling on two tracks which provided both the way and the means to its destination. But if the train decided it didn't need the tracks, that they impeded its progress and decided to jump them, we know what would happen. The train would forfeit the ability to move even one inch forward. All progress would cease. Reaching any particular destination would be "out of sight."

The same applies to life's forward direction. If we imagine that we can get along without the directives of God's Word, opting to go it alone, we will creep along. Progress will be minimal in the pursuit of freedom from character defects.

Getting Your Eyes Fixed on the Goal

When runners set out on a race, they keep their minds, their eyes and their bodies fixed on the goal. This is also true in the moral race of life. Of course, everyone battles with his or her particular defects, and yet, the goal is the same. From the Christian point of view, the greatest goal in life is to be Christ-like. In doing God's will we must do more than just adhere to certain rules and regulations, and certain moral precepts. Rather, we must follow Christ and allow the Holy Spirit to empower us with a new achievement, increasing the dynamic of our love. This love, the Apostle Paul tells us in his letter to the Corinthians, is supreme, the greatest impulse He can unleash in our lives. But again, love is not just a spiritual virtue, but a Person—Jesus Christ, Who comes to live within our deepest, innermost being, releasing his power into every aspect of our lives.

"How does this all happen?" June said with a wistful sigh. She was struggling to make the A.A. program work for her, but had real difficulty with the Sixth Step. The more she struggled to deal with her defects, the more she felt bogged down. It was like taking two steps forward and three steps back. And she was discouraged. She had begun the Christian life, but still grappled with what it meant to turn your will and life over to the care of God.

"It does seem at times that we are making little progress," I confessed. "But I have found that yielding to Christ is a process, as well as a definite decision at a certain point in our lives. We must yield daily to the living Christ and allow Him to enter fully. There must be a complete takeover, a conquest of our wills. You know, if you were to come to my front door and knock, I would obviously invite you in. But if I left you there while I busied myself in the kitchen with the supper, you'd have every right to ask, 'What kind of host are you?' I should invite you inside my house, and make you feel completely welcome and at home. That's the way it is when we let Christ take over. He can't address our defects if we don't invite Him into the kitchen, the living room, the bedroom or the recreation rooms of our lives."

June smiled, and I could see a sense of hope shining through her eyes. "You make it sound so simple, Cal," she replied, "but then, I guess that's what the A.A. motto, 'Easy Does It,' is all about."

"Exactly," I replied. "This is what the Christian lifestyle is all about, and remember what Jesus promised—'My yoke is easy and my burden is light' (Matthew 11:20). He's not out to complicate life, but to release divine energy to make necessary changes. When we make our hearts into Christ's home, it has to be absolute. The more we do this, I've discovered, the more the old defects begin to drop away. But this must be my conscious objective as a Christian. This certainly holds true for alcoholics. God wills that you and I become increasingly Christ-like in character. It's the old displacement theory we all learned in grade-nine science. If you fill a cup with water the air is displaced. Now, if you tried to get the air out by reaching into the cup and trying to grab it, you'd never do it. But as the water moves in displacement occurs. The air flows out naturally. So it is with Christ, the more we allow Him in, the more He displaces the old life."

"You know," June responded, "that makes me think of the trees just outside my bedroom window. I've often noticed in the Fall, when the leaves begin to change and drop off, that some of them hang on. Not even the bitterest winds can unfasten them. They resist tenaciously. But in the Spring when the sap flows again, I've noticed that it moves into the branches and twigs, and pushes the old leaves off effortlessly."

"What a great illustration of what happens in us spiritually," I replied. "Some of those bad characteristics in our lives have a way of holding on as tenaciously as those leaves. But as we permit the life-giving 'sap of Christ' to flow more and more into us we will find Him pushing off those nasty habits—that impatience, those obnoxious ways of speaking and thinking, that hard-to-control temper. Such is the power of the living Christ when we allow Him to flow, making us into special, sanctified people."

I have always been helped by the writings of Henry Drummond, the great nineteenth-century naturalist and theologian—especially by his little book, *The Greatest Thing in the World* (love). As we determine to do something about our defects of character, he challenges us with this thought: "To become Christ-like is the only thing in the world worth caring for, the thing before which every ambition of man is folly and all life's achievements vain."

The Bible teaches that everyone should be engaged in this effort. Increasingly filled with Christ's Spirit and sanctified by his love, we not only change personally, but we affect society. The immediate societies of our family, our working relationships, our A.A. fellowship, our church, become centers of love and spiritual satisfaction. Not that this happens in any final or perfect way, but God seeks to move us toward it in love. When we do not allow Him to free us from defects of character, we thwart his desire for us personally, and therefore corporately.

The biblical outlook on life is that the world was made for man, and we are made for God. God's purpose for creation is fulfilled when a man, a woman, lives for Him. Probably God has more plans for his creation, but certainly nothing exceeds his desire that we seek Him, find Him and become like Him. This sanctifying, special purpose of God that sees life as unique, gradually takes place as we willingly yield to Him and surrender anything in our lives that robs Him of his plan and purpose for us.

I remember so clearly the dialogue I had with a university student who had become an alcoholic and was desperately trying to find sobriety. But as his desire to be sober tussled with his desire to go on a drunk, he recognized that he was hanging on to drinking. In the back of his mind, he felt he could drink, maybe on the weekends, or once a month, or some special occasions. The struggle played havoc with his studies. Often he had to miss classes for a day or two while he sobered up from these casual bouts of drinking.

"You know," I said to him, when he turned to me for help, "you remind me of a little boy left in the living room one evening while his parents said goodnight at the front door to their visitors. When they were out of the room, he noticed a beautiful vase by the fireplace with a long, elegant neck. He grabbed it, wondering what might be at the bottom. He pushed his fist down and felt a nickel on the bottom. He grasped hold of it, but as he brought his hand up, he discovered that the neck of the vase was too narrow for both his hand and the nickel. As he was just about to break the vase, his parents came back into the room. Realizing what was happening they 'flew' over to him, got hold of the vase and persuaded their son to drop the nickel. When he did, they turned it upside down and the nickel dropped out. They gave him the nickel, but they had the vase."

"You're like that, Don. You want to hold on to the 'nickel of drinking,' and all the while you are risking your most precious possession, namely your life and possibly your career."

Don needed a greater love than alcohol to invade his life. God's love creates goodness, and the desire for goodness harmonizes us with God's creative purpose. The evil that works in us (and in the world) attempts to defeat this purpose. But when Christ-like living becomes our primary goal, we find ourselves being crowned with a sense of joy and success. The first Olympic runners, who won the crown of myrtle leaves, kept their eyes on the goal and crossed the finish line with a real sense of achievement. At the end of every day, God wants us to experience that sense of well being. This race is run, one day at a time.

Much Ado About Nothing

Critics of Christianity sometimes complain that the sacrifice made by Jesus to free us was useless extravagance. After all, they say, who was He dying for? Just a few puny creatures on an inconsequential planet called earth. How can God possibly confine his purpose to such an insignificant location? Why would He concern Himself with how we human beings live? The Psalmist, in one of his poems (Psalm 8), voices these sentiments when he exclaims, "What is man that you are mindful of him, or the son of man that you should visit him?" In other words, How can God really care what we do with our lives? Does it really matter if we try to eliminate the character defects that mess up our lives?

Such a question often follows from a faulty understanding of God's character. It confines its perspective of the universe to its immensity, and our comparative insignificance. But we have to realize that the God Who made the vast universe has not only created the fantastically big, but also the infinitesimally small. Science has found flowers in the Sahara Desert so small they can only be seen through a microscope. Yet these flowers boast exotic colors and display delicate design.

True, the universe is material, as are we human beings. But we are also spiritual beings, and that makes an infinite difference. The highest expression of God's will is not displayed through millions of galaxies in outer space. No. His greatest concern rests on his created children. He was willing to create harmony with them. Thus, He calls us to live free from the defects of character that hinder his high purpose for us and for Him. And the death of Jesus was not too high a price to realize that purpose. It provided the means to experience freedom from sin and new lives dominated by love. The Apostle John penned these beautiful words: "Greater love has no man than this, than a man lay down his life for his friends" (John 15:13). And God loved us even when we were not his friends. The Apostle Paul reiterated the same truth when he wrote to the Romans, "God commended His love toward us, in that while we were yet sinners, Christ died for us" (Romans 5:8). This demonstration of perfect love not only reconciles us to God, but also inspires us to yield our lives to Him, allowing his love to free us from all that hinders our moral and spiritual growth toward holiness and uniqueness.

Ah, The Mystery of Life—Is It So Sweet?

Another factor we often deal with as we struggle to rid our

characters of defects relates to the mystery of life.

"Why," we often ask, "are there so many ups and downs, so much suffering, so much indifference, so many perplexities which baffle explanation?"

Norma put this question to me as we met together for a regular counseling session. I knew that with her it was not theoretical. She had suffered the loss of a son, killed in a car accident by a drunk, hit-and-run driver. The tragedy ruthlessly forced her to confront her own alcoholism. She had joined Alcoholics Anonymous, and while it helped her in many ways, she still needed someone to listen to her express doubts and bitterness.

"It's so easy to let the cloud of despair and cynicism overshadow us," I replied. "What's the use anyhow? Why all this effort to improve, when again and again we fall victim to life's tragedies? Why not just throw in the towel and eat, drink and be merry? This seems like a practical solution to the dark side of life. It's a common avenue of escape. Life's so short, why not just yield to our baser instincts, and let the chips fall where they may?"

"That's the way I felt for some time after Tom was killed," Norma replied. "It eventually forced me to face my own lifestyle and realize that drinking was not the right solution. But even though I've been sober for more than a year now, I still find it hard to cope with the challenge of Step Six."

"That's perfectly natural," I responded. "We can deal with life by burying our heads in the proverbial sand and pretending that nothing really matters. Some resort to prolonged anger and curse fate for life's seeming unfairness. Some great thinkers recorded how they grappled with life's bewildering puzzles." I then got up, went over to my bookshelf and pulled out a book that contained a few lines from Omar Khayyam. I read them to her:

> Ah, Love? Could you and I with Fate conspire
> To grasp this sorry scheme of things, enter
> Would we not shatter it to bits—and then
> Remold it near to the heart's desire.

I then picked up the New Testament on my side table, and

turned to Paul's letter to the Corinthians. "I believe Paul shows us how we may have victory," I said, "because he knew what it was like to grapple with situations that could have destroyed him. Listen to this. 'We are often troubled, but not crushed. Sometimes in doubt, but never in despair. There are many enemies, but we are never without a friend. And though hurt at times, very badly, we are not destroyed' (2 Corinthians 4:8-9, J. B. Phillips Translation). He could talk this way because Christ had suffered and died, but ultimately triumphed. This for me is always the key."

God wills the development of character, but this cannot happen without some pain and suffering. All growth in nature points to this fact. Think of a beautiful pearl necklace. We marvel at its exquisite charm. But how were these pearls produced? As the oyster encounters the grains of sand lodged under its shell, it seeks to eliminate the discomfort they cause by excreting a white substance to coat them, gradually creating a pearl. I believe character forms this way. The "grains of sand" in our own lives, our character defects—from debilitating habits to distorted attitudes—mar and often seek to destroy us, but the Spirit of Christ, in conjunction with our wills, secretes the gift of love and a life of beauty forms. It happens all the time—I've seen it.

Surrendered daily to the power of God, we will make fresh discoveries about ourselves. Worrywarts will have to learn how to trust. People who fly off the handle easily need to control their tempers. Even people who commit more serious crimes of murder, rape and theft generally want to be free from such destructive behavior because they intrinsically know life is not meant to be lived that way. Studies made of incarcerated men and women show this to be true. No one wants to go through life defeated by attitudes and habits that rob them of real happiness.

If a person has attained a certain success, he or she needs to pray for indulgence toward those sitting on the ladder's bottom rung, wondering if they can ever really make their lives different. Everyone needs to practice tolerance with those struggling with change. We need to remember the oft-repeated A.A. cliche: "There go I, but for the grace of God."

Honest Facing of Self

When Dorothy wanted release from her character defects, she discovered that they didn't disappear because she was hanging on to them. She enjoyed her pet defects. She resisted change, even though she wanted it—a strange contradiction.

Many of us can identify with her struggle. When confronted by our lust for power or deep desire to control, we often dig in our heels. When challenged to practice morality, not limping from one sexual experience to another, we resist what we call "reasonable demands." After all, we do have to do something about our physical urges.

Yet self-deception needs to be shaken. Love of the status quo needs to be re-examined. Some people seem determined to perpetuate their character defects, such as anger, self-righteousness, self-indulgence because it makes them feel better, at least on the surface. We all rationalize much of our behavior to justify our actions. So much of life is riddled with envy, yet how often do we determine to be free from it? Procrastination, a most insidious defect, is excused as being, "just me." We can will to do good, as the Apostle Paul recognized, but we are also pulled in the opposite direction. He was honest enough to write, "When I would do good, evil is present with me."

Bill was making good progress in ridding himself of character defects. We often discussed the process.

"Have you ever noticed," he asked, "how, if you think you've mastered a major defect of character, you often become complacent about your minor weaknesses and neglect them?"

"I guess we think that we'll never be perfect anyway, so why go on trying to get rid of every defect? Spiritual sloppiness is what I call it," I remarked.

"I suppose a higher level of perfection might be attainable in some areas of life, but certainly we alcoholics have to realize how unattainable that is."

"And yet," I commented, "even despite the fact that none of us can ever measure up to the morality expressed in the Ten

Commandments, or the Sermon on the Mount, the tension to strive for the highest and the best remains. It's the other side of the coin. Life is such a paradox, isn't it?"

"I suppose the important thing is being in touch with ourselves," Bill went on. "Nothing is worth having without some measure of effort. I have discovered that all I needed was sincere, day-by-day surrender. I've also discovered that the more I eliminated negative character defects, the more inner happiness I experienced. I guess we've just got to decide whether we want to be happy or not."

"I guess it's like the tortoise and the hare," Bill went on. "As we move from point A to point B, we can either make steady progress, or just drag our feet. In Aesop's fable, the hare dashed forward, then he slackened off. The tortoise persevered slowly, but kept going and won the race."

"That's a good way of putting it," I reacted. "What do we want to be like, the tortoise or the hare? If we postpone dealing with our defects, they will just undermine us, especially our sobriety. And being sober is something the sincere recovering alcoholic wants desperately."

"Take action," Bill said, as he responded enthusiastically, "that's the slogan for success."

"Right on," I replied. "That's what the Sixth Step tries to get across. Don't be content with yourself. Purpose in your heart that changes have to be made, and then surrender to God's power. It's the only way to go."

CHAPTER SEVEN

STEP SEVEN: Humbly asked Him to remove all our shortcomings.
Alcoholics Anonymous

TRACK ONE: The greatest friend of truth is time, her greatest enemy is prejudice, and her constant companion is humility.
Charles Caleb Cotton, 1780-1829

Humility and How I Achieved It

I kidded with a friend on one occasion and asked her if she had ever read my book, *Humility and How I Attained It,* with fifty illustrated pictures. We laughed at the absurdity of having such a book published, but soon afterwards we agreed that many people speak and act this way.

In Step Seven of the Alcoholics Anonymous Twelve-Step Program, the need for humility is stressed. It lies at the heart and soul of any progress we make in ridding our lives of harmful habits and attitudes. But in order for us to demonstrate this basic attitude, we need to understand its true nature and how it can be expressed in daily life.

One evening a group of A.A. people were enjoying one another's company socially. During the conversation, someone started taking inventory of one of our fellow members.

"Have you ever noticed," said Bob, "how much Harry is so proud of his humility?" Everyone laughed because we all knew that pride and humility cannot coexist. You can't have them both at the same time.

Cathy spoke up. "I guess we're all like Harry sometimes. At least, I know I am. I begin to make progress getting rid of some particular fault, and before I know it, I'm patting myself on the back, thinking that I am really somebody, just because I have begun to minimize this shortcoming."

We all agreed with Cathy that pride can so easily infect our lives, keeping us from really discovering ourselves. No humility can be achieved without popping the balloon of our self-centered pride. Overcoming our faults and shortcomings demands a spirit of humility, with God getting the credit for any of the changes in our lives.

As you begin to work the Seventh Step, you realize that it cannot be achieved without the practice of healthy humility. Not only do you have to admit your inability to manage life positively because of alcohol addiction, but you must also continue adopting the A.A. lifestyle to make humility possible. This demands a constant dependency upon God and abdication from the throne of prideful self-congratulations as we meet life's emergencies and temptations.

True and False Ideas about Humility

Many images may flash into our minds whenever we begin to think about this particular virtue. It may be the Uriah Heep image of Charles Dickens' famous novel, *David Copperfield,* that I've described in a previous chapter as an oily, conniving bookkeeper always wringing his hands and exclaiming, "I'm an 'umble man, Master Copperfield." Of course, as you get to know him, you realize that he was only fooling himself. He reeked with pride and self-righteousness. This phony brand of humility is the antithesis of true humility.

Some people think humility means weakness—allowing other people to walk all over you and refusing to stand up for yourself, the door-mat variety. But true humility does not allow people to push you around and rob you of your God-given dignity. Meekness or humility does not imply weakness, but courage to face up to faults and failures, not running away from the challenges they present.

What's Behind Our Pride?

The development of science in the nineteenth and twentieth centuries has contributed much to that unreasonable confidence we now have in man's ability to solve every problem, despite its shape or size.

I remember a conversation I had with a university student who had just begun his spiritual journey and was trying to dispel some of his religious prejudices.

"It's amazing," Doug exclaimed, shaking his head, "how I used to think that human reason could solve all the problems of humanity. And even now, I still find myself slipping back into that way of thinking."

"It's not easy," I replied. "We have all been inoculated with the prideful claims of science. As you know, it boastfully asserts we will ultimately overcome every human problem. It will only be a matter of time."

"I used to believe that way too," Doug responded. "I didn't have the slightest doubt that science would one day fulfill all our needs. I could just visualize the time when happiness and contentment would flow like a mighty river over all the world, and everyone would be swept into ultimate satisfaction. What a pipe dream! That was before I realized the shambles of my own life. Science couldn't help me one bit. I then began to wake up to reality."

"You're not the only one, Doug, who has swallowed all this fantasy about science. Our whole society is riddled with it," I replied. "So many of my own philosophy books boast about this in vulgar optimism, deifying the accomplishments of scientific technology. Tragically, many alcoholics have bought into this theory, deceived like most people in this science-dominated society."

"Of course," Doug continued, "we shouldn't downplay the terrific achievements of science. I will always be grateful to God for using science to help solve many of the problems that curse mankind."

"Oh yes," I agreed, "science has helped us find cures for disease, ease the drudgery of mundane tasks and has produced so many material comforts. Science certainly deserves much credit and commendation. Its only harm comes via its boast that it can solve everything. That's when pride takes over."

One great accomplishment of Alcoholics Anonymous is its success in exposing science's inability to overcome alcohol addiction. Life has become such a total disaster at this level for so many people, that the benefits of science can only record their bankruptcy. Most alcoholics I know have dreamed of ultimate happiness and then when it didn't materialize, they turned to other possibilities, primarily the bottle. This only produced frustration that culminated in excessive drinking, blackouts and despair. Nothing brought ultimate satisfaction. The debilitating effects of alcohol destroyed any possibility of success and happiness. Most alcoholics discover this by bitter experience. Science can only shoot blanks at destructive drinking patterns.

Lack of Understanding

Until an alcoholic realizes this, he or she will continue to be confused. The only ammunition is a humble spirit that seeks a Power greater than itself. Without true humility, alcoholics will develop a false humility that will open the door to moral and spiritual failure. At this point of despair there are no human answers. Their cries to God for help indicate the first signs of humility. When a person makes material satisfaction paramount, he or she will ultimately reach rock bottom. Science, with all its benefits, cannot rescue them.

Humility and Morality

Dorothy was an alcoholic brought up on the philosophy of no moral absolutes. Everything was relative. Right and wrong depended upon circumstances. When she came into A.A., she found difficulty with the Twelve Steps because they seemed too rigid. She believed moral values should be more flexible.

After an A.A. meeting one evening, we talked about the challenge of developing a solid basis for an ethical lifestyle.

After listening to her complaints about the apparent rigidity of the Twelve-Step Program, I said to her, "How do you think we can achieve a vital relationship with God, if we continue to live by inconsistent, flexible values? If we acknowledge the reality of God, as A.A. does so emphatically, how can we go on living as though no divinely inspired rules could guide our lifestyles? I feel that as long as we want to be in the driver's seat of life, our religious and moral beliefs will only be superficial and constantly changing. That can hardly promote stability. If you have an unrealistic understanding of what behavior God requires, you never can achieve consistency. How would you like to ride in a jet piloted by someone who didn't care what controls he used as long as he used them sincerely?"

Dorothy smiled. She could see the point, although she wasn't convinced that this applied to moral standards too.

"It takes humbling on our part," I insisted, "to acknowledge that God has the right to distinguish between right and wrong. If we refuse his direction, we really aren't taking Him seriously as God, and we certainly, in my opinion, would be clueless as to how to prescribe our own recipe for happiness."

I went on to share, from my long experience in counseling alcoholics, how often I'd watched them suffer mental anguish, making little progress spiritually, because they refused to let God direct them morally and spiritually. Holding on, as some of them did, to the old ideas about achieving happiness, they endured repeated humiliation. Only when they 'fell off the wagon' continuously, did they admit their total failure. In this state of humiliation, they took the first steps toward achieving day-by-day sobriety. They had to discover that they couldn't go it alone, and they had to constantly yield to God's will. But God's will is not some nebulous, airy-fairy concept, but a concrete course of travel, just like that of a train running from Vancouver to Halifax. God, through the Ten Commandments and the Sermon on the Mount, reveals how to live in harmony with Him and one another.

Some alcoholics find it hard to "make it" because they think of these moral, spiritual standards as negatively attempting to control a person's life, degrading their humanity or individuality. But unless we view these divine regulations as steps toward freedom, life will be difficult. Humility plays a critical role as we mature, gradually eliminating characteristics that mar our lives.

The Beginning, Not the End

One mistake often made by alcoholics as they begin to admit their powerlessness over alcohol is their failure to understand that this first act of humility does not represent the climax of their new life, but its initiation.

Robert had taken his Fifth Step and struggled with the relevance of the remaining steps. He was becoming aware, however, how often we nurture our old attitudes and behavior patterns, despite their deleterious effects on others. With urgency in his eyes he asked, "How can you lower the level of your moral and spiritual deficiency? It often seems like an impossible goal."

I admitted that it sometimes seemed hopeless. We have practiced our bad habits such a long time that we feel we will never overcome them regardless of how hard we try, or how much humility we struggle to achieve.

"Robert," I said, "regardless of how impossible it seems, we must commit ourselves to making spiritual progress. We simply can't give in and stand still. This may seem like a 'heavy' for the struggling alcoholic, but you can't escape it. I know you like to lift weights. Do you remember how much pain you endured when you first started? You began to use muscles you didn't know existed, and I'll bet that you felt like 'throwing in the towel' dozens of times. But as you continued week by week, those muscles gradually toned up, and before long you no longer felt tempted to give up. I'm sure you have heard more mature A.A. members say, 'It get's better.' If you take the steps necessary for recovery, even though you may drag your feet at first, you will find that change takes place slowly but surely. As we yield to humility, we will discover that performing God's revealed will becomes a way of life."

In order to incorporate God's way of living into their lifestyles, many recovering alcoholics meet regularly with an A.A. member of good sobriety. This person will sympathize with your struggle, but also encourage you not to give up—to "hang in there." You will experience the satisfaction that comes from replacing negative characteristics and conduct with good choices and habits. As I said earlier, you'll eventually be able to say with the old black preacher, "I ain't what I ought-er be, and I ain't what I'm gon-er be, but thank God, I ain't what I use-ter be."

Don't be Afraid to be Deflated

Because most of us have so much pride, we resist the challenge of change. As our spiritual understanding sharpens, however, we will become more cognizant of how much more "needs to go" from our lives. Whenever an honest friend points out something that needs changing, instead of resisting, we will begin to realize the benefits of having our egos deflated from time to time. This is the only route to humility. Instead of avoiding the pain of struggle, we will accept it, knowing that as we humble ourselves, God will empower us with stamina to accept life's challenges. His power will also enable us to face temptations without constantly yielding to their control. But if we allow our pride to resist the pain of change, we will always be on the run. And sooner or later, our character defects and shortcomings will find pseudo solution in the bottle. This comment often attempts to justify our self-centered behavior: "Oh, well, I'm not a saint and never will be."

Green Lights and Red Lights

Incumbent in learning to drive a car is knowing the difference between the green traffic light and the red. One means advance, the other means stop. Both these lights work in the A.A. Twelve-Step Program. On one side a green light encourages us to progress, using the truths of the program. But on the other side, the light will be red. It will say "stop." Stop running away from the need to change. It will challenge us to consider our old style of life and the results of dishonesty and pride. But listening to the inspirational testimonies of people making the program work for them will bring glimmers of hope. Humility, many have discovered, is contagious. You will not be able to continue flaunting your pride and self-sufficiency in the presence of those discounting theirs. It will eventually become obvious that the practice of humility handles the conflicts of life far more constructively. Through the love of God displayed in an A.A. meeting, you will become sensitive to the green light—its positive directives and challenges—and to the red light, with its warning.

Altering Our Ideas About God

Many people harbor negative concepts about God. They imagine Him as Someone Who wants to rob them of all individuality, forcing them to conform to his will in a high-handed, compulsive way. As we begin to discover humility, our attitudes toward God, the Higher Power, will begin to alter.

John had been an unbeliever most of his life. He had not thought through his agnosticism intellectually. Rather, he had picked it up from his home atmosphere where neither of his parents had anything but the vaguest idea about God's existence. John's longing for something more took him on an extensive search that included the misuse of alcohol. But his excessive drinking only substituted disaster for the inner satisfaction and well being he sought. When one of his drinking buddies discovered sobriety through A.A. and encouraged him to join one of the meetings, he was reluctant. But eventually his curiosity got the best of him. He wondered how A.A. had changed his friend Peter. After attending the meetings regularly for some time, he willingly admitted that his life had become unmanageable because of alcohol. At this point, he reached out for help from God, the Higher Power. At first he felt comfortable with the idea that the A.A. Group was that Power, but gradually he began to see its inadequacy.

One evening I had been asked to speak at the A.A. meeting I often attended, and in my talk I said something about the personality of God. Somehow this touched John and he sought me out during the coffee hour.

"I've been an atheist, I guess, all my life," John confessed, "but now I am beginning to see that I will only maintain the sobriety I'm experiencing, if I trust a Power greater than myself. Does that Power have a personality, as you said tonight in your talk? You seem to have something I wish I had, Cal."

"You've certainly begun to find God, John, as soon as you admitted your need for sobriety," I responded. "The humility you expressed at that time has now brought you to the threshold of another discovery. The Higher Power is at work in your life, that's for sure. But the more you yield yourself to Him, the more He can reveal Himself to you. And as you do that, you will realize that God has personality and can be known in an intimate, personal way. You surely have noticed how many people in A.A. have changed for the better, and almost all of them give God the credit. The more you open up to the truths shared in this meeting, the more real God will become. You will find yourself being drawn into a personal knowledge of Him."

"I used to think that my unbelief was basically intellectual," John responded, "but recently I have started to see that it was mostly environmental and very much a matter of pride. The actual fact is that I haven't wanted Him, or anyone else for that matter, to interfere with the management of my life."

"Right on," I replied, "you've made a great discovery. But even people who have been brought up with the belief that there is a God also have had to discover that He was something more than just a concept. To know God as a Personal Higher Power must be experiential. All of us—alcoholics or not—have to discover that God is not our bellhop. He wants to do much more than carry the burdens of life that are too heavy for us. I know many people only turn to God when their problems demand it. But this is 'using' God, a form of pride. In so many words they are saying, 'I need you right now, but as soon as I get this problem solved, I'll be on my own way again.'"

"What I'm hearing you say Cal," John said, "is that God must be discovered at a much deeper level than most of us realize. I think I hear you saying that He must be our constant Friend. Like a Pal.

He wants to share Himself with us at every point along the road."

"You're so right, John," I went on. "Even Jesus was totally committed to the realization that without God, nothing could be achieved. On one occasion He said, 'apart from me you can do nothing' (John 15:5)."

"Just talking to you, Cal, has made me see that God won't force Himself on us. He won't try to talk us into believing in Him," John continued. "I have to humble myself and reach out to Him, and then He will give me the power to deal with my shortcomings. I'm just beginning to see how destructive my self-centered ego has been. I have a feeling that there is a new road for me to travel on, or maybe I need to stop driving down the dead-end road I'm on, and get onto the road that will lead me to a personal knowledge of Him."

"That's what humility is all about John," I responded. "It's recognizing that if anything positive is going to happen in your life, He must be part of it, not in a minor way, but in a major way. If you will take the first six steps of A.A. seriously, you will eventually ask, 'What kind of a person do I want to be? Is living in peace and harmony with others something I really want to strive for? If so, then I am really going to need God. Not some vague, nebulous God, but Someone who is personal, real and concerned.' This Seventh Step helps widen our vision and takes off the blinkers. We've got to humble ourselves and ask Him to dispel our shortcomings. As we yield to Him personally, we will find Him doing it."

Conclusion

As we sum up Step Seven, we must realize that through much of life, we have been dominated by fear. The fear of change in particular. On the one hand, we have been deluded to think that we would lose something we really wanted if we became too humble, but on the other hand, our pride has also kept us from seeking it. Most of our fears can be eliminated if we allow God to invade our lives. The words of Jesus' disciple John, also tell us how: "Perfect love casts out fear" (1 John 4:18).

The humbling of ourselves before the God of infinite love can set us free, not only from alcohol addiction, but from every fear that has dominated our lives, destroying our inner happiness. The power of God is the power of love, and the more we have of that power, the more our shortcomings disappear.

STEP SEVEN: Humbly asked Him to remove all our shortcomings.
Alcoholics Anonymous

TRACK TWO: Humility is the most difficult virtue to achieve.
Shakespeare and the Stoicism of Seneca
by T.S. Eliot

The basis for the Seventh Step in the Alcoholics Anonymous Program derives, like all the other Steps, from a biblical and specifically Christian understanding of life. The theme of humility, emphasized by the Seventh Step, threads through the entire Bible. Some biblical characters failed to practice it, while others did grasp its significance.

Jesus Christ serves as the supreme demonstration of this virtue which was also reflected in the lives of those who followed his teaching and example. At first, the disciples of Jesus were proud, arrogant, impulsive, narrow-minded and self-centered men. They hated their enemies—the Romans who controlled their small, impoverished country. They despised their religious leaders, who seemingly had betrayed their country to Rome. They disdained the Gentiles, classifying them as "dogs," the worst description they could attach to another race.

But when they began to follow Jesus, their misconceptions of life spilled over into their attitude toward Him and his purpose among them. It led them to lofty thinking about their place in his coming kingdom. "Allow us to sit beside you on your throne in your Kingdom," (Matthew 20:21) two had asked, "one on your right hand, and the other one your left."

"You don't know what you're asking for," Jesus replied, knowing full well that his kingdom was not like earthly power and authority, but a spiritual reality, characterized by love, humility and service. The pride of these men blinded them, at least at this point, to the need for humility.

One disciple distinguished by dominating pride was Peter. He wanted Jesus to raise an army, vanquish the Romans, and establish a Kingdom where he and the other disciples would rule with Him. When Christ told him that it would be necessary for Him to suffer and die before this kingdom could be inaugurated, he replied arrogantly, "This shall never happen to you Lord" (Matthew 16:22). He experienced severe rebuke from Jesus, Who clearly saw in him the pride that marks us all.

But after the crucifixion and resurrection, this proud, boastful man was transformed by the power of Christ's love on the Day of Pentecost, when the Holy Spirit entered the lives of all the disciples. As a result, Peter could later write in his first letter to Christian friends, "Be clothed with humility" (1 Peter 5:5).

Many verses in the Bible encourage us to practice the spiritual art of humility. But I want to focus on these particular words of Peter, who saw the importance of this virtue for victory over the downward pull of sinful human nature.

In using the words "be clothed with humility," Peter drew attention to a virtue that T.S. Eliot claims is one of the most difficult to achieve. The word "clothed' in the Greek language describes the white apron every slave wore as an outward sign of bondage to the Master. Doubtless, Peter used this particular word remembering that incident in the Upper Room, just before Jesus was arrested and taken away by the Romans for trial and execution (John 13:4-10). At the end of the meal now called the Lord's Supper, Jesus got up from the table, put on a white towel or apron, knelt before each of his disciples and washed their dusty feet. When He came to Peter, this haughty, self-righteous disciple refused to let Him continue. He no doubt reasoned that Jesus was Master and Lord, and from his perspective, it was inappropriate for Him to take on the role of a menial servant. He was shocked to think that Jesus would stoop to such an act. In no uncertain terms, he told Jesus that he would never let Him do this for him. Responding to this prideful display, Jesus made it clear that his refusal would forfeit his share in the future work of his kingdom. "You have no part with me," Jesus said. Only then did Peter concede and allow Jesus to wash his feet also.

Now, as a man empowered by the Spirit of Christ to proclaim

the Gospel and Lordship of Christ, he knew the important role of humility in the life of the Christian.

What Does It Mean to be Humble?

From a Christian perspective, what does it mean to practice humility? Firstly, it does not mean denying your abilities. It does not mean that you pretend you are worthless or incompetent in your area of expertise. A person may practice humility and still recognize his ability in any number of areas.

As you examine the Gospel record, notice that as soon as Jesus finished washing his disciples' feet, He returned to the table. He then said to these men whom He was trusting would advance the cause of his kingdom, "You call me Master and Lord, and you are quite right, for that is exactly what I am. If I therefore, your Lord and Master, have washed your feet, you ought also to wash one another's feet" (John 13:14). Observe that Jesus knew Who He was and, in this humble act of service, He did not overlook this fact. Christian humility does not keep you from recognizing your abilities, talents and characteristics. An accomplished musician capable of evoking great emotion and pleasure, need not think that he or she is the same as a student still studying conservatory music. To do this would be false humility. He must simply not flaunt his talent, nor adopt an attitude of superiority.

To recognize your own personal worth is to begin recovery from self-centeredness. Tragically, many people suffer from a lack of affirmation, be it from family members, teachers or friends. The resulting development creates a negative, self-depreciating attitude.

When I began to counsel Alice, she was suffering from a nervous breakdown. I worked hard to help her appreciate herself. She was brought up in six different foster homes as a child and, in one of them, the foster father sexually abused her when she was twelve. She described herself as "trash." Even when she became a Christian, having accepted the forgiveness and love of God, she still could not think well of herself. It took constant affirmation before she began to believe that she was a person worth loving. Again and again, I emphasized that she was not "garbage." She was somebody.

If Christ had come to suffer and die for her, she could not go on thinking she had no value. Her false humility had to be overcome by the Christ Who loved her unto death, and accepted her unconditionally for who and what she was. Alice, ably talented as a painter, constantly depreciated her ability, until the power of Christ through the constant nurture of Christian friends, broke through. She began to believe she could paint, and paint well.

If people can perform a particular job, hobby or sport well, they should be comfortable admitting it. Paul the apostle encourages his fellow Christians not "to think more highly of themselves than they ought to think" (Romans 12:3). By this, he did not mean they were to think less of themselves. Self-depreciation only encourages negative thinking, which must be overcome. To be humble and of lowly mind means accepting the truth about yourself. Our gifts and abilities are to be recognized, but not boastfully. When we affirm ourselves, we can more readily recognize the gifts and strengths of others, who may even perform better than we can. Granted, you may be much better than I am in sports, singing or business management. Should your ability, then, make me feel unhappy and down about myself? Certainly not. In humility, I can give thanks to God for your talents, and still go on appreciating what I can do at my own level of achievement. As someone has rightly observed, "One molehill may be a little higher than another, but both of them are equal distance from the sun." A friend of mine told me about his seven-year-old son who, when he was told at school by his teacher that the sun was some ninety-six million miles from the earth, asked, "Is that from the downstairs or upstairs of my house?" The old saying, "Comparisons are odious," still rings true. Yes, people can out-perform each other but when we as individuals learn to clothe ourselves with humility, donning it each day like a coat or dress, we can appreciate our own abilities and at the same time give thanks for the gifts and expertise of others.

Humility—the Key is Service

Christian humility does not entail putting yourself down, but rather getting your eyes off yourself. Begin by thinking about what you can do for others. The "white apron" of service may be worn over a beautifully embroidered dress or over a pair of blue jeans. During World War I in Russia, the Tsarina and her four daughters served alongside fellow nurses in a military hospital. They all wore the same uniform despite their higher rank. Underneath their nursing uniforms or aprons, however, they wore expensive clothing. At the coronation service of King Edward VII, the Archbishop of Canterbury preached on the biblical text, "I am among you as one who serves" (Luke 22:27). The highest vocation of everyone, be they kings, queens, or just ordinary people, is to serve others. But this service must be rendered with true respect for the person being served. It must not be done condescendingly. Unfortunately, some wealthy countries serve the needs of Third World peoples without regard for their dignity as persons.

Humility—Don't Draw Attention to Yourself

Service to those less fortunate than yourself must be done without drawing undue attention to yourself. The doctor in Lloyd C. Douglas' famous novel, Magnificent Obsession, served the needs of many needy people in the utmost secrecy. He didn't want people adulating him, so he kept completely quiet about his good deeds. Most of us fall short of his example. All too often we want recognition for what we have done. But the more that the Spirit of Christ takes hold of us, the more we serve without "the left hand knowing what the right hand is doing" (Matthew 6:3).

Alexander MacLaren, the great Scottish minister of the last century, has written these thought-provoking words, "It will usually be found that people who think of themselves more highly than they ought to think are often slow to use for their brethren their abilities of which they are so proud and you may be sure that the people who think humbly of themselves are generally most ready to help those who are in need of help." Humility and service go together.

The Greatest Inspiration to Serve Humbly

What inspires love and humility more than anything else was

the self-effacing love Jesus Christ displayed in his incarnation and death on the cross. In writing his beautiful letter of joy to the Philippian Christians living in northern Greece, Paul described this supreme illustration of humility. He wrote:

> Let this mind be in you, which was also in Christ Jesus
> Who although He was God, thought it not robbery to be equal with God
> But made Himself of no reputation, and was made in the likeness of men
> And being found in fashion as a man, He humbled Himself, and became obedient unto death
> Even the death of the cross
> For this reason, God has highly exalted Him, and given Him the name which is above every name
> That at the name of Jesus, every knee should bow and every tongue confess that Jesus Christ is Lord, to the glory of God the Father.
>
> Philippians 2:4-10

Christianity exalts this spirit of humility. Jesus' example has provided the inspiration and motivation behind the Seventh Step. To humbly overcome all our shortcomings requires divine power. As the Spirit of Christ takes hold of you, He will set you free from the burden of your sin and guilt, which has dominated and controlled your life. The "fruit" of humility appears as we relinquish ourselves totally to Him and participate in the process called Christian growth, overcoming our shortcomings to increasingly reflect the character of Christ.

CHAPTER EIGHT

STEP EIGHT: Made a list of all persons we had harmed and became willing to make amends to them all.
Alcoholics Anonymous

TRACK ONE: It is part of the cure to wish to be cured.
Seneca

Separating the Men from the Boys, the Women from the Girls

Alcoholics Anonymous insists on restitution as fundamental to complete alcoholic recovery. As someone has rightly said, "It separates the men from the boys, yes, and the women from the girls." As we begin to assess our past behavior, we will discover that our relationships with significant others have been badly damaged. It is, however, not enough to ask for God's forgiveness alone. We must be willing to get rid of self-condemnation, only possible as we honestly face the hurt we have caused others. Then, we must actively seek appropriate reparations. It won't be easy, but it will access maturity as a recovering alcoholic.

Wishing Won't Make It So

As we begin to seriously face the harm we have caused others, we may desperately want to make everything right again. But confession, while indispensable, does not constitute full restitution. We have to walk the second mile. The chapter, "How It Works" in The Alcoholics Anonymous Big Book, strongly emphasizes taking no shortcuts and avoiding half measures. Not only will we gain sobriety, but we will achieve the peace of mind we lack. Our alcoholic behavior has harmed many people, so our selfishness and thoughtlessness cannot be ignored. Atonement (at-one-ment) will only take place when we humbly confess it and make amends where we can. The moral log jam in the river of life needs clearing. Afterward we can experience the inner purification at the heart of any understanding of forgiveness.

Don't Get Bogged Down

Often only in the context of Group Discussions does the need of taking the Eighth Step surface.

"That's a tall order," Jake moaned after the Step was read, and the group began to delve into the meaning of making amends. "I think it's unreasonable to insist that every mistake we have made against other people must be atoned for."

Almost everyone in the group nodded their heads.

"Well," I said in response, "it sure seems like hitting below the belt, but rationalize as we may, we can't sidestep the issue."

"But Cal," Jake continued, "you've got to be kidding when you say that we must 'make up' with everyone. There're just too many people to remember."

"Nice try, Jake," I retorted, "but you can't get off the hook that easy. Don't let yourself get sucked into that self-justification mode."

"Yes, but can we actually be held responsible for what we did when we were 'plastered'?" Audrey chimed in.

"You're getting bogged down in the problem," I said. "You've got to see what's in store for you if you take this step to heart. The greatest source of peace comes not only when we experience God's forgiveness, but also that of fellow human beings. Horizontal relationships must be restored as well as the vertical one with God. No progress can be made in good sobriety until we review our guilty past with ruthless honesty. We must submit our wounded consciences to thorough examination. Remember, that's what we did when we took Step Four. We moved into first gear, as far as initiating inner freedom, but we mustn't stop there. Step Eight challenges us to double our efforts and deal with unresolved past sins."

"I can't bear the thought of doing it," Bob piped in.

"I know how you feel," I responded. "Opening up the old festering wounds is not a pleasant experience, but it is essential to expunge the poisonous puss of self-condemnation buried in our subconscious minds. Some people resist this surgical process, but let's encourage each other to undergo the operation and facilitate complete healing. Our thoroughness will determine the measure of our emotional and spiritual cleansing. This makes all the pain and humiliation worthwhile."

Don't Blame Others

As an alcoholic attempts to make amends honestly, his first priority is to forgive others. We all know how defensive we can be. It always seems like someone else's fault. We want the other person to initiate the necessary apology. But if we take that attitude, we will never discover what we have done to break down the relationship. You may think you have the right to harbor resentful feelings, but this will only delay the process of dealing with your own personal defects.

Be in touch with yourself. As the well-known A.A. cliché, goes, how can we point a finger at the other person when four fingers are pointing back at us? What about yourself? That's the real issue. Sick emotional reactions typically prevail between fellow human beings. Our many weak spots in character make us vulnerable. The alcoholic by his or her behavior, often pinpoints the weakness in others.

The wife of an alcoholic sat in my office one evening, weeping vociferously. When she finally got control of herself she blurted out, "He always gets the best of me. I can take his drinking most of the time, but if only he wouldn't shout at me, I could bear it. When he lashes out at me, I lose control and say terrible things I never meant to say."

This situation recurs again and again. Recipients of an alcoholic's abuse often reach the breaking point. The alcoholic then uses their weaknesses to justify his or her actions, and defend his behavior patterns.

"My wife's a bitch," one alcoholic said to me with fiery eyes. "Her temper is something else."

He never stopped to consider that he triggered this weak spot in her emotional makeup. The alcoholic's destructive behavior only multiplies the personal suffering of those left to cope with it. Instead of resenting his or her actions, the alcoholic needs to ask forgiveness for initiating the misery caused to family and friends.

Another Hurdle to Jump

When we honestly pursue reconciliation, we must also repent—be willing to change. We must face wounded persons and talk about our own character defects, not theirs.

One alcoholic friend said to me, "The best thing my wife ever did to me was to kick me out. When I began to realize that she couldn't and wouldn't take any more from me, I realized I needed to change and sober up. I needed this 'kick in the pants' to make me realize that I needed her forgiveness, even though at the time, she was not prepared to give it."

He harbored no resentment and was quite repentant. He showed the humility discussed in the last chapter. Engaging Step Eight means seeking out the person we have sinned against and verbalizing our feelings. Obviously, it takes courage to write a friend or a loved one we have hurt, or to sit down with a person who has given up on us, and confess our personal contribution to their emotional pain.

A young man participating in a recovery program I was supervising in the Union Mission For Men in Ottawa said to me one evening, "If my dad could only have opened up and told me how he felt about his drinking and what it was doing to our family, we could have had a good relationship—he just couldn't."

In my opinion, he probably just wouldn't. Pride gripped him too strongly. Even if we repress our sub-conscious life, we can't repress our sins against others forever. They raise their ugly heads and demand attention. We "chicken out" at this point and say, "I don't know how to put my feelings into words." The challenge is to try. Some people avoid confrontation by saying that this backward look into the past isn't constructive. But actually, it precipitates potentially stronger relationships with alienated friends or loved ones.

Trying to Get Off the Hook

Making amends, however, may create some peculiar difficulties. Because no one was apparently hurt by our drinking, we may feel that lets us "off the hook." Wrong.

We may not have noticed anyone in our families distraught by our drinking. Debts were always paid. Home life wasn't upset too much, as far as we knew, because often we drank somewhere else. Our social reputation didn't seem undermined, because most of our drinking was undercover. Most people didn't appear too upset by the odd drunken weekend. No one seemed upset because our social behavior was unacceptable. So all in all, we didn't need to apologize for anything we had done while drinking.

I can remember Joe saying to me, when he began to struggle with this particular Step, "It's so difficult for me to own up to what other people said I had done, when I wasn't conscious of doing anything wrong. I always remembered the bad things done to me, and this always gave me plenty of 'reasons' to drink. It was like a flash of light searing across my mind, when the truth crashed in on me that I had every reason to ask their forgiveness for the misery I caused them while drinking. When I made this breakthrough, I knew I had to get right with those I had hurt. It was like escaping a dark prison, where I had been bound in self-pity so long."

Forgetful Minds

Facing our need to make amends reveals how fleeting our memories actually are. We have failed to consider what our drinking amends, in most instances, our unwillingness to take honest inventory as Step Four challenges was dropped as irrelevant. Many people have told me that they never gave it the time of day. Their memory seemed to be totally obliterated. Only when the alcoholic honestly examines his or her conscience can this repression of moral deficiency surface. Our emotions have either become so desensitized that we have ignored the pain we caused others, or we have stubbornly refused to face what our persistent drinking was doing both to us and those closest to us.

I remember counseling a teenage girl at a high-school camp I was directing. She was crying her eyes out with anger and frustration. She loved her father on the one hand and yet hated him on the other, because he seemed totally blind to the hurt he had caused his family for many years. I told her to go home and start demonstrating love toward him, trying to remember that he was an emotional cripple. At first she felt she could never do this sincerely, but she promised to try. Some months later she came to me with a bright smile on her face exclaiming, "I can't believe it, but he actually asked me to forgive him."

What's Good for the Goose is Good for the Gander

Making amends with others must also be coupled with forgiving ourselves for all our mistakes and failures. It precedes reconciliation with others. If we can't forgive ourselves, we will find it next to impossible to ask forgiveness of others. Without forgiveness in our own troubled consciences, our attempts to make amends will likely be superficial or simply peter out. It requires in-depth thinking on the alcoholic's part, and in this thought process repressed emotions will undoubtedly surface. We will begin to see things for what they are. We will begin to forgive the inner child of our past, denied affirmation by a father or mother; we will begin to forgive the buried teenager in us struggling for acceptance, and feeling that drinking with our friends would do it; we will begin to forgive the repressed bridegroom in us, full of insecurity as we entered marriage hoping that our mate would give us something we couldn't find. Once we begin to forgive the repressed inner self, asking forgiveness of others will be much easier. As Susan demonstrated love toward her insecure, repressed and unloved father, whose life was badly distorted, her love freed him. He began to forgive himself, and then to seek her forgiveness. When I met him some months later after I had counseled Susan, he blurted out happily, "I feel free."

Take Off Your Blinkers

The misconception that we haven't harmed anyone needs to be faced squarely. Harm can't be confined to physical abuse, although that occurs in alcoholic families. (Plenty of wives and children can show you black eyes and bruised bodies.) It doesn't just involve the accidents we've caused, the temper tantrums, the persistent lying, the irresponsible way we've spent money on booze instead of the family or the moral unfaithfulness that marred our marital relationship. You can't stop there. Harmful behavior has dynamics far more subtle.

"He's so stingy," one wife confided. "I can't believe his miserly attitude toward money. He doesn't seem to know the meaning of the word 'generous.' "

One nineteen-year-old fellow, whom I sat with having a Coke after a football game, said to me, with hot tears streaming down his cheeks, "I don't think he ever came to one of my games." This negligence in keeping appointments has created more hurt than anything I know.

"Grouchy—that's the only way I can describe him," a family of four told me as they tried to adjust to their father's behavior. "You have to tiptoe around the house as though you're walking on eggs. He has no sense of humor—he can't see the funny side of anything."

"You wouldn't believe the favoritism he practiced towards us kids," one girl in her twenties said to me, as she tried to address the sibling rivalry between her and her sister caused by their father.

"When I got out of the house, after living there for seventeen years, I felt as though I was coming out of prison. You can't believe how deep our resentment got as Dad dominated everything we did. He threw his weight around, depriving us of making choices for ourselves," said a woman now in her forties still having difficulty emotionally from these childhood and adolescent experiences.

"The drinking bouts were nothing compared with the sad-sack, gloom-and-doom spirit that hung over the house after my husband came off a big drunk," a good friend in Alanon (an organization for those who have alcoholic relatives and need emotional support as they struggle to be positive about the alcoholic's behavior) told me. "The physical or verbal abuse was easier to take."

These examples represent hidden abuse behind the lives of those who live with an alcoholic spouse or parent. In most cases, the alcoholic responsible was oblivious to what was going on.

Get With It—Honesty is a Must

The rigorous honesty required by the A.A. Twelve-Step Program proves difficult for many alcoholics to put into action.

"I was so insecure," I heard Norm confess one evening at his regular A.A. meeting. "I just couldn't own up to what I had done, partly because I couldn't see it at first. I was so blind. It was a big step—no, an enormous step of courage and faith—when I actually said to someone in my family, 'I'm sorry. Will you forgive me?' "

But when honesty does surface, we must not only address obvious infractions but also the hidden ones. God will not let us discover too much at a time. He will gradually make us aware of everyone who has been affected by our drinking.

I remember how hard it was for Doug. After doing some reading in the Twelve-Step Recovery book, he said to me, "I can see now that I have to go back as far as possible even though, in some cases, I can't rectify much of what I've done. But wherever possible, I know I must deal with all the situations contributing to breakdown in my relationships. I can at least begin by asking God to forgive me and making things right in my heart. But I also know that I have to seriously face each person and discover, by God's grace, how I have caused unhappiness in their lives. I know I can't be trite or superficial about this. I must go right to the core of things. There's no other way."

"Doug," I reminded him, "as a believer in God, I know you can rely on Him to help you remember. Just pray the words of the Psalmist centuries ago, 'Search me O God and know my heart, and see if there be any wickedness in me, and lead me into the path of life' (Psalm 139:23-24). As you confess all you've done, He will help you release all stored-up self-condemnation that you may not realize now but that you know is there. Along with this, God's healing love and grace will flow into your heart. But one thing you must remember—this analytical process must be done without any external pressure from others. No one can force you into it, or put a guilt trip on you to do it. Another thing—exaggeration of any facts only opens the door to deception. You must tell it like it is, and not embellish. You need to be honest *and* objective. Keep in mind that the inspiration to follow the Eighth Step will likely come from other A.A. members who have completed the process themselves. They will probably be unaware of their positive effect upon you. As you respond to their lead you will find the impetus to take the same step."

In the long history of spiritual awakenings, sincere seekers willingly deal with their specific sins. This leads to reconciliation between people separated for long periods of time.

After reading the history of spiritual renewal in Nigeria where Christianity had been practiced for a number of generations, I was deeply impressed by their method of restitution. A director of the Women's Association confessed publicly to pilfering church supplies over the years. She justified it by saying that she did not deliberately steal. She reasoned, "I'm the head woman, and as such, I have certain privileges others don't have." But when she faced her thefts, she knew she could not rest until she had restored everything she had taken. And so, she took a large basket filled with rice and returned it to the church supply room.

As a result, the wife of one of the house servants confessed to taking eggs from the pantry. Her guilt became so severe that she returned what she had taken with the words, "It is not enough just to confess this. I want to give an egg for every egg I have stolen."

Another man with only a few francs confessed that he had taken a New Testament and had not paid for it. He justified it by saying to himself, These white men have plenty of money. Why should I be concerned with a few francs? But now he made amends by returning the amount he owed for the book.

To be effective, Step Eight has to be radical—no half measures, especially if we want reconciliation with God and ourselves. If we courageously embark on this Step, our conscience will make us feel young again. It will restore relationships—well worth the effort.

STEP EIGHT: **Made a list of all persons we had harmed and became willing to make amends to them all.**
Alcoholics Anonymous

TRACK TWO: **Listen, I will give half my belongings to the poor, and if I have cheated anyone, I will pay back four times as much (Zacchaeus).**   *Luke 19:8*

Restitution—Biblically Based

The principle of Step Eight in the A.A. Program originates from the Old and New Testaments. During Old Testament times, the Israelites—God's people—were constantly admonished by both their prophets and sacred writings to reconcile their offenses and make appropriate restitution. Consequently, they would be free from the guilt that ensues from the breakdown of relationships.

If He Can Do It, I Can Do It

A pertinent story from Luke 19 illustrates the importance of making amends. Zacchaeus, a prominent man in the Jewish community, was considered an outcast by most people because he cooperated with the Roman government to collect heavy taxes. These tax collectors, called publicans, were employed to collect a set amount for the government. They were authorized to collect as much more as they felt they needed or wanted as personal income. This occupation, called "farming out the taxes," was often pursued by unscrupulous men well known for dishonesty and greed. Victimized by their injustice, the people hated them. The religious leaders despised them because they collaborated with the Romans in violating the laws of God, without regard for others.

Hobnobbing with the Outcasts

Zacchaeus the publican was an outcast, particularly from the perspective of the religious establishment. Jesus aroused suspicion because He did not conform to their understanding and practice of God's laws. They especially decried the company He kept, as did others. They saw Him associating with the undesirables of society, whom they called "sinners." One said, "Look, He eats with publicans and sinners," a totally unacceptable posture for someone proclaiming the Word of God. If He really was from God, they reasoned, how could he hobnob with blatant violators of his law?

But Jesus did not allow his ministry of love to be affected by their self-righteous assessment. He said to the people, perhaps with a touch of humor, "I did not come to call righteous people, but sinners to repentance" (Luke 5:32). Dazzled with their own brand of morality, these men remained blind to their faults and deaf to the message of hope in Christ. Sinners, on the other hand, knew their shortcomings and welcomed the possibility of change and spiritual renewal. Jesus came to alleviate the consciences of those longing for freedom from sin.

And the Walls Came Tumblin' Down

Zacchaeus lived in the famous town immortalized by Joshua. He and the armies of Israel marched around the strong walls of this ancient city (dating back to at least 700-900 B.C.) and they fell down, thus enabling the Israelites to capture the city and invade the land given to them by God. But greater walls had to come down when Jesus visited this famous city. As He approached the town, large crowds gathered along the highway either to welcome Him or catch a curious glimpse of this famous prophet and healer. Curiosity overcame Zacchaeus and he resolved to find a way to at least see this Man he had heard was rejected by the religious class, just as he was. Because of his short stature and the dense crowd, he decided to climb one of the many sycamore trees lining the highway and thus enjoy a ringside seat. He wouldn't be deterred by outward circumstances.

Something happened that day to make the walls of guilt, shame, hardness of heart and insensitivity to human need come tumbling down. As Jesus travelled the dusty road, he suddenly stopped right under the tree where this hated government agent crouched among the leafy branches. Looking up into the tree, Jesus saw this hated man and said in a clear, winsome, yet commanding voice, "Zacchaeus, come down from that tree. I would like to eat with you today." The man must have been bowled over with astonishment, but without a moment's reluctance, he scrambled down the tree and prepared to welcome Jesus into his, no doubt, palatial home. He must have been filled with consternation and fear. Why did this Man want to visit him? What was he after? What demands would he make?

The doors of Zacchaeus' home opened. A meal was served as the host sat bewildered by Jesus engaging in conversation with his publican friends. The quality friendship shown by Jesus, his acceptance—even of those the religious leaders rejected—his words of affirmation, his invitation to seek more than money broke every barrier down. Zacchaeus became cognizant of his need. His pride shattered. He wanted to change his lifestyle and face the sins he had justified for so many years. As the supper concluded, he felt compelled to rise from the table where he had been reclining and make an open, straightforward confession. "Whatever I have taken falsely I will restore. Yes, if I have taken anything from anyone unjustly, I will return him four times what I took." This was a complete reversal. His changed heart led him to promise restitution to those he had robbed.

Undoubtedly, Jesus knew this man's heart. He saw the walls of self-love crumbling, and a new freedom emerging. Without ado, Jesus simply affirmed what happened. "Today," he said, "salvation—liberation, freedom—is coming to this house." Jesus knew that this naturally follows when a person confesses his sin and promises to make amends where he or she can. He knew that new possibilities for positive relationships could now develop between Zacchaeus all those he had wronged.

Restitution is Where It's At

With grace of God at work in this situation, no words of

condemnation were spoken. No chastisement for his dishonesty and greed. Grace in action caused Jesus to sit at the table of this social outcast and compel this hated Roman tax agent to face himself. His long-suppressed conscience emerged, and he knew that he had to make amends. He knew he had to return what he had taken from his countrymen through extortion. The power of love broke through as Jesus simply accepted the hospitality of Zacchaeus' table, and allowed himself to be served. Zacchaeus saw a dimension of life that touched his heart and changed it. The goodness of God in Jesus Christ, as the Apostle Paul states in Romans 2:4, led him to repentance. And now, this internal change motivated him to practical action. He must make amends for his wrongdoing.

What it Means to be Liberated

The open confession of Zacchaeus that he would restore whatever he had wrongly taken led Christ to react positively. He said for all to hear, "Today, salvation has come to this household."

It was a day of new beginnings. Jesus then went on to declare that He came "to seek and to save that which is lost and to give his life for the sake of others" (Matthew 20:28).

The word "salvation" or "save" is narrowly defined today. To be "saved" in biblical times meant to be liberated from the old life of narrow, self-centeredness that only robs us of inner personal freedom. Salvation rescues us not only from the power of our sin, but also frees us to make amends to others and serve them in love. Jesus continues to set us free today, by giving Himself to us in love, a love that culminated in his sacrificial death. The power released in our lives emancipates us from our warped understanding of what it means to be happy, and from our narrow self-centeredness.

A powerful story from the life of the great Italian painter Raphael illustrates further. On one occasion he was visited by the older artist and sculptor, Michelangelo. The younger Raphael was working on a particular canvas with a theme too big to be contained within the narrow limits of the frame. After looking at the painting for a few minutes, Michelangelo took a piece of chalk, and scribbled across the canvas the Latin word "amphilus" which means "larger, bigger." In so doing, he alerted Raphael to begin again, but with a much larger canvas to do justice to the chosen theme.

Jesus Christ does this for us when He begins to liberate our lives. Across the canvas of life, narrowed by self-absorption and sin, He writes the words "larger, bigger." This is what "salvation" means. It expands our lives into new dimensions, where we can make amends for wrongdoing and thus widen the possibilities for fresh, new relationships.

Convicted, But Not Condemned

The dynamic love of Jesus convicted Zacchaeus of his wrongdoing, but did not condemn him. Rather, it opened a door through which he could enter into new life. This produced hope for the restoration of right relationships with those he had treated unjustly. He faced his own moral failure for the first time and he knew it needed rectification. Amends had to be made, money had to be returned. Long years of crooked behavior had to be straightened out.

When the Spirit of Jesus Christ overshadows us, we discover that He doesn't condemn us, but convicts us to step in a new direction. We get right with parents we have ignored. We build bridges of understanding and acceptance with children. We face our alienated spouses and we deal with marital conflicts. We return what we have taken from employers. When salvation works its way into our lives, we embark on the road to reconciliation.

All this happens when we hear the Word of God and act upon it. To hear is to obey. Convicted by the words of Christ, we move into action. One of Christ's most powerful parables centers around two men who built houses. One was erected on a flimsy foundation of sand and collapsed when the rains descended. The other was built upon a rock and withstood the full blast of nature because its foundation was solid. From this story, Jesus teaches that spiritual renewal not producing character change represents a house built upon sand. But when true character transformation has occurred, new abilities to deal with the storms of life surface. Self-effort doesn't save us, but rather God's saving grace that creates a hunger for righteousness. This is fundamental to understanding the implications of God's love. As our Savior, He not only saves us from the condemnation of past sin, but sets us free from a careless attitude to life that ignores the need for reformation in our actions. The Book of Hebrews speaks of Christ "saving to the uttermost," or completely delivering us from the guilt of every action that has undermined our relationships with others.

A Savior, Not a Moralist

The unique approach of Jesus to Zacchaeus distinguishes Him as unique among moralists, who tell you what you have to do, but offer no power to accomplish it. A long history of preachers in the Hebrew Christian tradition have pointed out accurately the national and personal sins of people, but they have offered no power to initiate reconciliation. Sometimes change does take place, but not for long. In the thirteenth century, a great preacher in Florence called Savonorola, soundly denounced the sins of society. He inspired the lawless Florentines to burn many of their worldly books and trinkets, and give up many immoral actions and entertainments. But it lasted only a year. Finally the people turned on Savonorola and burned him at the stake. John Calvin's powerful denunciations of degenerate Geneva compelled the people to reform in significant ways. But it lasted only a few generations. Moralistic revivals do not have "lasting power." Something more is needed—only the all-accepting love of God for the individual creates permanent change.

This happened in Zacchaeus' home. Jesus did not preach any moral tidbits to this hated tax collector. He did not lecture him on the need for honesty. He did not compel Zacchaeus to look at his character and examine his ways. This took place naturally, as the grace of God working through Jesus enabled Zacchaeus to respond freely. The subtlety of Jesus' approach is much more effective than the head-on, direct approach of the moralists. William Wordsworth, in one of his poems, speaks of the "truth breathed with cheerfulness."[1] The gentleness of Jesus' approach won the day in Zacchaeus' life.

The Inspiration to Make Amends

This kind of approach enables the alcoholic to begin making amends. My wife and I had two alcoholic friends. After they began the Christian life, they still had a strong attachment to their wine. Whenever we were with them socially, they always wanted us to drink with them. We simply said, "Go ahead, but we're not too fond of wine." Nothing was said about their need to give up drinking. Gradually, they became less and less attracted to wine and their habit dropped like feathers off a molting duck.

Change Through Exchange

One obvious feature of Christ's ministry was his rejection of legalistic observance of laws, even though given by God. He knew that people don't change by being scolded or harangued. His approach was change through exchange.

As previously mentioned, if you want to get air out of a glass you don't grasp after the invisible, illusive substance. Instead, you fill the glass with water. As the liquid comes in, the air goes out—the law of displacement. We've also discussed the following example. In the Fall you often see a tree with a few yellow leaves still hanging on despite relentless winds. Throughout the winter, they tenaciously hold on to the branches. But in the Spring, when the new sap surges up the trunk into the branches those dead leaves are just pushed off. As the new life comes, the old life goes.

Jesus and John the Baptist display these distinctions. The one, in a loud, clamorous way, called upon the Israelites to change their ways. Many of them were baptized to signal their intention to obey the laws of God. He appealed to men's hearts on the basis of fear and self-preservation. Their repentance was, unfortunately, only temporary and short-lived.

---

1. *A Choice of Wordsworth Verse*, R.S. Thomas, P. 33.

Jesus, however, introduced people to much more permanent and dynamic change. It radically departed from the old way of responding to people's sin. He gave people the privilege of friendship, accepted them as persons and by the quality of his friendship and the graciousness of his words, He enabled them to begin again. This kind of attitude can't help but create a desire for a new way of living and deliverance from destructive habits.

When Jesus sat at Zacchaeus' dinner table, the quality of his friendship and the understanding He displayed made this man feel inwardly guilty and recognize his need to make amends to those he had injured. He made a decision to change, motivated by unconditional love. The power that enabled him to relinquish his dishonest lifestyle came from Jesus' acceptance of him as a person. This provided the dynamic to make lasting amends.

Love Conquers All

Friendship with Jesus Christ creates genuine goodness in a person's life. His interest in us not only turns us away from an old and unfulfilling life, but produces a transforming relationship grounded in genuine friendship. In the Gospels, Christ is called the Friend of sinners. The magnetic power of his all-accepting love produces an inner desire to change. This change leads to new relationships with people previously alienated by our behavior.

CHAPTER NINE

STEP NINE: **Made amends to such people whenever possible, except when to do so would injure them or others.**
Alcoholics Anonymous

TRACK ONE: **The hearts of good men admit the need of atonement.**   *Homer*

Now is the Hour

"As soon as I get some sobriety under my belt," Harry said to me, "I've got to clean up the mess I've created. But it will take time."

Step Nine introduces us the the importance of using discretion when seeking reconciliation for our past actions, and developing a sensitivity for the right time to act, or not to act. As the writer of the Book of Ecclesiastes writes, "There is a time . . . ." and then he lists various possibilities. "A time to love, a time to hate, a time to be born and a time to die, a time to plant and a time to uproot, a time to kill and a time to heal, a time to tear down and a time to build, a time to weep and a time to laugh, a time to mourn and a time to dance, a time to scatter and a time to gather, a time to embrace and a time to refrain, a time to search and a time to give up, a time to be silent and a time to speak, a time for war and a time for peace" (Ecclesiastes 3:1-8). Certainly the Ninth Step highlights the words, "a time to be silent and a time to speak."

"When do you think I should open up and tell my wife all the garbage in my life?" Garth asked me. He has been sincerely working the A.A. Twelve-Step Program and wanted to go all the way. "No short-stops for me," he said. "I want A.A. to affect my whole life, not just my drinking."

"Well," I replied, "I know that your wife seems like number one on your list. But you need to approach it slowly. The recovering alcoholic should come to grips with several groups of people as he or she reflects upon past behavior, while at the same time considering the effect it will have upon them. As soon as sobriety has been maintained for a reasonable amount of time, we can approach some people immediately. Others should be approached more cautiously. Still others we would only hurt more deeply, if we shared intimately with them. These people are best left alone to deal with their emotions by themselves or with the help of a friend or counsellor."

"I see what you're driving at," Harry responded, "but somehow, I feel in my guts that I've got to start first with my wife, and probably my kids, too."

"I know you're eager, Harry, to make things right with the family, but you've got to think clearly before you rush in. No question the serious recovering alcoholic wants to initiate as much reconciliation as possible. And their drive may compel them to tackle people head on, particularly with those families of alcoholics who intend to sober up with the help of A.A. Some aspects of our behavior may require apologies as soon as possible. These people will observe our enthusiasm as we tackle the challenge to remain sober. But in my own approach, I think we should delay making amends until we have attended many meetings, and have studied the Big Book carefully. Our families need to see our words being backed up by actions that authenticate them."

Harry quietly reflected on what I said and then responded, "Well, don't you think it's better to get things off your chest? After all, it's a lot better than what happens after a bout of drinking and the disaster that usually follows."

"Of course," I replied, "it's only normal to want to make things right, if possible. But confession at first may only reflect your admission that you need to change. Change should be tackled step by step, not in one big jump. Opening old wounds may be too painful to express at first. After all, you must make sure your confession actually helps your relationship with the family, and doesn't just alleviate your own self-hate and guilt."

"I see what you're driving at," Harry agreed. "I guess I'll just have to take it slowly. After all, we don't act like saints overnight, if ever."

Actions Speak Louder Than Words

Making restitution with our fellow employees requires the same approach. Some people at work have had close involvement with our drinking behavior. If we stop drinking, they need time to adjust. At first, they still probably think our decision won't last, like a New Year's resolution, broken a few days afterward. As people see the outward change A.A. is making in our lives, they will accept apologies far more readily for the dysfunction caused by our alcoholism. Better to start out by paying old debts, or fulfilling broken promises. Our positive behavior will soften the hearts of those most severe in their denunciations. Few sayings are truer than "actions speak louder than words." People we have hurt deeply need to see changes in character before they can respond positively to our verbal assertions. The change comes first.

The Need for a Balanced Approach

As we see our relationships with those we have offended improve, we may be tempted to go overboard trying to make things right. As Bob sat in my office one evening feeling quite dejected, he admitted to going too far too fast.

"I feel like I've been a fanatic," he groaned. "I should have let sleeping dogs lie."

"One thing you probably have to learn, Bob," I said, "is that confession, at first, only signals your need to change. After a few weeks it can take on deeper confidences. Rehashing the old hurts may be too painful at first, especially for the ones we've hurt the most. They may not want you to pull off the scabs of wounds they believe are healing quite nicely. I've found that an aggressive approach never works."

"I guess what you're saying, Cal," he responded, "is that as we lay our cards on the table, some of the cards need to be hidden for awhile.

"Right on," I replied, "and above all, it is important to get beyond remorse—a negative form of repentance. Remorse never changed anyone. It reeks of self-pity. Wringing one's hands in despair does not allow God to lead us beyond self-condemnation. On the other hand, positive repentance always leads to change, true humility, and authentic love for those wounded by our behavior."

The Underlying Motive for Change

As we begin to open our hearts to another person only one motive should predominate—love. Without this cardinal virtue, complete revelation of our past could only result in radical disintegration of our already tenuous relationships. Particularly if we have cheated on our spouse in extra-marital affairs. As this kind of exposure proceeds, we must be careful not to undermine the third party. Many people involved in adultery have sincerely repented and we need to be careful to protect their reputations.

Other problems, delicate in nature, must be approached thoughtfully, but with courage. Misuse of company funds requires a good measure of wisdom. Our reparations must not jeopardize our families' security. They have already suffered with lack of funds. Along with discussing these matters with our sponsor, we must earnestly seek the guidance of God. If we determine to be a channel of love, the wisdom to carry it out in a healthy way will be given. Restitution doesn't come easily and has no ready-made solutions. With hearts motivated by love, however, we are heading in the right direction, and God can be trusted to guide. If panic generated by fear overtakes us, only the invasion of divine love can overcome it. That is made clear in John's first letter, "Perfect love casts our fear" (1 John 4:18). We must not fight against fear, but rather, open our hearts to God's all-pervasive love. This love will enable us to make amends at all costs for the benefit of others.

Overcoming Self-Condemnation

"I don't feel I have any fear in sharing my past with my wife and family," Roy confessed. He had severely damaged his relationship with his family over the years but somehow the power of their love for him was still winning out. Now sober, he was trying to be honest with himself, working hard to make the Twelve-Step Program work for him. "What I don't think I am going to be able to do," he said, "is to forgive myself. How am I going to overcome this hang-up, Cal?"

"Knowing your family, Roy, as I do so well, I think you can trust them to accept you without too much difficulty. But I know what you mean when you say that forgiving yourself is a big hurdle to jump. As I reflect on this common weakness, I have begun to get some insights. Firstly, we have no right to distort our emotional life and put ourselves through the screws. You cannot atone for your misconduct by crucifying yourself. All you can do is face yourself honestly in the sight of God."

"You're really helping me, Cal, to see that forgiving myself is a possibility," Bob responded.

"Yes," I replied, "God will apprise us of the hurts our drinking has caused. No superficial considerations will do. We must be willing to get down to the nitty-gritty of what has really happened. But as we do this honestly and courageously, our reflections will surface many repressed emotions. Then we've got to decide what to do with them. Are we going to put ourselves through the mill, hoping to expunge our guilt? Are we going to go on some futile pilgrimage? I don't mean to a religious shrine, but to those places where we have sinned against our loved ones, and then grovel. Forgiving ourselves can only come about when we accept that God by his love and grace has already forgiven us. If we reject that forgiveness, we are still unbelieving and want to do it our way. The words that Jesus spoke from the cross to the soldiers who were crucifying Him have to be assimilated. He said, 'Father forgive them, they know not what they do' (Luke 23:34). If you really apply those words to yourself, you will lose your attitude of self-condemnation. You are acting in faith to believe what God has said about you. If you take Him seriously, you will find Him absorbing your sins into Himself, the way blotting paper absorbs ink. This transference of your sin and misdeeds onto Him will occur. It will enable you to renounce the no-win predicament of self-depreciation. It's the only way to go."

STEP NINE: Made amends to such people whenever possible, except when to do so would injure them or others.
Alcoholics Anonymous

TRACK TWO: If you come to the altar, prepared to give a gift to the Lord, and there you remember that your brother or sister has something against you, leave your gift in front of the altar, and go and make peace and then come and offer your gift to God. *Matthew 5:24*

Step Nine emphasizes openness and honesty, leading us to action that rectifies broken relationships. Believers are encouraged to initiate change that results in the positive transformation of any of them. This action originates from the teachings of Christ and will result in spiritual and physical recovery.

I was leading a Bible study for A.A. members who had found Christ as their High Power. We were studying the Sermon on the Mount and came to the section where Jesus gives specific instruction on how to reconcile ourselves with those alienated from us (Matthew 5:24).

Bob, one of the newest members of the group and an avid Bible reader, piped up, "I think that Jesus wasn't the only One Who advocated getting right with people you've hurt. I think I read the same thing in the Book of James yesterday. He tells us that we are to confess our faults one to another in order to be healed (James 5:16)."

"You're perfectly right, Bob," I replied, "but I am sure that his inspiration came from Jesus. You must remember that the twelve apostles spent three years with Him, and undoubtedly reflected his teachings. Both Jesus and James clarify that hiding is fruitless. No rationalization, no cover-up. We must be up front with one another to build bridges of reconciliation."

Another new member of the group, Mary, feeling awkward and uncertain about her lack of knowledge, hesitantly asked, "Cal, what do you think those words of James imply? Does it mean we have to put it right with everyone? I think some things I've done are best forgotten. I can't see myself opening up to some people I know. They would be too hurt and things would go from bad to worse.

"I know what you're driving at, Mary," I replied, "and you notice from the Ninth Step, that this kind of confession should only proceed if we know it won't make things worse. But having said that, we mustn't use this as an excuse. We must remember that the Christian life not only consists of a personal, life-changing commitment to Christ, but it must also affect everyone else in our lives. It's not just a matter of you and God, but rather, God, you, and your relationships—family, friends, and others. We are all tied together in the bundle of life. Whatever affects you affects me, and vice versa."

Nothing Completely Private

No longer can we delude ourselves that others need not be concerned with our lifestyles, actions and attitudes. True, some of my actions concern only me. I am the only person who can deal with them, especially negative or destructive ones. But on the whole, the assumption that my sins are mine and mine alone is false. Many of my sins have affected the lives of significant others. I must be willing to mitigate the subsequent breakdowns. For some behaviors I am responsible only to God. But on the whole, most of my faults affect others as well as myself. Christian teaching recognizes our responsibility before God for what we have done to ourselves and to others.

Life binds us intricately to one another. Like a body, what happens not only affects one part, but every other. Ingrown toenails make the whole body wince in pain. Likewise our personal lives. To be free from the pain of a guilty conscience, I must be willing to confess my sin openly, not only to God, but also to those I have sinned against. This, the Apostle James assures us, leads to inner healing that affects my body's health too.

The Potential for Restoration

Healing, the hope of confession, naturally results from restored relationships. Many of our physical aches and pains often relate directly to unresolved bitterness and resentment caused by unforgiveness and unwillingness to make amends where possible. But the Gospel challenges us to accept the forgiveness of Christ so that we can make things right with others. The teachings of Jesus emphasize the need for right relationships. Christ came to be the Great Reconciler. He desires that we deal not only with our sin against Him, but also with anything that hinders us from reconciliation to each other.

Worshiping in Spirit and Truth

A primary characteristic of the Christian life is worship. But many Christians handicap their worship by not clearing the obstructions between themselves and other Christians. Many receive Holy Communion, for example, where love and forgiveness are symbolically extended, while animosity and resentment still fester in their hearts. This completely contradicts Christ's teaching. In the great Sermon on the Mount, Jesus addresses the problem. He says, "If you come to the altar, prepared to leave an offering to God, and there you remember that your brother or sister has something against you, leave your gift at the front of the altar, and go at once and make peace and then come and offer your gift to God" (Matthew 5:23-24). In other words, right relationships supersede worship or good deeds in importance. Reconciliation, making peace with others, prepares hearts for meaningful worship. Without it, our worship reduces to mere ritual.

Adhering to the Right Order

Christianity subscribes to a hierarchy of actions. Some take precedence over others. For example in a monarchy, kings and queens come first, then princes and dukes. They are followed by counts, barons, knights, etc. But the opposite applies to the Christian life. Jesus taught: "He who would be greatest among you must be servant of all" (Mark 9:34). In the process of understanding, the simple and obvious teachings must be accepted first. The more advanced, complicated, and difficult truths follow. This recurs in all branches of knowledge. Simple arithmetic precedes learning advanced geometry and calculus.

Until we apply the basic rules of reconciliation, we cannot proceed with the higher obligations of Christian living. Many accounts in the Bible describe those who wanted to occupy the more exalted positions before completing initial and primary obligations. On one occasion a mother requested that her two sons, disciples of Jesus, have "front row" seats in the coming Kingdom (Matthew 20:21ff). She wanted one to sit on the right of Jesus, and the other on the left. This request was voiced in the presence of other disciples, and they responded indignantly. Jesus used the opportunity to outline the order of his kingdom. He reminded them that before the kingdom could come, they would have to start on the bottom rung of preparation. If they wanted to be princes in God's new order, they had to become child-like. Again, we see Peter bragging about his loyalty to Jesus. "I am ready to go anywhere with you, even to prison and death," he affirmed (Luke 22:33). But when Jesus faced his greatest trial in the Garden of Gethsemane, boastful Peter was fast asleep, forfeiting Jesus' call to, "Watch and pray that you enter not into temptation" (Mark 14:38).

Before we take to heart the primary issues of Kingdom living, we all too often preoccupy ourselves with secondary ones. We eagerly seek the secrets of the Kingdom before personally surrendering to Jesus as Lord. So often we claim to practice Kingdom principles but fail to confess our need for forgiveness and grace. Often we want change between us, friends or family members we have hurt, circumventing our need to make amends. As someone has amusingly noted, Christians can become so heavenly minded that they are no earthly good. If we want fellowship with God and each other, we must be willing to start on the "ground floor" before ascending to upper realms of spiritual insight.

For example, Jesus paints the picture of a man responsible in his worship of God coming to the temple to make an offering. But just as he reaches the altar, he remembers a conflict with his brother. What should he do about it? Jesus says that before he goes any further in his worship, he must go from the sanctuary at once, and make his way to his offended brother. There he must ask forgiveness and do anything that is necessary to make amends. When this is done, then he has the right to return to the temple and engage in worship with a pure, sincere, uncontaminated heart (Matthew 5:23-24). In other words, restoration is preeminent. Worship, though of great importance, must be preceded by reconciliation. Otherwise, as I said, previously, it reduces to religious ritual.

Corrie Ten Boom, the famous Dutch Christian writer and speaker, tells how God taught her forgiveness in her book, *The Hiding Place.* At the outbreak of World War II when her country was overrun by the German army, her family helped many Jewish families escape to England. They eventually were caught and sentenced to some of the worst concentration camps set up for political prisoners. Her father died within one week and soon after her sister contracted tuberculosis. Corrie went to the head nurse of the hospital, seeking a bed for her sister and was cruelly refused. Within six months, her sister died and her body was thrown into a human dump heap. Corrie was left alone to endure further Nazi atrocities.

After the war, Corrie wanted to get as far away from Germany as possible. She traveled in North America speaking to student groups about the love of God in Jesus Christ. Engaged in this ministry, she was convicted by the Spirit of God that He also loved the Germans, despite what happened to her family and the Jews. At first she resisted this Inner Voice, but eventually she could not repress it. She returned to Germany.

One evening, as she spoke in a certain city, she saw a lady in the audience she thought she had met, but she couldn't remember the circumstances. After the meeting, Corrie spoke to the chairperson pointing out the lady in the crowd and asking her name. "Oh," said her friend, "that woman used to be the head nurse in Dachau concentration camp during the war." Immediately Corrie recognized her. Hatred and animosity welled up in her heart. She knew it was wrong and returning to her hotel room, she got on her knees before the Lord and asked Him to give her the ability to forgive this woman. He did. Rising from her knees, she found the phone directory and telephoned her. She asked her over for tea the next day. The woman responded, "You mean you want me to come and have tea with you, knowing who I am?" "Yes," replied Corrie, "I want to get to know you better." What resulted from this act of forgiveness on Corrie's part? Within a short time, this former head nurse of a concentration camp, disillusioned and bitter, entered the Kingdom of God. Why? Because the words of Jesus are true: "Blessed are the merciful for they shall obtain mercy" (Matthew 5:7). We learn that it is impossible to serve God and, at the same time, retain a spirit of bitterness and unforgiveness. Amends must be made—a fundamental of spiritual growth.

Jesus gives a second illustration with a touch of humor. "Imagine," He in effect says, "a person trying to get a splinter out of another person's eye, and yet all the while there is a large beam of lumber protruding from his own eye" (Matthew 7:5). His first concern should be to attend to his own condition, before helping out his friend. Jesus exaggerates for a reason. Often, we point out someone's trivial misconduct, while ignoring major faults of our own. Self-examination must come before we speak critically about someone else. Before analyzing someone else's conduct, we must rigorously review our own attitudes and behavior. So often we accuse other people—coworkers, friends, neighbors, family members—of their faults, but fail to criticize our own attitudes and conduct. It is a common fault. We constantly need to ask the Holy Spirit to teach us how to handle our shortcomings before addressing those of others.

I find the words of the hero in Bazil King's novel, *The Side of Angels*, pertinent.

"I've stumbled on to a great truth. It's that man's first occupation is not with others, but with himself. It's not to put them right—it's to be right on his own account. I was so busy casting out other people's devils that I had forgotten all about my own. I've been so eager that my neighbor's garden should be trim and productive that I'd forgotten that my own was overrun with weeds."

The Apostle Paul defines a basic Christian principle: "that which is spiritual is not first, but rather that which is natural" (1 Corinthians 15:56). First and foremost we must attend to our need for forgiveness before we can move on to the higher obligations of Christian living. Truth and honesty about ourselves lead us to the Christ of the cross Who died that we might be rightly related to our heavenly Father. A person must begin in square one before moving on to the additional pieces of life's puzzle.

The Psalmist asks himself a primary question in Psalm 15: 1-3. "Lord," he prays, "who can ascend up to your Holy Hill?" And then he answers his own question. "He who walks uprightly and works righteousness, who speaks the truth in his heart, who no longer slanders his neighbor with his tongue."

The ability to adopt this lifestyle does not come naturally. We need the invasion of a Higher Power—the power of God Himself. Only He can assist us with our needs first, and then empower us to establish new relationships with those whose lives we have damaged. Make amends in your own heart first and then sincerely move toward others to make things right.

CHAPTER TEN

STEP TEN: **Continued to take personal inventory, and where we were wrong, promptly admitted it.**
Alcoholics Anonymous

TRACK ONE: **Make yourself an honest man, and then you may be sure there is one less rascal in the world.**
Carlyle

Progress—Good and Bad

Life can well be described as an exciting adventure, especially when working out the principles that make for personal happiness and inner contentment. The Tenth Step in Alcoholics Anonymous calls us to persevere in making its program a regular, consistent part of our daily lives. It challenges us to "hang in there," despite how we may sometimes feel as we struggle to achieve the stability of character that comes from discipline and practice.

In one of my most stimulating A.A. Discussion Groups, we focused on how to follow the Fifth Step. The group was made up of mature A.A. members, who had progressed in their sobriety to the point where they could discuss their weaknesses without being threatened. One evening we talked about our need for daily evaluation.

"What do you think is the key to growth?" John asked. His struggle to find stable sobriety had been long and often filled with disappointment.

"I believe it centers in our willingness to examine our strengths and weaknesses together, in order to make spiritual progress," replied Mary.

"That's not easy, but I guess it's absolutely necessary," John responded.

"Well," I piped in, "we can take heart, I feel, that many before us have worked hard to develop character and we can learn from them. Self-examination becomes much easier if we follow the example of others who have not given up simply because everything didn't fall into place right away."

"Yes," Dorothy said, "I guess the saying, 'practice makes perfect' still rings true. We can't stand still in our personal growth. We either move forward or backward. We have to be willing to purge our lives of habitually negative elements, and that requires constant dedication."

You Can't Stand Still

Every alcoholic I know has discovered, often by sad and painful experience, that if you indulge yourself in a drunk today, you can't escape the consequences tomorrow. These hangovers, however, take a variety of forms—they don't all come from taking a drink that leads to a drunk. If we indulge in self-pity or irrational anger, we will reap a physical and emotional payback. Peaceful living emerges only as we avoid the causes of self-condemnation. Morbid introspection doesn't cure us. We must determine to correct our mistakes and failures. As we rigorously examine our character and habits, the door to change will open. This "moving ahead" will produce a feeling of success. We will experience a sense of peace and hope for a better future.

Obviously, not all inventories are taken the same way, although the principle of self-examination remains. We can check up on ourselves as we move through the course of a day. Whenever feelings of frustration, impatience and anger emerge, we can stop and question ourselves. "Say, what's going on here, anyway?" Before retiring to bed, take a few minutes (or even longer) to look back over your day, evaluating it as honestly as possible. It helps to monitor the process continually and not run away from life the way you're living it. Look at life as a balance sheet, with assets and liabilities. Inventories can often take place between friends or with a sponsor. After an A.A. meeting, over a cup of coffee in an informal atmosphere, we can share with another sensitive person. Look at your progress (or lack of it).

Take time to "get away from it all." You can take in a conference or go some weekend to a monastery or retreat center, where prolonged, in-depth evaluation can be made quietly, without rush or interruptions. Quiet meditation can bring to light some areas of our subconscious struggle that we may not be facing honestly.

Self-Examination—Is It Really Necessary?

At first, you may think that continual self-examination sounds too depressing. Despair may threaten to overwhelm you. To curtail its effects, remember that God hasn't given up on you yet and never will. Feelings of futility and a "What's the use?" mentality will diminish. Practice will make this process easier. Happiness will increasingly emerge when we, in the words of the Bible, "lay aside the weights and sins which so easily beset [take hold] of us" (Hebrews 12:1).

Beth, whose sobriety was increasing, blurted out one evening in our Discussion Group, "I just can't seem to take an effective inventory. I need some basic insights to help me."

"I don't want to sound like a Mr. Know-It-All," John responded, "but I go at it this way. Every time I feel I am just about to fly off the handle over what some person has said or done, I try to zero in on the problem, recognizing that I may not be reacting to the person but something in myself. It probably means I still have some unresolved resentment. I see it as the emotional garbage I haven't dealt with yet."

"Yes," interjected Maude, "but don't you have to deal with your own feelings of anger first? Furthermore, isn't there such a thing as positive anger?"

"Quite right," John replied, "certainly there is a place for what I call creative anger, but all too often our anger is negative and basically destructive."

Almost everyone in the group nodded.

"Negative anger," John went on, "is often just the tip of the iceberg of some unresolved bitterness. Having 'good' anger means being sure you're not blaming some previous event or alienated person who has hurt you in the past."

"Well, I know that alcoholics are probably among the most hurt and disappointed people in the world," Beth responded (having listened carefully to the whole conversation). "This certainly provides fuel for the fire of any angry disposition. I know that I sure have a short emotional fuse."

"You're talking about me when you say that," Mary said, deciding it was time for her to share her feelings. "I have found that an uncontrolled outburst should be judged in the light of the misery it can create for hours—even days afterwards. My emotional jags of up and down often result from my negative reactions. I go on an emotional binge, with all its feelings of condemnation. Indulging my character flaws of jealousy, anger or self-pity do nothing but rob me of inner happiness. But what can we do about it?"

"I guess that's what this discussion is all about tonight," I joined in. "We're all becoming aware of how necessary it is to do an on-the-spot inventory. As life is being lived day by day, I need to develop a 'stop, look and listen' attitude. This is the only way that I can control life's experiences, rather than being controlled by them. We need to be constantly evaluating ourselves on how we react to life's ups and downs."

"I've found that my greatest battle at this point is in the area of self-justification," Mary said. "If I am willing to acknowledge my faults rather than justifying them, I know I've come a long way in not acting negatively. That means, for me, that I need to work at practicing self-control and honest analysis of my behavior. If I don't, I feel like throwing up my hands in despair. There doesn't seem to be any reason to carry on."

After a general assent from everyone in the group, we turned to interpersonal conversation.

"Let's go back to the topic," Beth blurted out, restoring some "law and order" to the group. "I'm sure we all agree that everything in life should be approached creatively, not destructively. Perfection may be the ultimate goal, but as we all know from the Big Book and from personal experience, we're not perfect people. We're just stumbling heavenward. That means we all need to be patient with ourselves and others."

The Key to Developing Self-Control

Is it realistic to think that we can develop consistent self-control? This question begs asking as we grapple with our wild, ungoverned natures that love to get their own way. We all know the difficulty of reacting rationally when life "blows up." Words dart thoughtlessly, and before we know it they have pierced hearts. How do we restrain ourselves so that quick tempers, dogmatic assertions and sweeping statements can be curtailed? The self-control required will not come automatically.

Step One can help us here. Not only must we realize our powerlessness over alcohol, but we must also recognize we are powerless to enact good behavior. We must constantly yield our lives to God, depending upon his resources through prayer and meditation. A.A. people must honestly believe they can't "go it alone." Only with God's power can we experience some measure of victory at this point.

As we progress, we must guard against self-exalting pride. When we recognize our inability to achieve success at this level, turning to God in our helplessness will release supernatural spiritual energy. It will enable us to make our inventory and rise above the downward drag of self-centered behavior.

Seriously studied the last thirty to forty years, alcoholism has been diagnosed not just as a physical problem, but essentially an emotional one. Most alcoholics I have counselled would agree that their alcoholism expresses their emotional illness. As counseling processes proceed, this eventually becomes obvious. Malfunctions usually originate in the home. But, as healing takes place and as forgiveness and acceptance of others occurs, memories of painful experiences surface, eager to be healed. As this healing takes place, power for day-by-day living comes. The subsequent self-discovery radically changes your whole life. It calls for a new approach, a willingness to commit ourselves to this essential principle: I must be willing to change my attitude toward myself and others. As we set the rudder of our wills in this direction, the power of God will steer us in the right direction.

Not Demanding the Impossible

Moving in this direction, we can release people from the high and almost unreasonable expectations we place upon them. We will exchange harshness for kindness and understanding, making allowances when others fail to measure up. If we earnestly pray the words of the Lord's Prayer, "Thy Kingdom Come," God will enable us to be more courteous, kind, just and loving.

What Makes a Daily Inventory?

As each day ends, record some of your impressions. This exercise has proven valuable for self-examination. Remember that life has its positive and negative elements. Many people wince about taking a daily inventory because they view life so negatively. But don't confine your self-inventory to your mistakes. Instead, concentrate on giving thanks for obvious progress and our good reactions to life's challenges. When defeat produces a sense of failure, do not emphasize it. At the least, do not divorce it from the positive, constructive events happening in your life. Every alcoholic knows that the tragedy of his or her drinking led them to A.A., and that was one of the best things that ever happened to them.

Making an Honest Appraisal of our Motives

"I find it hard to be honest in my daily inventory," Joan confessed to me in one of our counseling sessions. "I never seem to know whether my motives are sincere or phoney. I'm always asking myself, Why am I doing this? Why am I saying this?"

"Well," I replied, "motives are not easy to discern because we all hesitate to examine ourselves daily. I have found that I can only deal with the mistakes of life only if I ask God to show me what underlies my behavior. I've made some progress in understanding my moods of jealousy, fits of temper and unforgiveness, but only as I have asked God to reveal them. I realize that I can't come to any understanding of my motives purely on my own. I can only know myself as He is allowed the right to point it out to me."

"How exacting an examination of your behavior do you have to undertake in order to have light shed upon your motives?" Joan questioned.

"I have found," I replied, "that I will be tempted to rationalize and explain away my behavior if I do not first ask God to reveal what I should be learning about myself gradually. If you feel threatened when your true motives are exposed, you need a lot of courage to be ruthlessly honest. By reflecting on why you are critical of a certain person, you will likely understand it gradually, if you are willing."

"I know what you mean," Joan smiled. "I'm just beginning to discover that what I don't like about someone else is usually one of the things I don't like about myself. Sometimes when I've tried to teach someone in the family a lesson, I've begun to realize that what I'm doing is actually punishing them—getting even with them."

"Yes, and even when we slump into a depressed mood or even illness, it can be another devious way of getting sympathy," I replied. "It's amazing how all of us are riddled with self-justifying acts and constantly battle with them."

"I used to think that self-righteousness was confined to religious hypocrites, but I'm beginning to realize that we all have to admit to it," Joan responded.

"Admitting this, Joan," I said, "is the only way to free ourselves for growth in humility. Good and happy living grows out of our willingness to face our own faults and undergo correction."

"I take great comfort in the words, 'God isn't through with me yet,' " Joan laughed.

"There's no doubt," I responded, "that a serene conscience only comes as we search our own hearts in the light of God's never-failing love and light. We must not push our bad behavior into our subconscious, where it can only fester and produce more inner conflict. As Step Ten puts it so well, 'We must be willing to take a personal inventory and, where we are wrong, promptly come to grips with it.' "

STEP TEN: **Continued to take personal inventory, and when we were wrong, promptly admitted it.**
                                                   Alcoholics Anonymous

TRACK TWO: **One thing I do, forgetting those things which are behind, and stretching forward to those things which are before, I press on toward the goal unto the prize of the high calling of God in Christ Jesus.**
                                              Philippians 3:13,14

The Necessity of Progress—The Right Kind, That Is

The Christian Faith teaches that the dynamic of life demands a willingness to constantly judge our thoughts and our actions. Step Ten in the Alcoholics Anonymous Program incorporates this thinking from New Testament Christianity.

The byword of Western civilization until the end of the World War II has been "progress." Four major events, however, precipitated the collapse of this idealistic viewpoint. They were the two World Wars with the Great Depression of the thirties sandwiched between. Finally the dropping of the hydrogen bomb on Hiroshima abruptly corroded the concept of man's perfectability.

Amazingly, however, the vulgar optimism of the late nineteenth century and early twentieth century has hung on tenaciously. The attempt of Hitler's Nazi government to exterminate the European Jews should have eliminated its possibility. Without a Christian understanding of human nature, we can quickly slide into barbarism. The disintegration of communism in many parts of Europe starkly evidences that civilized progress can only be made when it centers around the preeminence of God. Only this focus can guide human nature in a positive, progressive direction.

To guarantee this progressive development, human nature must be spiritually based. Yet, as we know, many kinds of spirituality claim our allegiance today. From my study of various spiritual philosophies, I want to relate what I believe will enable us to develop in our personal understanding of our essential human nature, as well as the nature of the Higher Power (whom I chose to call God as revealed in Jesus Christ).

Basic to our understanding of who we are as human beings is what Christ taught: people cannot live by bread alone, but only by that living Word of God that proceeds from God Himself. No doubt, many good changes have occurred in the history of society since the Middle Ages. We have only to review the social development of Western society during the last century to learn about them. We all benefit from scientific and technological development. Even the forces of nature have been brought increasingly under man's control for good.

But has it refined human nature? Do we have more appreciation for the spiritual values taught by Christ, or have we degenerated morally and spiritually? Have the people capable of putting a man on the moon or curing disease increased their concern for the economically and politically deprived? Have the problems associated with crime, alcoholism, drug addiction and sexual abuse decreased? Has our knowledge about the universe and this particular planet enhanced our spiritual life and relationships to one another and God?

If we do recognize this blatant discrepancy, what is the solution? What laws of nature should we be discovering to improve our lives? What new levels of harmonious living should we be achieving for life to progress constructively? Perhaps reviewing the lifestyle of a progressive, spiritual man of the first century will offer some insight to guide us.

The Apostle Paul—He Has So Much To Teach Us

Writing to Christians in the ancient city of Philippi, the site of Europe's first Christian church, this spiritually transformed person shared how he was ordering his life. From a Roman prison he wrote, "This one thing I do, forgetting what is past, I press toward the mark of the high calling of God in Christ Jesus." In this dynamic, positive statement, we can receive power to progress in our lives.

Paul had purpose. The words, "this one thing I do," show us a man determined to move in a certain direction-toward Christ. But why Christ? Because in and through Him, he experienced a revelation of love that set him free from the burden of his sin and radically transformed his character. As a self-righteous leader, he knew firsthand how pride can fracture personal relationships. Only through the humility of God becoming a man in Jesus Christ and adopting our human nature to serve and then die on the cross could he hope to make any spiritual progress at all. Paul knew how to waste God-given energy on what brings little or no satisfaction. But now he can boast about the highest possible purpose—the only one that satisfies. He encouraged the Philippian Christians to seek a relationship with God through Jesus Christ in order to direct their lives aright.

Going Somewhere

As we look at human life and society, could anything be more obvious than our lack of direction? Many people reflect the attitude expressed in Thomas Wolfe's book, You Can't Go Home Again. He writes, "accepting the inevitable truth that human growth does not proceed in a straight line toward its goal, but compares the development and progress of mankind to the reelings of a drunken beggar on horseback." In Tennessee William's famous play, *A Streetcar Named Desire*, he has Blanche saying, "Maybe we are a long way from being made in God's Image, but . . . there has been some progress made. . . . Such things as art, poetry and music . . . such kinds of new light have come into the world. . . . In some kinds of people some tenderer feelings have had some beginning. That we have got to make grow! And cling to, and hold as our flag. In this dark march toward whatever it is we're approaching . . . Don't . . . don't hang back with the brutes."

Everywhere we look we see people, young and old, with no clear direction for their lives. Those on the top of the social ladder continually search for satisfaction in what money can buy and leisure affords. But what stimulates this feverish search for satisfaction? Nobody seems to know. What is its ultimate purpose? No one can be certain. Take a look at the middle class, eagerly striving for the top, seeking for meaning in materialism, yet satisfaction eludes them.

What about the working class? Life seems narrow in its horizons. People spin out the daily routing of their work-a-day world, with no more hope than more fringe benefits and temporal security. Is life just a meaningless series of work, TV, sports and weekend excursions?

The way most people live today contrasts starkly with the goals Paul set for himself. He knew what life was all about. The center of his existence was simply, "For me to live is Christ." He wanted to achieve Christlikeness—not by his own efforts, but by depending upon the Holy Spirit. His passion to understand more of Who Christ was and how to appropriate what He represented governed his lifestyle. His pursuit made him progress to the life that is truly life and climaxed in the realization that not even death could deter him.

Detachment from the Past

A healthy detachment from the past evidences significant spiritual growth. Paul writes, "Forgetting those things which are past" (Philippians 3:13). Many people, especially alcoholics, are tormented by the events of their past. The memory of what they have done, particularly what has created guilt perpetually overshadows them. If ever a person could have been enslaved by his past, Paul could. He participated in the martyrdom of the first Christian, Stephen. He spearheaded a drive to round up Christian believers from all over Asia Minor, bringing them to trial for betraying the heritage of their Jewish faith. He could have been traumatized by his memories.

But instead, he overcame his guilt because he really believed that God had forgiven him. Grace had taken him beyond his sin into a new life of freedom. He now pressed forward, knowing that he could only commit his failure to God and his mercy. In the light of his overpowering love revealed at the cross, he could discover even more of God's goodness and guidance.

How can we achieve victory over the negative aspects of our past? Is it really possible? Perhaps it is only wishful thinking, like fantasies without hope of materializing. So often, our minds drift back to those marks of self-centered living, and they seem to hinder our progress into the future.

But someone might argue, Isn't there a place for remembering what we once were and did? We have also experienced many bright days in our past. What we have learned in our past can help us live today. Human history, bad and good, teaches us much. Could we make progress spiritually without remembering the lessons of past failures?

Many of us can identify with the great Scottish writer, Robert Louis Stevenson, who once wrote, "The past is myself. In the past is my present and in the past is also my real life." Someone has rightly said, "Poor is the man who has no yesterday."

However, Paul did not turn from this. Rather, he refused to allow the past to pain him, to prohibit him from starting again. He warned against its ability to erase our confidence for the future. So many people fear that what happened to them in the past will recur. Therefore, for the sake of what life should be today, we must not allow the past to dominate us. A German philosopher, Neitzche, has written, "Forgetfulness is a property of all action." How tragic when people allow the fears of their past to keep them from a confident entrance into tomorrow.

Excessive recollection of what we once were or did seriously impede Christian progress. Often when people testify about what God has done in their lives, they revel in the day of their conversion, but fail to acknowledge what God is doing in their lives now. I know Christians paralyzed because of their past failures. They cling to their old ways, fossilizing the traditions and customs of their forefathers. The spirit of conservatism chokes their spiritual energy. We must ask God to set us free from any attitudes that constrain us, beliefs that rob us of progressive faith and block the flow of creative living. Paul urges us on to new possibilities as we face the future unafraid.

In his famous allegory of the Christian life, John Bunyan writes about Christian who was overwhelmed by his past faults, sins and waywardness. The burden threatens to crush him. But the divine injunction comes to him, Forget it. The memory of past sins has no power to lift us out of ourselves, no ability to heal our hurts, no inspiration to move us beyond ourselves. I am encouraged by the words of the poem that says,

> Let us forget the things that tried and vexed us
> The worrying things that caused our souls to fret
> The hopes that were cherished long, still denied us
>   Let us forget
> Let us forget the little slights that pained us
> The greater wrongs that rankle sometimes yet
> The pride with which some lofty one disdained us
>   Let us forget.
>
> *Author Unknown*

Spiritual Growth —Working At It Continually

Spiritual growth also happens when we determine to keep working at it. Paul never points to a time in Christian development when we can say, "I've arrived," "I've made it." On the contrary, the challenges keep coming as we press on towards the goal. In the so-called secular world, people recognize the necessity of constant effort. If you want to grow in knowledge, you must constantly read and study. If a farmer wants good yearly crops, he plans for the future. "Nature," writes the famous German poet and philosopher Goethe, "knows no pause and places a curse on all inaction." In archery, you must pull the bow back as far as you can stretch your arms, if you want the arrow to go the greatest distance. All great artists, musicians and writers realize that only consistent effort will produce accomplishment. Progress rejects the "laid back" approach because of the laziness and indifference it generates.

If you have ever read Napoleon's biography, you will notice that throughout his career, he gave his all to whatever he undertook. Emerson wrote of him, "Having decided what was to be done, he did it with all his might and main. He put out all of his strength. He risked everything and spared nothing, neither in munitions, nor money, nor troops, nor generals, nor himself."

What is true on the secular scene, must be equally true on the spiritual. Effort is essential, like it or not. Otherwise, we will stagnate. We may cringe at this because so often we prefer laissez-faire attitudes and recoil from constant struggle. The A.A. slogan, "Easy Does It," does not insinuate that no effort is required to maintain sobriety. It simply means that as we trust God, our highest Power, we can rest secure that we will make it, one day at a time. Paul compares the Christian life to a runner who has set out on his course enthusiastically. We are meant to be runners. We will not only be unfaithful to God, but also to ourselves if we fail to give it all we've got.

During the last two centuries, change, for the sake of making progress, has blossomed in popularity. Tragically, however, its humanistic basis precludes any interference of help from a Superior Power. Society has yielded to the belief that happiness can be achieved by self-effort alone—the ultimate modern misconception.

The Christian faith, however, unequivocally divorces itself from this presumption. Progress comes only as we trust in God and search his Word for spiritual assistance. We do not depend on the machinations of blind, impersonal fate, nor upon our education credits—not even on our sincere determination. We cannot do it on our own, but only by daily drawing upon the power of prayer, Bible meditation and reading as well as dialogue with other strugglers. We primarily depend on God, as we yield our wills, zeal and spiritual pursuits to Him. These basic ingredients combine to promote steady, day-by-day progress. Paul encourages not only his fellow believers at Philippi, but also all those who set their hearts to develop spiritual strength, knowing they have escaped the condemnation due them. As they look to the Christ of the cross and the resurrection, He will cultivate a deeper appreciation of who we are in Him, and all we can accomplish because of his love for us. When we complete the glorious adventure of this life that unfolds before us, we can rejoice knowing that we gave the Christian life everything we had.

CHAPTER ELEVEN

STEP ELEVEN: Sought through prayer and meditation to improve our conscious contact with God, praying only for knowledge of his will and the power to carry it out. *Alcoholics Anonymous*

TRACK ONE: Meditation is the life of the soul. Action is the soul of meditation. *Francis Quarles, 1592-1644*

Separating the Men from the Boys—the Women from the Girls

George had fifteen years of sobriety under his belt. His drinking years had taken their toll and left their mark on his health, yet everyone in Alcoholics Anonymous would probably have said that he was doing well. He had recovered his family, his job, and above all, his self-respect. He was coping, but . . .

The more George progressed in his sobriety the more he felt spiritually empty. This wasn't obvious at first, although it took him a long time to turn his will and his life over to the care of God. But eventually, he surrendered and let God take the "driver's seat" of his life. He had begun to do some serious reading and was realizing that alcoholic recovery included more than just sobriety, significant as that is. He longed for satisfying spirituality. Something was missing.

One evening, at George's regular A.A. meeting, I was asked to speak. I decided to talk briefly about the Eleventh Step, that emphasizes the need to move on to "improve our conscious contact with God." The means for realizing this deeper awareness comes through prayer and meditation. In my talk, I used the words of Francis Quarles, an English writer of the early seventeenth century.

Reflecting on the spiritual life, he discovered the importance of prayer and meditation. Thus he had written, "Meditation is the life of the soul. Action is the soul of meditation."

These words struck home in George's mind. He had heard about the need for taking this Eleventh Step from A.A. friends, as well as from talks at A.A. meetings but that night it registered. He wondered if his ignorance of prayer and meditation created his spiritual emptiness. These two dimensions had escaped him, although he had prayed desperately when he was drunk. After his sobriety took hold, he prayed only for others in difficulty, for people struggling with life's many problems. Rarely, if ever, did he pray for himself, imagining this an exercise in humility—after all, others were in more need than he. But in my talk, I stressed the importance of communication, not only with others, but above all with God. I reasoned that if God is personal, as the Bible teaches, and as many in A.A. have discovered, then we should cultivate our relationship with Him. Communicating with God begins the life of the soul, and inspires us to action.

Following the meeting, George wanted to talk and so we set up a time and place.

"I just can't imagine a busy person like me, getting down to meditating," George confessed. "I can hardly take time to read the newspaper. I don't know how I would ever get into a pattern of meditation. And yet, I know I need something more. Perhaps this is where it's at, and I've just been missing it."

"Well, you can see," I replied, "that Alcoholics Anonymous emphasizes that we must work at the Steps, and not give up before we've got involved with all of them. People today are too actively involved. 'Do, do, do,' is what we hear constantly. We get the idea that to start meditating you'd have to drop out of life and become monastic."

"That's the image that flashes into my mind the moment I think of meditating and praying," George agreed. "I like to be busy and yet sometimes, especially on weekends, when I can relax, I realize that my life overflows with hobbies, engagements, club activities, and A.A.—to say nothing about my work. But I must say that in spite of the busy-ness of life, I get much satisfaction out of it. Yet, as I say, something is missing."

"It's great to discover that over-activity hinders the pursuit and development of spiritual life," I responded. "That's the reason why prayer and meditation bottoms our list of priorities. It's too bad that most people think spiritual disciplines belong to ordained clergy. We think we can benefit from their prayer life vicariously. But letting this mode of spirituality prioritize our lives seems like a pipe dream."

For a long time, we talked about people who come into A.A. as agnostics. It takes them time to get beyond the A.A. Group as their Higher Power. Despite all attempts to show them the reasonableness of believing in a personal, loving God, they cling to their distorted misunderstandings of God's existence. They don't even believe communication with Him is possible, even though A.A. encourages us to believe in Him and draw upon his power and love.

But down the road, A.A. agnostics begin to come to faith in Him. Their struggle with agnosticism wanes, and the light of faith begins to dawn. Religious prejudices and bigotry, along with legalistic religion, often keep the agnostic from considering the truth. Pointing to all the human suffering, cruelty and injustice in our world, they sincerely ask, "How can there be a God in this kind of world? Life seems to lack meaning and God seems well-hidden, if there at all."

Not everyone, of course, has an agnostic spirit when investigating A.A. and the possibilities of sobriety. A few will acknowledge some kind of deity because they realize that nothing in this world could exist by itself. A bookshelf suggests a carpenter, a piece of music directs us to a composer, and oil rig points to a skilled mechanic. So it is with the universe. Nature and the intricacy of the human mind and body suggest the existence of a Power easily called Creator. But conclusive proof that a personal God loves and cares for us still rests in the realm of uncertainty.

For some people in A.A., to suggest that a Personal Power exists and that we can communicate with Him, love, serve, and obey Him seems too much, especially considering the enormous problems of humanity. They need to experiment with a Supreme Power, to prove that He lives and makes Himself available to us. But what is it that opens the door to such a possibility?

"I can see prayer being necessary for those in desperation," George continued as we wrestled with the meaning of the Eleventh Step. "I know from my own experience that in spite of my agnosticism, when I reached out to Him, I found He was there. That experience terminated my scoffing and scepticism. I became sold on the idea that there is a Supreme Power, Whom I'm not ashamed to call God anymore."

"It's that searching for God with all sincerity that makes it possible to find Him as a living reality," I said. "And when that happens, you know that prayer is real. After all, prayer is just talking to God—to a God Who is there and Who can hear. You begin to realize that communication with Him is just as vital to life as food, light and love. Without these the body suffers. And without prayer, the spirit dries up but, fortunately, doesn't die. It keeps signaling its presence, as does a hungry stomach."

"For a long time now," George said, "I've been feeling spiritually stagnant. Do you think it might have anything to do with my failure to draw upon the inner power released through prayer?"

"As I have just said, George," I replied, "denying the body food simply pictures the spiritual starvation that takes place in our souls when we neglect basic spiritual needs. We have to discover, as so many others, that no real existence can be meaningful and satisfying without a personal communication with the God Who longs to enter our consciousness. The need for creative living as well as the need for forgiveness and grace spring up when we acknowledge God's existence and that He longs for fellowship and harmony with us. But one thing we must keep in mind, George," I continued, "is that prayer and meditation are not just academic formulas for contacting God. Meditative prayer always involves self-examination. We see this from a number of the other Steps in A.A. We must be open to reviewing our lives in the presence of God. When self-examination combines with prayer and meditation, they produce a pattern of life that creates simple trust and confidence in God's will. As Step

Eleven says, along with prayer and meditation, should come a desire to carry out his will in daily life. This willing obedience produces the inner security our souls long for."

"I found when I was doing Step Four and then went on to Step Six and Seven, that I had plenty of dark spots in my life—some I was totally unaware of—until I began to sit quietly and take stock," George responded.

"You've already begun to discover, George, that prayer and meditation will not only expose those dark areas, but promote healing," I replied.

"You're so right, Cal, but as you well know, it isn't easy to humble yourself sufficiently to face our failures and the hurt we've caused. But I guess it's the only way to receive the forgiveness God wants to grant. If I could only get down to the day-by-day business of mediation and prayer, examining my lifestyle, submitting my mind to change and renewal, I know I could make great strides in spiritual growth."

"Remember, George," I replied, "not just to catalogue your dark side. Each of us has a measure of goodness, even though buried and sometimes denied. Many people get so down on themselves that they find it hard to see the good that comes from God, of course, the Source of all goodness. Even those spiritually renewed often hesitate to acknowledge their positive qualities. They feel that humility comes from downgrading themselves. They seek to mitigate the pride that has become increasingly evident to them. But self-examination includes seeing the good as well as the bad. Exposed to the sunlight of God's truth, not only do the dark areas of unresolved hurt, resentment and sin begin to surface, but also the good we accomplish by God's grace."

George sat quietly for a moment, reflecting on what I had said, and then responded, "I remember a small discussion group I once chaired, where I tried to get members of the group to list their good points or strengths. Everyone had a difficult time trying to think of anything positive to say about themselves, but they eagerly recorded all their negative points. It really was a sorry situation."

"Well," I responded, "this only illustrates what many people, even in Christian circles mistakenly understand by 'the depravity of man.' True, human sinfulness makes it impossible for any of us to build bridges to God. But that does not negate the possibility of doing anything good. A mother taking care of her child, a friend sticking up for his buddy, a father helping his son with a bank loan—these are good. But none of us can win God's acceptance by doing them. God does not accept us on the basis of our goodness, but rather on the basis of the love and grace He freely gives because of Christ's death on the cross. Trying to earn his favor by good deeds only deepens our uncertainty. How good do you have to be to be good enough for God? God's favor cannot be achieved by our human goodness, perpetually deficient in meeting his perfect standard."

Meditative Prayer—How It Helps Make Deeper Contact With God

Step Eleven challenges us to seek more intimate communication with God. Allow me to share some of my own discoveries at this level.

First, a wealth of meditative literature available today helps us deepen our day-by-day relationship with God. I have found that regular use of this literature stretched my understanding of God. Many people whose spiritual life originated in the Church find the devotional books available a great help toward spiritual growth. But the roots of many people in A.A. deny this possibility. How can they begin to progress in this direction? Before we can meditate, we must ask, What is meditation? The answers come to us from different quarters. We simply need to start reading the many books on prayer and meditation. This is what I call "priming the pump." These spiritual books suggest how to start our own reflections, our own prayers. One such book entitled, *The Imitation of Christ*, was written by Thomas à Kempis, a man in the fourteenth century who discovered how to make God a personal part of his life. Now available in modern English, it can be read much more easily. In the twelfth century, St. Francis of Assisi left the wealth and security of his father's home in Italy to become a wandering monk, ministering to the needs of the poor and sick. His simple, uncomplicated trust in God's daily provision and presence, has greatly inspired many. When asked by the Pope why he wanted to start a new monastic order and what its governing principles would be, he forgot the sermon he prepared to impress him. Instead, he launched into a spontaneous prayer that revealed the essence of spiritual life as he saw it.

> Lord, make me an instrument of thy peace . . . .
> Where there is hatred let me bring love.
> Where there is wrong, may I bring the spirit of
>   forgiveness
> Where there is discord, may I bring harmony
> Where there is error, may I bring truth
> Where there is doubt, may I bring faith
> Where there is despair, may I bring hope
> Where there is darkness, may I bring light
> Where there is sadness, may I bring joy.
> Lord, may I seek to comfort rather than to be
>   comforted
> To understand, rather then to be understood
> To love, rather than to be loved
> For it is in self-forgetting that one finds himself
> It is by forgiving that one is forgiven
> It is by dying that one awakens to Eternal Life.
>
> Amen

Thinking about the meaning of words like these will undoubtedly increase your own sensitivity to God's presence and to the needs of those around you.

Another avenue is to study particular biblical subjects. Most Gideon Bibles found in our hotels or motels list them as does the Good News Bible found in Bible Society outlets. The listings include such subjects as desiring inner peace, anxious for your family, when friends seem to betray you, discouragement, worry, boredom, bereavement as well as others. Sometimes taking a hymn book and allowing the solid truths of the words wash over you can be most refreshing in the meditative process.

Above all, prayer and meditation must not be hurried. Take time to engage in them thoughtfully. Don't question the concepts they represent during these times. The spiritual insights of others have been tried and proven in their own lives and now you can be the beneficiary.

I like to compare meditation to suntanning. As you lie quietly on the beach taking in the ocean's seemingly endless reach, you can contemplate the vastness of God's universe. Quietly resting, you can hear Him speaking truths you may never have considered before. This can be life-changing. Just as the sunlight changes the color of your skin, the truths of God, received through meditation, can transform you inwardly. His love releases you from negative thinking, leading you into more positive approaches to life. Seek to tap the boundless resources of God stretched out before you like the ocean.

Meditation? It's Not Me

Some of you may think this meditation business is not you. You have never done anything like this before, and you would feel weird doing it. You may think it too farfetched. It's hard to imagine yourself lying on some sandy beach, gazing out to sea and thinking about God.

That may be, but A.A. challenges you to let go of your prejudices, your fears, and let something new happen to you. Do you remember all the fantasies you had when you were drinking? A little more than farfetched I venture. You may be sober now, but don't you often let your mind wander, thinking about the possibilities that could be just around the corner? Using your imagination to create new possibilities is not bizarre. In fact, unless you exercise faith about your future, you may never realize your dreams, your secret longings. Planning for the future is not only a common exercise but also a wise one. The creation of architectural designs precedes new construction. A teacher uses imagination to prepare appropriate education materials. Meditation also prepares you for future action. As you quietly reflect on spiritual goals, you set in motion the inner drive to make it happen—to go for it. So it isn't as absurd as you may think to lie on the beach, gaze at the open ocean and imagine the limitless power of God available for you.

As you absorb the truths of St. Francis' prayer, or some passage of Scripture, you may find yourself longing to apply them. You will want to channel God's love and hope to others. As you dwell on what it means to love, to understand and to forgive, these attributes will be nurtured within you. The truth will give you power to change. As we use our imaginations creatively, looking to God in faith, we will be amazed by the harmony we will experience, both with God and with others. Meditation and prayer help make it possible. Idealizing for the future will enable you to review your past and say with confidence, I am going to move on. I am setting the rudder of my will to improve my conscious contact with God. This will steer you in new directions and inspire you to welcome changes like friends.

STEP ELEVEN: Sought through prayer and meditation to improve our conscious contact with God, praying only for the knowledge of his will and the power to carry it out. *Alcoholics Anonymous*

TRACK TWO: He meditates on his [the LORD'S] law day and night. *Psalm 1:2*

Meditation and Prayer —They Mean Many Things

The conviction of Alcoholics Anonymous that prayer and meditation can improve our conscious contact with God originates in the Hebrew Christian Faith. Many kinds of prayer and meditation are practiced by the adherents of religions and philosophies, but Christianity is credited for A.A.'s insight into what these two spiritual exercises can accomplish. Throughout this book, the God revealed in Christianity and spoken of seven times in A.A. can enter into intensely personal relationships with us. From the beginning of our realization that a Power greater than ourselves exists (Step Two) to a God capable of controlling our wills and lives (Step Three), the prevailing principle taught by A.A. (for those who have eyes to see it) is that our relationship with Him must not be static. We were born to grow in knowledge and understanding. We must not rest easy in what we know of Him today. We must continually discover more about his love, grace and power. Step Eleven reflects this concept—keep on improving your conscious contact with God.

What does prayer mean? It points to One with Whom we can communicate, Who can enlighten our consciousness with a revelation of Himself. What does meditation mean? It encourages us to think about God, to surrender to his will and be empowered to love even as He loves. Meditation kindles deeper desire to do his will, and releases the spiritual energy to do it. Accordingly, Jesus was primarily a Man of prayer and meditation. His teaching and actions display his close contact with his Father, Who empowered Him with love not only to teach, but to undertake the miracles that marked his ministry. He embodied the truth expressed in Psalm 1.

The person who takes the time to meditate and pray will enter into life that is blessed indeed.

What then does it Mean to Meditate?

A number of images surface from the Hebrew language to illustrate this concept. One image means "to chew the cud." As a cow lies quietly in the pasture, it regurgitates its intake of grass and subjects it to a finer digestive process. Crude, you may say, but it paints an accurate picture of meditation. Taking time to "chew the cud" of God's Word makes it part of us. As we ingest these ideas, they release energy to yield every aspect of our lives to the will of God.

Another aspect of meditation includes creative thinking. Not all thinking is meditation, but meditation always involves our minds, our thinking process. To meditate means to think deeply.

Still another aspect of meditation centers around the Hebrew words "to sing, to murmur, to mutter." This latter word, "mutter," is what meditation came to mean in the English language. It means to turn something over in your mind, to brood over, to muse upon in one's thoughts, to actually mutter out loud—perhaps under your breath. In Eastern countries, Muslims and Jews are often seen walking along the streets talking to themselves. They are meditating—muttering thoughts that have arrested their attention. Only in the West have we introduced the practice of silent meditation.

How do we practice prayer and meditation suggested by Step Eleven? Ideas activated in our minds as we reflect on the Scriptures, or any other spiritual literature should be "chewed over." They need to be "muttered" out loud or silently to ourselves. In other words, our new ideas about truth need to become part of us, just as food becomes part of our bodies. In so doing they can positively effect our character and conduct.

Meditation and Prayer—They Change Our Self-Image

Some years ago, we had a conference in our church, called

"Faith at Work." Our special speaker was the well-known Christian writer, Rosalind Rinker, who brought her sister along as a resource person. Both of them stayed in our home for the weekend.

At this particular time, my wife, Alice, was significantly depressed. She felt she was failing as a wife, mother, Christian and friend. Just about everything echoed, "I'm falling short." She felt unloved by the people around her, and primarily by God, making her feel even more guilty.

One evening she had an opportunity to share how she was feeling with Rosalind and her sister. After hearing Alice's self-description, not just her words, but more importantly, her heart, Rosalind's sister related an experience she had some years before. It reflected Alice's situation.

She had been experiencing rough times and felt like a loser. She also felt bereft of both satisfaction and fulfillment. Then someone suggested to her that she meditate upon the words of the well-known children's chorus, *Jesus Loves Me*. As she did this, she emphasized each word. (1) JESUS, the Son of God, the Savior, loves me enough to die for me. (2) Jesus LOVES me—not like, or endures, or puts up with, but actually loves me unconditionally with no strings attached. (3) Jesus loves ME, with all my faults, failures, sins, my ups and downs, my lack of self-esteem—He loves me. She typed up these words on little pieces of paper and pasted them all around in her home. Over the stove, the bathroom sink, her own vanity, her clothes closet. Throughout the day as she moved about her home, she reflected on the meaning of these words individually. She took time to let the truth sink deeply into her mind. Gradually, her mood and her attitude toward herself began to change. She started to accept her humanity, her imperfections and her abilities. She began to see herself as a person God loved, and that initiated a desire to love Him in return. Meditation facilitated the process. She practiced it as she went about accomplishing her household tasks. Disciplining her thoughts as part of her daily routine, she discovered that the truth had set her free.

Alice began to do this and over a period of a few months Alice's attitude about herself began to change. A new self-image took form.

She began to love and accept herself, and became increasingly a channel of love to others, especially to those grappling with poor self-esteem themselves. Such is the power of regular meditation.

Facing the Truth

The Christian understanding of prayerful meditation does not teach us to let our minds go blank, and then reflect on those words or ideas surfacing from our subconscious minds. Rather, it focuses our minds on significant truth that God wants to reveal to us. Jesus saw this when He said, "The truth shall set you free" (John 8:32). It is fundamental to the meditative process. When we read the words of some particular biblical passage or some Twelve-Step words and allow them to impact our open and receptive minds, we will experience truth producing changes in our lives, lining up our wills with the will of God. We will find ourselves set free from self-hate, negativism, despair, lust and unforgiveness—the power of truth in action.

The psalmist did this when he meditated upon the law of the Lord, day and night. Poetically, he was saying that he constantly allowed his mind to be influenced by the truth of God's Word. It was not merely a dry, academic, logical or matter-of-fact acknowledgement of the truth. Rather, he was reflecting the inner satisfaction that gave him moral and spiritual vigor to face life's challenges. He made meditative prayer an integral part of his life, not just something confined to its circumference.

Most religions place strong emphasis upon the importance of meditation and prayer. This universal concept has helped many people experience the reality of God's presence. But since Christianity inspires the Twelve-Step Program of Alcoholics Anonymous, people in A.A. who profess to be Christians eagerly incorporate this important principle into their lives.

Transcendental Meditation, popular for many people today, teaches its adherents to meditate on a secret word or idea—a mantra—which is a Hindu concept. In Christianity, the "mantra" comes from the Bible. For example, you could reflect on the meaning of the words "grace," "peace" or "salvation." Begin for a few minutes each day. As the benefits become more obvious, you will do it for longer periods. I have found the following biblical passages particularly uplifting.

I can do all things through Christ who strengthens me.   *Philippians 4:13*
Lo, I am with you always.   *Matthew 28:20*
I will never leave you nor forsake you.
                                                                Joshua 1:56
If we confess our sins, God is faithful and just, and will forgive our sins and cleanse us from all unrighteousness.   *1 John 1:9*

Another helpful method of Christian meditation is to read a passage of Scripture slowly and thoughtfully, allowing the Holy Spirit to activate some word, phrase, or idea. Record the message you get in a spiritual diary. Memorizing verses that have touched you personally will store up truth in your mind that the Holy Spirit can bring to your consciousness when you particularly need them—times of temptation, discouragement or even times of rejoicing. These words will guide and uplift you as your face particular circumstances.

Jesus used Scripture in a similar way when He was tempted by Satan with three tantalizing concepts. Each time, He refuted these suggestions using the Scriptures God brought to his mind. I have personally found this to be an important part of my own meditation. Again and again, God has called to my mind memorized verses that applied to a current situation. I have found for example, that when I have to make a decision I am tempted to vacillate and be upset and anxious. The verse, Isaiah 30:15, most often comes to my mind with great force: "In quietness and confidence shall be your strength." Meditating upon the truth of that statement, centuries old, and yet eternally true, gives me the stability I need to grapple with significant decisions.

Meditation guarantees, as A.A. says, an improvement of our

conscious contact with God. Its uncomplicated practicality will increase our desire to do the will of God, and thereby make us more like Jesus in word and deed.

Tragically, many professing Christians and people in Alcoholics Anonymous have neglected to "plug into" this most important aspect of spiritual growth. The power of God, ever available, only comes to us as we take time to pray and meditate.

In the latter part of the nineteenth century when electricity was discovered, many people remained skeptical. They prepared to go on lighting their candles and oil lamps, unwilling to experiment with something as intangible as electrical energy. Amazingly this electrical power, that brings so much benefit to our modern lifestyles, existed in the universe for millions of years unused and untouched before it was harnessed.

Why then, should anyone be skeptical about the inexhaustible store of spiritual energy proceeding from the heart of God, capable of doing as much in our lives morally and spiritually as electricity has done for us physically. Because God is love, as the Christian faith teaches so consistently, He willingly releases it into our lives through prayer and meditation. We can then pass it on to others using his strength. In the process, we will grow in the knowledge and understanding of God, especially as revealed to us in Jesus Christ. Knowing Him will empower us to face every situation in life and live in helpful, constructive relationship with each other.

CHAPTER TWELVE

STEP TWELVE: Having had a spiritual awakening as a result of these steps, we tried to carry this message to alcoholics and to practice these principles in all our affairs. *Alcoholics Anonymous*

TRACK ONE: A Christian is a beggar, telling another beggar where he can find food. *D.T. Niles*

You Can't Keep a Good Thing to Yourself

"I didn't think I would ever get to the place in my sobriety, where I would be willing to go on a Twelve-Step call," Mary said to me, as we discussed the remarkable change in her lifestyle after being in Alcoholics Anonymous for two years.

"It's hard to keep a good thing to yourself," she continued. "Sharing the discoveries of your life with others, especially people struggling to find sobriety, certainly leads to inner joy."

I couldn't help remembering the night I visited Mary, accompanied by Evelyn who had heard of Mary's need and had asked me to come with her. Although Mary fought for years to confine her drinking to social occasions, now its fury was threatening to take her job. She had no alternative but to phone the local A.A. office for help. When we went to see her, she wasn't yet convinced that her drinking was as bad as her boss and co-workers said. Yet, she did admit that her life was becoming unmanageable because of alcohol. We spent the evening discussing the results of her drinking and before we left her apartment, she agreed to come to an A.A. meeting and listen although she wasn't sure she really needed it. If it didn't make sense, she wouldn't return.

Two years later I could hardly believe the transformation that had taken place. She had not only found sobriety, but she had become an active member of a Twelve-Step Discussion Group. Our friendship had developed from that. Applying the truths of the A.A. Program to life, she began to see its message of hope couldn't be kept to herself. It had to be shared. But she was reluctant to become involved personally at first because she felt the "old timers" were more qualified, and she was too immature in her sobriety. But eventually, she volunteered to go with Dan (in charge of the A.A. office) to visit a person who phoned in for help. That visit made all the difference.

"There's nothing that makes you happier than helping someone find the truth that opens the door to hope. I can't help but think of the words I read in one of the Gospels, 'Freely have you received, freely give,' " Mary said later. "Sharing the program of A.A. with a suffering alcoholic has to be one of the greatest privileges I've ever had, especially when you've experienced the power of those truths yourself."

Words Without Actions are Meaningless

The Twelve-Step Program of A.A. climaxes in the challenge of sharing with others in need of help with their alcoholism. But before you can do that, the Twelve-Step Principles have to become a living reality in your own life. Words without actions are nothing. You have to experience a spiritual awakening. People contemplating whether they need A.A. or not may feel that the word "awakening" has no meaning for them. But as they experience the power of God changing them through the application of the Twelve Steps, they will learn what it means. Their personal experience in A.A. will enable them to reach others spiritually bankrupted by alcohol and the problems its creates. They want to share their hope with others. The reality of personal healing causes you to reach out to others in need and show them that A.A. works.

A person who has experienced recovery through the entire A.A. Program will eventually want to get involved in Step Twelve. They will have already discovered that submission to God and his power creates the ability to accomplish what was once impossible. The inner self has been renewed by truth, love and release from addiction. Being a new person creates a fresh awareness of life's possibilities. Instead of living on a dead-end street, with no future but destruction, they have discovered an inner awakening that opens up new pathways of service. They want to be involved with others in need, and there is no end to that.

How Does It Happen?

How does a person become involved in the ministry of Twelve-Step work? It happens as a person experiences what it means to take hold of God, the God Who has inspired the Twelve-Step Program of A.A. and begins to let his love and truth flow through him. Not only are you freed from alcohol addiction, but a new desire to share also begins to emerge. You don't seek it but you receive it as you yield to God and his purpose for your life.

To live out the truths of the Program, you must understand what the Twelve Steps attempt to teach. You examine what A.A. insists can be experienced and digest the basic principles. As you do this, motivation comes to share these truths with others.

What are those basic principles? Let's take a quick review.

Step One. You realize you have come to the end of your rope, with no place to go—except up or out. As you acknowledge your inability to cope with alcohol and face up to its power over you, you reach out for help in desperation. You admit your powerlessness, and that your life is in shambles because of alcohol.

Step Two. The power to overcome alcohol addiction does not lie with you. It comes from a Power greater than yourself that brought this universe into existence. We call this Power God and his working in you will restore your life to the pattern He intended. Only by admitting our need for this Power can we begin to experience victory over our own powerlessness.

Step Three. As we yield our stubborn wills to God and open our lives to his love, He can release his power into us. This submission is fundamental to any in-depth recovery. God does not require that we fully understand Who He is when we make our surrender. He simply wants us to start where we are in our understanding of Him, and go on to know Him better (Step Eleven).

Step Four. This step calls us to be honest with ourselves at every level, analyzing what alcohol has done to our moral, physical and spiritual lives. We need courage to do this because we so often hesitate to study our reflections for fear of what we may see. Yet an inward look is essential for full recovery.

Step Five. This Step links to the Fourth. We must tell God, ourselves and another person the exact nature of our alcoholic lives. This step will never be taken adequately unless we have been completely honest with ourselves in Step Four. Confiding in another person will humble you but it will also facilitate hearing the forgiveness of God from human lips.

The remaining seven Steps encourage continual confession and spiritual growth, climaxed by sharing with others the hope that Alcoholics Anonymous can bring. These activities comprise the lifestyle of a recovering alcoholic. As these steps become part of the fabric of life, our habits change and our character transforms. We move from a nebulous belief in God and we transcend the A.A. Group where we have sensed the presence of God in group consciousness to the realization that God can be known intimately and personally because of his love and grace.

What Happens When You Share?

The desire to share the message of hope with other victims of alcohol abuse follows naturally from applied A.A. principles. Gratitude springs from your heart without outside pressure. Not just experienced by the "old timer" in A.A., this thankfulness also flows from the new person discovering the greatness of God's power. As the message of hope is shared, it deepens our conviction that we have found the answer in this God-inspired program. Even when

A.A. members still question their progress and grapple with character defects, sharing with another person gripped by alcoholism strengthens their own sobriety. Encouraging a suffering alcoholic to get involved with A.A. intensifies your own belief that you have stepped into a way of life full of promise for the future. Sharing enables you to know that nothing can hold you back from growth and spiritual development, except pride and laziness.

A.A. members who have inaugurated all Twelve Steps will tell you with enthusiasm that the road to joy is the road of sharing.

Bob and I were having coffee after an A.A. meeting and he was telling me of a Twelve-Step call he had just made, and how he had taken the person to an A.A. meeting. "To see someone discovering hope has got to be one of the most exciting things in life," he said to me with enthusiasm.

"Yes," I replied, "and this is particularly true, Bob, when you see not only the alcoholic recovering, but also their families. In fact, as alcoholics regain their self-respect, they begin to believe they have a place to serve in the community. What a sense of purpose!"

"Have you ever noticed," Bob asked, "how even sharing your own personal testimony in an A.A. meeting almost feels like doing a Twelve-Step call? It kind of gives the person whose attending for the first time a sense of hope."

"That's very true," I replied, "but sometimes an A.A. member, too shy to speak at a meeting, can be encouraged to do a Twelve-Step call along with another person on a one-to-one basis. But whether at an A.A. meeting or a person's home, sharing the message is what's important."

When You Seem to be Wasting Your Time

When you are helping an alcoholic face the need for sobriety, at times your conversation may seem irrelevant to the process. For example, a practicing "drunk" may try to sidestep the issue of sobriety by engaging in long accounts of family history. This may appear on the surface as unrelated to the immediate problem. You may feel that you're simply wasting your time, that the person isn't really interested in managing his drinking problem.

Being a good listener, however, is part of the Twelfth Step. The truth doesn't always dawn upon a person instantly or easily. It may take some time to break through. Sometimes a Twelve-Step caller may become discouraged when the person he has been visiting relapses into drinking. The time and effort spent on such a person seems to be in vain. Yet faith in the future outcome must not be abandoned. Determine to "hang in there" with the person, despite feelings of failure. In the end, you will win out.

What to Avoid

One danger of involvement is the temptation to become possessive of the newly recovering alcoholic. If a person you have been helping has a "slip" and goes back to the bottle, you are tempted to take it personally. This may produce feelings of anger and futility. Be careful not to set yourself up as a professional counselor, ready with advice on every subject. When the advice is not taken, we can sometimes be slighted. Patience must prevail.

Confidence in the recovering alcoholic must also be rebuilt. Many practicing alcoholics come from backgrounds devoid of trust. The concept of trusting someone almost eludes them. They've given up on everyone. Assign tasks to newly recovering alcoholics such as making coffee for the meeting, greeting at the door, washing up or setting up chairs. Their efforts will build confidence, as well as self-esteem. This aids recovery, and reminds the Twelve-Step person that spiritual growth and maturity take time. The growing pains of self-esteem are hard-won, much like bringing up children.

Remember that A.A. is not just a matter of applying the principles of the Program to a drinking problem. It also includes living out those principles in all the day-by-day experiences of life. Drinking too much is only one of them. In the case of the alcoholic, the experiences will include not only himself or herself, but also the home, the children and work. When a recovering alcoholic rejects alcohol as an answer to their problems, they must discover other practical solutions. Alcoholics Anonymous may openly receive the new person, but what about the family? The recovering alcoholic needs to be reminded constantly that it takes time to rebuild broken relationships. The lost job may never be recovered. The former boss may never be willing to give you another chance, especially with a history of repeated failure. The newly recovering alcoholic still needs help dealing with these issues.

The Relationship Between the Twelve-Stepper and the Sponsor

The person who does a Twelve-Step call and gets a person to start attending an A.A. meeting may not necessarily continue a relationship in any close or intimate way. The alcoholic needs help finding a sponsor who can help in the long process of recovery. Coping with the many-faceted circumstances of drinking's aftermath needs constant support and caring. Life has its ups and downs. How can a person learn to deal with the "downers" without resorting to booze? The sponsor can encourage the alcoholic to believe that with God, all things are possible. The long-time member of A.A. has the privilege of helping the newcomer practice the principles of A.A. "one day at a time."

No responsible A.A. member—sponsor or Twelve-Step caller—can ever claim perfection in this area. Everyone struggles with life and its problems. An alcoholic can easily make mistakes and blunder, without necessarily resorting to a drink. Sometimes progress can occur so quickly that the recovering alcoholic feels like saying, "I've made it." The sponsor must warn that self-satisfaction always stifles growth. Recovering alcoholics may begin to feel that they don't need A.A. anymore. The Bible warns against this dangerous misconception, "When a person thinks he stands, beware lest he fall" (1 Corinthians 10:12). When a person neglects his or her relationship with God and the principles of the A.A. program, the temptation to return to drinking lurks on the horizon. Only by daily asking for God's strength in faith can anyone deal with the struggles of life. The message of Twelve-Step Recovery does not end in sobriety. Sobriety only opens the door to new possibilities to live life the way it was intended. We need all the help we can get.

STEP TWELVE: Having had a spiritual awakening as a result of these steps, we tried to carry this message to alcoholics and to practice these principles in all our affairs.   *Alcoholics Anonymous*

TRACK TWO: I am not ashamed of the Gospel of Christ, for it is the power of God unto salvation to everyone who believes.   *The Apostle Paul, Romans 1:16*

The Power of God

Throughout our study of the Twelve Steps, the Higher Power has proven central not only to our sobriety but also to every other problem. We have also learned that the power of God, referred to seven times in the Program, is love—the highest power. We have also discovered, especially in our consideration of Step Three, Track Two, that the power of God's love is fully revealed in Jesus Christ. He came among us, loved us, gave Himself for us, forgave us, and now, because He is the Risen Lord, He can impart his life-giving love to us. If we have been taking the Twelve Steps seriously and opening our hearts to Him, inviting Him to live in us, we have the motivation for sharing our faith in his power with others. The Twelfth Step tries to affirm this. Having experienced spiritual renewal, having come alive in our inner-most being, we now eagerly want to help others discover it too.

While I was directing the Union Mission For Men in Ottawa, Ontario, we had a weekend conference with men from Harvest House (a drug rehabilitation center in Ottawa), the Salvation Army, as well as the men from our own Rehabilitation Center, who wanted freedom from drug and alcohol addiction. We invited the director of one of the Missions in Pennsylvania, Captain Rod Rochelle, to be our speaker. Rod had experienced, firsthand, a remarkable deliverance from double addiction. This had come about, first through Alcoholics Anonymous, and then later, in his conversion to Christ. As a realistic and relevant communicator, he shared how his life had been transformed by the power of God's love in Christ. As he concluded his first message, he asked the men to close their eyes, and imagine the cross with Jesus hanging on it. He then asked them to imagine Jesus inviting them personally to come to Him. After the prayer, he said that the men who wanted additional counseling could stay behind. About six men responded. One of them was a young man, Al, who had been an alcoholic in his early teens. He had come to the end of his rope and longed for a new beginning. That night he prayed that the power of God's love would come into his life and set him free—changing him where necessary and releasing new ability to live a better life. It began his spiritual awakening. During the next two years, he had two slips, but the power of Christ overcame all the negative power trying to reinstate his old way of life. He was discovering by experience that the person "in Christ" is new—a new creation—and that the old things are passing away, and everything is becoming new.

Love in Action

As a recovering alcoholic, Rod wanted more than anything else to see addicted men and women set free. He took action to do this because the power of God is love in action, the fundamental premise of Christianity. We want to tell others about the possibility of being transformed by that love. The good news of God's love in Jesus Christ is not merely an intellectual theology, even though it appeals to the minds as well as the heart. It does not merely appeal to the emotions either, even though it touches the deepest chords of our emotional nature. What the Apostle Paul asserts from his own encounter with Christ is that the power of God brings liberation—or salvation, as the New Testament puts it. Its message, filled with power, offers a life of power—the power of love.

Dynamite Plus

In the Greek language, the word for power is "dunamis." We derive our English words such as "dynamite, dynamo, dynamic" from it. They all express power, either in nature or in human personality. We need to grasp the significance of this word as it relates to the reality of love. Few words have suffered as much distortion in meaning like our modern word "love." For most people it refers almost exclusively to sexual love; others imagine that they can win love by what they do for others. Therefore, everyone, especially alcoholics, needs to discover the radical nature of this love that originates in God. We cannot win or merit his love. Rather, He gives it to us unconditionally. When this kind of love invades our lives, we are stimulated to share it with others in words as well as actions.

Today, so many people are harassed by forces seeking to control them. Others are driven by uncontrollable desires; others are tortured by the mysteries of life and death that rob them of happiness and inner security. In the midst of this spiritual slavery, the power of God's love can break through, to release freedom in all its dimensions.

When Love Took On Humanity

Christian conviction asserts that this unconditional love of God took human form in the Person of Jesus Christ. At the beginning of Jesus' life on earth before He was acclaimed Savior and God by his followers, what is the first impression that comes through from the New Testament documents? The first people who encountered the personality of Jesus were awestruck by his power. The disciples believed God had anointed Him. One Roman commandant felt drawn to Him as one to be obeyed. An ordinary man engulfed in business pursuits responded to the call of Jesus and he left his desk to follow Him. Those who were diseased received healing, those worried and fearful became calm. Something about Him drew people who longed for a more meaningful life. Only the self-righteous, religious leaders brimming with spiritual piety resisted the impact of his personality and teaching. Even as He was crucified at the hands of the decadent Roman government, a soldier exclaimed "Truly this was the Son of God." The power of his personality compelled the early Christians to go everywhere with the message of his love. This missionary spirit makes Christianity vital and living and inspires imitation by A.A. Members of A.A., recovered from lives of alcoholism through the dynamic message of The Twelve Steps, enthusiastically share with others what they have experienced.

You Can't Keep It To Yourself

Testimonies given by those touched by the powerful reality of Christ abound because they can't keep it to themselves. For example, Napoleon, a mighty nineteenth-century French conqueror, once commented on the influence of Jesus: "I can gain but a wavering influence over the man whose ear and eye I can catch. This man, vanished for eighteen hundred years, still holds the characters of men as in a vice."

The story of Christianity, despite all that mars it, reflects how love can make ordinary people live extraordinarily. From the beginning, especially after Christ left this world for the next and granted the power of his Spirit to his followers, this amazing spiritual energy has transformed people and society. Responding to the power of Christ, people have exchanged weakness for strength, hatred for forgiveness, indulgences for self-control. The galaxy of history reflects shining examples of men and women made new in Christ. They did not boast of perfection, nor were their lives entirely put together. But they discovered a new life in which the old was deferring to the new, making life more than worthwhile. Throughout their lives they couldn't help but share this spiritual awakening with others. This is how Christianity expanded into every part of the world, just as A.A. has, from a few people in 1935 to the millions freed from alcoholic addiction through a Power greater than themselves. And because of this, "you couldn't shut them up."

Two Indispensable Ingredients

When Alcoholics testify about what Alcoholics Anonymous has done for them, two factors are indispensable. First, they must tell it "like it was" before they came to A.A. Then they must share "how it is now," as they live one day at a time. Likewise, Christians must point, first and foremost, to the reality of the resurrection of Jesus Christ, and secondly, they must share how that event applies to their lives and enables them to live a resurrected life.

I can never forget Harry, a man whose life had been totally wrecked by alcohol. In fact, he had been at "death's door" an a number of occasions. His doctor had told him that he had only a year to live if he didn't stop drinking. In desperation, he reached out for help, first to A.A. and then to a Christian friend who shared the reality of Christ with him. As he yielded to Christ and allowed Him to invade his life, he experienced a "resurrection from the dead." That is what he told me one evening, as we sat chatting about the amazing power of the risen Christ.

"I find that story in the Gospel of John about Jesus raising Lazarus from the dead, my story," he said. "Of course, I hadn't yet been buried, the way Lazarus was, but I sure was near to 'kicking the bucket.' When Jesus came to Lazarus' tomb and called out, 'Lazarus come forth,' I almost felt I heard Him speaking to me."

"Yes, I am sure that's what happened, Harry," I replied. "But did you ever notice from the story that when Lazarus came out of the tomb, he was bound head and foot with graveclothes wrapped around his body. The first thing Jesus said to the people standing around watching this amazing miracle was, 'Loose him and let him go.' Lazarus was unable to free himself. He needed some concerned friends to unwind those graveclothes. Until that happened, he was alive, but not free. I think the same applies to our conversion to Christ and our need for A.A. When we accept Him, we become spiritually resurrected, but we need other people, friends in A.A., sponsors, people in the Church, to help us enter into the freedom that awaits us. They help us get free from all the hang-ups caused by our alcoholic drinking."

"That's quite an insight, Cal," Harry responded. "It makes you realize how necessary they both are—Christ and A.A. or Christ and the Christian friends you make when you start walking this road."

And so we see, the resurrection of Jesus nineteen hundred years ago still affects our spiritual renewal today. When the Apostle Paul wrote to the Christians living in the city of Thessalonica in northern

Greece, he said, "If we believe that Jesus died and rose again . . ." (1 Thessalonians 4:14). In other words, as a result of believing in and experiencing the reality of these two facts, we have impetus to share our faith with others. Paul also recognized the centrality of the resurrection when he wrote to the Corinthian Christians, "If Christ is not raised, our faith is useless, and we are still in our sins" (1 Corinthians 15:14). Once a person realizes the importance of this historical event and begins to apply its truth, power is released like a fountain overflowing.

What is the source of this resurrection life? Christ Himself. Without any embarrassment Jesus pointed to Himself as the Way, the Truth and the Life. Christianity essentially portrays life and how it can be lived in the power of the risen Christ. Through Him, we can live together as brothers and sisters, having genuine concern for all those around us. The power of God's life expressed itself through the human life of Jesus. In what He said and did, we see what God's power can do—even in us, as our lives are joined to Christ by faith and acceptance.

However, belief in the historical event of the resurrection of Jesus, important and indispensable as that event may be, does not ensure salvation. A second ingredient must be added. That resurrection life must be expressed through us. In all its dynamics, love must be demonstrated through us. Otherwise, Christianity reduces to theological dogma, not living reality. His resurrection life in us gives us the power to go beyond ourselves to serve the needs of others, even those from whom we might naturally turn away.

Some famous contemporary Christians today have captivated the admiration of the world. Mother Teresa of Calcutta lovingly serves the needs of dying men and women lying about the streets of that great city. Jean Vanier loves the mentally handicapped and expresses his commitment to them as he establishes homes for them called L'Arche. Dick Simmons, a Presbyterian minister, founded a ministry for unvisited fellows in our North American prisons. We must make love our highest goal, as Genie Price, herself once an alcoholic, expresses in one of her books, *Make Love Your Aim*.

One of the most poignant speakers I've ever heard was Star

Daly, a man judged to be an inveterate criminal. After his last attempt to escape from prison, he was placed in the "hole" of solitary confinement. To keep him from damaging himself, he was chained to the prison wall, and only freed for meals. One night in sheer desperation, he cried out, "O Lord save me." In that moment, he had a vision of Jesus that so transformed him that when he was released from solitary six months later, everyone in the prison was astounded by the change in his behavior. He eventually became a nurse on the prison ward, where he had opportunity to help men unable to sleep at night. He used to go into their cells and sitting by their bedsides where they lay stiff and rigid, he would transfer from his mind the peace and love of Jesus. He testifies that he saw them lose their tension and gradually drift off to sleep like babies. In his book, *Love Can Open Prison Doors,* he has a chapter entitled "The Way of Holy Affection." where he writes these words:

> "What shall I write about next? What jottings shall I record on this rough pulp paper tablet? Is there anything more than love? Dare I write of anything less? But the best writing is living. Oh, living! That's quite another story. Old habits are strong. Man is notorious as a resister of the Highest. The pull is not an upslope but a down draft. But love understands however, and lingers, until the man grows weary and lets go. Tonight, as I run these prison wards, there will be plenty of time to live what I write. The right word at the right moment for the right man. Chatting with this one and that one. Just doing the loving thing, that is all. Each sick man is the nurse's chance. Each man must have hope stimulated tonite and his faith quickened. But greater than all is love."

Here was a man distorted by hatred, violence, alcoholism and drugs. And yet, under the power of Christ, he so transformed that he spent the rest of his life sharing with others the power of a love greater than all.

What Happens When Love is Released?

Love brings the dynamic to change. Like a plunging waterfall, it always seeks release. It inspires us to act, to dare, to do. It not only transforms, but blesses others. But it cannot be hoarded like a private possession. If so, it degenerates into self-love, the antithesis of agape love—unconditional love.

For example, if my wife gave me a bottle of after-shave lotion for my birthday it becomes my personal possession. Now every morning as I finish shaving, I can look at the bottle and admire its lovely amber color or its fascinating shape. I can say, "Wasn't Alice kind and thoughtful in giving this to me, especially when she knows how much I like this brand?" I look at it, but never use it. Is that the purpose of after shave? Of course not. I must uncap the bottle, pour some of the lotion into my hands and splash it all over my face. The scent not only pleases me, but also others around me.

The analogy applies to God's love in Christ. Through the gift of his Son, Jesus Christ, He has released the fragrance of his love into human life and society. Many people admire the life of Jesus. They hail Him as the finest man Who ever lived. They value his moral and ethical teaching. They are captivated by the quality of his self-giving. But they never apply that power to their lives and therefore, they cannot release it to work in the lives of others.

Throughout the history of Christianity, doctrine—correct belief—has been emphasized. This assuredly has its place, but in the final analysis, God wants our beliefs to become the flesh and blood of our daily lives. All too often, professing Christians have been too passive in their faith, too restrictive in their application of it and too selfish. Whenever people in need have looked to us for assistance, we have been calculating. We get involved only when it fits our schedules. How often, when moral and ethical change were demanded, instead of joining forces with others, have we drawn back in cowardice or indifference? When William Wilberforce decided to do something about the horrendous slave trade in England, he launched out in love, motivated by the freedom Christ gives. For forty years he fought for its abolition. But many

Christians in England resisted his efforts, or simply ignored his cause. They continued to nurture their own private religious lives.

When the power of love grips us, we cannot contain it. It must be expressed in the totality of life. The mark of Christian discipleship is love. Jesus said so emphatically, "This is the way all men [people] shall know you are my disciples, if you have love for one another" (John 13:35). When captured by the love of Christ and brought into spiritual renewal, we naturally pass on this message of love, forgiveness, grace and hope to others. We find ourselves eager to practice the principles of Christian living, in the spirit of love.

Years ago, I subscribed to a little magazine called Fellowship. One issue published a poem by Peggy Bond that made a profound impression, not only upon my mind, but also upon my actions. Let me share it as we wrap up this consideration of the Twelve Steps of the Alcoholics Anonymous Program in the light of Christian truth.

> All the frontiers are closed.
> There is no other country we can run to;
> There is no ocean we can cross over.
> At last we must turn and love one another.
>
> We cannot escape any longer.
> We cannot continue to chose between good and evil;
> The good for ourselves, and the evil for our neighbor.
> We must all bear the equal burden.
>
> At last, we who have been running away, must
>   turn and face it.
> There is no room left for hate in the world we
>   must live in.
> Now we must learn to love. We can no longer
>   escape it.
> We can no longer escape from one another.
>
> Love is no longer a theme for eloquence, a way of life
> For a few to choose who have a heart for it.
> It is the sternest necessity, the unequivocal ultimatum.
> There is no other way out.

There is no other country to flee to.
Everyone on earth must face his task now.

Alcoholics Anonymous parallels the Christian Faith like railroad tracks. A prayer, written by Rienhold Niebhur, the famous twentieth-century theologian, was adopted by A.A. from its inception. It represents the last spike in both tracks toward the goal of true freedom:

God, grant me the serenity to
Accept the things I cannot change,
The courage to change the things I can
And the wisdom to know the difference.